D0945345

INTERPRETING THE
WORD OF GOD

INTERPRETING THE WORD OF GOD

Festschrift in honor of
STEVEN BARABAS

Edited by
SAMUEL J. SCHULTZ
and
MORRIS A. INCH

MOODY PRESS
CHICAGO

© 1976 by
THE MOODY BIBLE INSTITUTE
OF CHICAGO

All rights reserved. No part of this book may be reproduced in any
form without permission in writing from the publisher except in the
case of brief quotations embodied in critical articles or reviews.

The use of selected references from various versions of the Bible
in this publication does not necessarily imply publisher endorsement
of the versions in their entirety.

Library of Congress Cataloging in Publication Data

Main entry under title:
Interpreting the word of God.

    1. Bible—Hermeneutics—Addresses, essays, lectures.
I. Schultz, Samuel J.   II. Inch, Morris A., 1925-

BS476.I65   220.6'3   75-43659

ISBN 0-8024-4092-4

Printed in the United States of America

Contents

Foreword

STEVEN BARABAS's self-effacing attitude, coupled with his diligence and effective ministry, made our work on this festschrift especially enjoyable. We invite Steve to assume the place of honor, interrupting his characteristic search for the lowest seat.

Our genial colleague took his education at Princeton, made Phi Beta Kappa and graduated magna cum laude in 1937, received the B.D. in 1940, and the Th.D. in 1948 with a major in New Testament and minor in theology. Prior to joining the Wheaton College faculty, he gained teaching experience through offering Greek at Princeton, a year of evening instruction with the Albany Bible School, and a summer at Nyack College. Steve postponed an earlier invitation to enter into full-time teaching, feeling the importance of gaining a pastoral background, and left that rewarding place of service reluctantly but not with regret. He ministered at the Ballston Center Presbyterian Church, Ballston Spa, New York, and since coming to Wheaton, has been active in pastoral supply and Sunday school teaching.

In 1950 Steve married Mary Jane Hendricksen, at that time a member of the Wheaton College Art Department. Mary Jane has been a kindred spirit these years of ministry. Two children, Dan and Kathy, have been the beneficiaries of their parents' love and devotion.

So Great Salvation: The History and Teaching of the Keswick Convention was published in 1952. Still an important work for the subject area, it illustrates the care and insight Steve brings to all his work. He was the associate editor for the *Zondervan Pictorial Bible Dictionary* (1963) and the *Zondervan Pictorial Bible Encyclopedia* (1975). Merrill Tenney speaks in glowing terms of his associate's contribution. "He is well read in theology," Tenney observes, and enjoys "a wide bibliographical knowledge." Steve

7

wrote and rewrote many of the articles, as well as giving his expert attention to the material which crossed his desk. Such words as "agreeable," "reliable," "helpful," punctuate Tenney's description of him and would be recognized by us all as characteristic of the man.

Steve also acted as editor of the *Evangelical Theological Society Bulletin* over a three-year span, associate editor for an additional year, chairman of the Spiritual Life and Standards Committee of Wheaton College for an extended period, and chairman of the then Division of Biblical Education and Philosophy of the college for a three-year term. He graciously accepted assignments as illustrated by our annual ritual of voting him in as recording secretary for the Department of Biblical, Religious, and Archaeological Studies.

Students will remember this professor as a mentor and friend. He gave unbegrudgingly of his time and counsel and perhaps seldom excelled more than in his directed studies. Younger faculty in the department especially looked to his sage advice and balanced approach to situations. Everyone in the college faculty recognizes him as a dedicated servant of Jesus Christ and as a cherished colleague.

For his part, Steve recalls, "Working with students has been a privilege and a blessing. I have never been seriously tempted to accept offers to teach elsewhere. In the same way that the members of the church at Ballston Center are still intimate friends . . . so my former students at Wheaton are very close to me." Drawing together his various associations and experiences, he quotes from the psalmist: " 'The lines are fallen unto me in pleasant places' " (Ps 16:6).

Our association with Steve Barabas has disproven the thesis that time must tarnish our good impressions. In a small way, we hope to express an appreciation to him through this volume and to assist all those who search the pages of Holy Writ for life's meaning, taking our cue in this latter regard from Steve's own life and work.

MORRIS INCH
Chairman
Bible, Archaeology, and Religion Dept.

Introduction

THE BIBLE is so simple that the least educated can understand its basic message and yet so profound that the best of scholars can never exhaust its full meaning. Unique in literature, the Bible is the divine-human communication that delineates God's Word to man in written form.

In this volume, we colleagues of Steven Barabas in the Bible, Archaeology, and Religion Department at Wheaton College offer some of our insights gained from teaching and sharing the Word of God in the classroom. To some extent, these contributions reflect the questions and problems that emerge as students become involved in studying the Bible at Wheaton, where the Bible is regarded as the integrating core for a Christian liberal arts education. Consequently, we recognize that the study of God's Word demands scholarship at its best in the content of a liberal arts curriculum.

Our hope is that this volume may provide stimulation and guidance for those who read and study the Bible as the Word of God. Scholarly research in biblical studies is considered only a means toward this end of knowing and understanding God. Repeatedly the reader will perceive our concern that at the heart of the Bible is the good news that man can have a personal and vital relationship with God.

Beginning with the divine promise made to Adam and Eve, the Gospel is enlarged throughout the centuries in a cumulative revelation culminating in the incarnation of Jesus Christ. The written record of divine revelation has come to us through numerous cultural and linguistic changes. Varied interpretations have been offered throughout subsequent generations as theologians have attempted to relate the divine message to the contemporary cultures.

Being removed by centuries and millenniums from the time of
writing, we are aware of our limitations to fully understand the
context in which the Word of God was given. Whatever insights
we offer from our study of the culture, history, languages, and interpretations that pertain to the writing and transmission of the
Bible are given with the hope that they will stimulate a construc-
tive approach toward interpreting the Word of God.

From the pages of the written Word of God come admonitions
and examples of God-fearing individuals who maintained a man-
God relationship. It is our prayer that each reader will ultimately
gain a greater understanding of man's personal relationship with
God. Toward this end, we offer these chapters.

SAMUEL J. SCHULTZ
Coordinator
Biblical Studies Division

1

Ancient Near Eastern Religion and Biblical Interpretation

by J. E. Jennings

The ancients saw more clearly, perhaps, What was really true, inasmuch as they were nearer to the beginning and divine origin of creation.

CICERO

For the invisible things of him from the creation of the world are clearly seen.

ST. PAUL

SEVERAL THEMES woven into the fabric of the biblical text have generated a disproportionate share of controversy among interpreters, especially in light of the study of comparative religion. Notable examples are the tree of life, the scapegoat, and the principle of blood sacrifice. The existence of certain resemblances in these motifs to some of the chief identifying marks of various primitive and pagan mythologies has been widely viewed as destructive to the biblical concept of revealed religion.

It is the purpose of this chapter, first, to discuss the principles which ought to guide our interpretation in these areas; and second, to examine briefly the three topics mentioned above, as well as three other matters related to ancient Near Eastern religion: primitive monotheism, the structure of the wilderness and Solomonic sanctuaries, and the cult of the "Queen of Heaven" in ancient Israel. The aim is not to attempt an exhaustive or even reasonably

11

complete treatment of each issue and its problems, but rather to seek to discover and apply principles fundamental to proper biblical interpretation in these and related matters.

In the past, the tendency has been to interpret such factors in the light of widely varying and compartmentalized schools of thought which reach conclusions often dictated by their presuppositions. Consequently, to the materialist, the Old Testament was studied in the context of "comparative mythology," and the total evolution of Israel's religion, according to the positivistic theory, was explicable in the light of the known stages of human religious development through animism, polydaemonism, totemism, idolatry, and monolatry to monotheism.

In an entirely separate compartment, the theologians and exegetes went about their work, frequently emerging with a pietistic picture of Abrahamic and Mosaic religion which was entirely pure of Babylonian or Egyptian elements and which was hermetically sealed from Near Eastern culture generally, inasmuch as it was revealed.

Neither of these views can be sustained in its entirety today. Both views—not just the theological—can be seen to have partaken of naive and literalist assumptions. This is true of the former scheme because of its reliance on a doctrinaire ideology of rigid developmental stages which are being seriously questioned by current scholarship. The artificiality of the latter view is equally apparent.

The principal factor in the breakdown of such self-assured results is the relatively recent and rapidly expanding rediscovery of ancient Near Eastern culture through archaeological research and its allied disciplines. The clear light of history can now be turned on to illuminate the Mesopotamian backgrounds of the patriarchs, Egyptian elements in the Pentateuch, and the interplay of Canaanite and Israelite religion in the period of the monarchy. If both reconstructions are impossible to accept today, it is not because of a major philosophical shift. Materialists are still materialists and believe in the total evolution of all religion; theists still believe in the existence of a personal God and the possibility of revelation. Christians further affirm that all Scripture is God-produced, and that as a supreme revelation, "God was in Christ, reconciling the world unto himself" (2 Co 5:19).

Thus it is still true that one's philosophical and theological presuppositions do indeed govern one's conclusions. The recognition of this factor is the indispensable starting point in any biblical hermeneutic. But the ideas of the old materialism posturing as a scientific understanding of the development of religion can have no place in an uncompromisingly Christian world view. God is, God acts, God speaks, God has revealed Himself in Scripture.

Both theologians and students of comparative religion are now forced, however, to develop interpretations of the biblical data which will take into account the new realities of archaeological discovery, to which fresh facts are being added every year.*

The required modification in viewpoint demands facing up to some hard questions. The question which can never be answered satisfactorily by an interpreter holding materialistic assumptions is, How can the unique elements in biblical religion be explained? The Bible is the world's greatest religious treasure because it is unique.

For the Christian, the question is the opposite: How can the similarities between revealed religion and pagan religion be explained? (A corollary question of great importance can be attached to this primary one, namely, What is the explanation of the origin and existence of pagan religion?)

To attempt a brief answer to the corollary question first, apparently pagan religion did indeed evolve according to patterns of development capable of being analyzed and understood. The mechanics of this process have been described by the materialist school. There should be no controversy here. Existence demands explanation. The evolution of religion is a fact just as the evolution of culture is a fact. (Perhaps some will prefer to use the term

---

*As the most recent examples of archaeological discoveries which have a bearing on the interpretation of biblical religion, two dramatic finds may be cited: (1) a Philistine temple at Tell Qasile (found in 1972-73), and a monumental horned altar (apparently apostate) from Israelite Beersheba (found in 1973). The excavator has identified it with the altar condemned in Amos 5:5. See Y. Aharoni, "The Horned Altar of Beer-sheba," *The Biblical Archaeologist* 37 (March 1974): 2-6; and A. Mazar, "Excavations at Tell Qasile, 1971-72," *Israel Exploration Journal* 23:2 (1973): 65-71.

development rather than *evolution* to escape association with the concept of biological evolution in the materialist sense.) Accepting the *fact* of development, and explaining the *mechanics* of progression, however, does not insure that the *cause* has been discerned. Here we must turn to an interpretative philosophy for an answer. Materialism posits some indefinable "force" always— though no one knows why—producing a higher level of development. Christian idealism asserts a more sublime and satisfactory concept in the biblical framework of thought by emphasizing the purposive acts of a beneficent and self-revealing God. Accordingly, Christian theology not only argues that it can explain pagan religions' origin and development better than materialism, but also that it can add insights not possible without revelation.

It is well known that scriptural writers intimate that false gods have a real existence and real powers perhaps attributable to demonic sources (Deu 32:17; Ps 106:37; 1 Co 10:20; Rev 9:20). In the patristic literature this becomes a positive assertion (e.g., Theophilus *To Autolycus* 10). It is conceivable, therefore, that all pagan religion is satanic in origin. This alone is not enough, however, to explain the knowledge of God, the concern with atonement, and the high moral tone of the developed religions. We must explain the good, as well as the bad, in pagan religion. The fathers also recognized this. In speaking of Seneca, for example, Tertullian declared, "He is on our side," implying acceptance of divine truth in pagan religion.[1]

It may be suggested that three principles, in a theological sense, are applicable to a basic Christian understanding of the evolution of pagan religion:

1. The doctrine of the *imago dei*.
   Man, possessed of an immaterial part, of a moral and spiritual sense, will by virtue of the Creator's design, inevitably seek to exercise himself in a religious way. Some of his religion will be true and right.
2. The doctrine of *general revelation*.
   Man can know two things about God from nature, Scripture declares: that a great power exists, and that this power possesses

"god-ness," i.e., deserves to be worshiped (Ro 1:20). Further, man can know something of the moral law because it is written in his own heart (Ro 2:15).

3. The existence of evil, and its personification in the demonic realm, together with the stamp of receptivity to sin in fallen human nature.

All of these factors taken together are perfectly capable of explaining ancient Near Eastern religion from its inception (in a fully organized fashion) in the neolithic period fertility cults to its culmination in the sophisticated henotheism of the late Roman Empire. The sublime language of Egyptian prayers and hymns, Egyptian religion's extremely high ethical concepts, the sense of moral responsibility of Babylonian religion, the existence of a virtual monotheism in certain periods, and a developed theology bearing some relationship to biblical teaching in Near Eastern religions generally, are all understandable in light of the principles of the image of God in man and the general revelation afforded to all men.

The matter has its negative side as well. In particular, the dark and superstitious dread of much of Babylonian sorcery may require a demonic explanation. Wizardry, necromancy, extispicy, augury, and astrology all arose alongside the commendable elements. To these evils may be added the enslavement to lust typical of Canaanite religion. But it is important to see that tracing the cultural and chronological development of religion merely explains its *course*. Theological insight is needed in order to explain its *cause*.

To turn to the more important issue bearing more directly on biblical interpretation, the question remains, How can the similarities between revealed religion and pagan religions be explained? Again, as in the previous question, the matter will ultimately have a theological resolution. Revelation is a unique act of self-disclosure. But the central problem of the symbiosis between much of Israelite cultus and Near Eastern religion remains unanswered by such a statement. Neither will an examination of the mechanics of cultural and religious syncretism alone suffice to enlighten the difficulty. A full solution also requires a simultaneous examination of the mechanics of revelation.

Cultural and religious diffusion in the ancient Near East is so readily apparent that it needs no elaboration. Similarly, the fact that the Bible was not composed and written in a vacuum, but reflects the crosscurrents of contemporary life, needs no demonstration today. And it is not strange, therefore, that diverse Near Eastern religious ideas and institutions appear intertwined in the warp and woof of the biblical record.

The revelational aspect has two parts, both of which will be helpful here: (1) a recognition of the distinction between general and special revelation; and (2) a recognition of the way in which God has chosen to reveal Himself historically.

Briefly, one can point out that numerous features of Israelite religion, such as the agricultural calendar, may have been the result of mere cultural development and diffusion alone. Other features, such as the ethical injunctions and taboos shared with other nations, could have been based on the general revelation common to all men. The most unique features, such as the disclosure of creation, of the divine nature as triune, and of the Messianic redemptive ideal as well as the *Paraclete* doctrine, require special revelation to fully explain them, despite comparisons with alien religions and claims that these concepts also evolved. At each stage, of course, it is possible that God did reveal through "borrowed" elements (or more precisely, infuse old cultural forms with new revelatory meanings). In fact, Scripture clearly indicates that this is exactly what happened. The agricultural calendar, to use the same example, was utilized in a context of revealed religious teaching. Thus, a general principle may be laid down: the factors held in common between Near Eastern cultures, yet displayed in a "Thus saith the Lord" context in Scripture, are to be understood as a part of *general* revelation, which are also *special* in that God chose to include their provisions in His specific revelation to the Israelites.

The second part regarding revelation is equally important. In attempting to understand how God has chosen to reveal Himself, it is instructive to observe in Scripture the interaction between cultural elements and divine teaching. A pattern may be detected. Whenever God utilized a previously existing cultural form to convey religious truth (as in the case of the comparisons between Hammurabi's law code and the Mosaic one), we may say that God deliberately intended to make a vehicle of the contemporary form for the purpose of effective communication and teaching according to the principle, "from the known to the unknown." To put it another way, God very frequently revealed Himself in harmony with the cultural patterns of the age.

This is perhaps true in the majority of cases, although not necessarily exclusively so. A corollary of this principle is that God may in actuality prepare the age to receive His message (as in the Messianic denouement), indicating that revelation is multifaceted (with active and receptive aspects) and therefore broader in its total impact than the narrow confines of the inscripturated Word. The fact that the Word is inscripturated does give it precedence over general revelation in terms of religious truth. It is thus more detailed, but no more true, than the revelation in nature, in the *imago dei,* and in history. We have in the Bible a divine commentary on only a fraction of the total span of history or of the multitude of historic events; but we may be sure that God has always been, and still is, active in history. If Jesus is the living Word, and the Bible is the written Word, then history is still "His Story," as Ethelbert Stauffer has maintained. A Babylonian or Egyptian idea, if borrowed and inscripturated under the divine inspiration of the Lord who created all men, is just as true as if it had fallen from the crystal air of Mt. Sinai and been inscribed on its red rock by the finger of God. Consequently, to see a conflict between scriptural particularism on the one hand, and cultural universalism on the other hand, is to construe wrongly God's revelatory activity.

In summary, the principles which should guide our interpretation are as follows:

1. A thoroughgoing theistic world view
2. A grasp of the factual data provided by Near Eastern studies, particularly in the area of comparative ancient religions, and including the concept of the diffusion and evolution of religious ideas and institutions within this cultural sphere

3. An understanding that some biblical traditions are mere cultural borrowing
4. Knowledge that some religious elements in the Bible which are parallel to other cultures are due to general revelation in nature
5. Knowledge that some religious elements in the Bible are due to general revelation in the *cogito* (based on the *imago dei*)
6. Realization that discontinuity in ancient religion and disharmony with God's special revelation is due to demonic activity as well as the fallen nature of man (which distorts the *imago dei*)
7. An understanding of God's revelation as typically occurring through contemporary cultural norms

With these ideas in mind, an examination of six selected problems is the next step in order to determine the usefulness of the approach suggested here.

THE TREE OF LIFE

Those studying Near Eastern archaeology and art history conclude that the motif of the tree of life is a thoroughly Mesopotamian one, displayed continuously on the iconography, and eventually becoming all-pervasive in oriental mythology.[2] The tree appears in Egypt, Syria, among the Hittites, and elsewhere, but nowhere is it as conspicuous as in Mesopotamia. Many of the cylinder seals and presentation *stelae* contain the sacred tree as the central element.

At Eridu the Sumerian Kiskanu-tree grew in the sanctuary of Apsu near the sacred pool in the temple.[3] A similar kind of tree (the black cedar) was important in the rites of Dilmun, the island of terrestrial paradise in the Sumerian myths. In the Myth of Adapa, a mortal is summoned before the lord of heaven, but is sent back to earth to die of sickness or disease in due course, because he refused the food of immortality. This food was presumably taken from the archetypal tree of life in the abode of the gods. These brief examples are sufficient to show that a terrestrial, tree-centered paradise located far away was a familiar theme in the Sumerian and Akkadian cosmology.

In the apocryphal book of Enoch, Elijah and other heroes had their dwelling in a distant Elysian region beyond the Erythraean Sea, where the tree whose fruit Adam and Eve had eaten to their shame was located. It was to be transplanted to the holy place beside the Temple of God in a future age (1 Enoch 28:1—31:6). In the final vision of the Johannine apocalypse, the tree of life is in the center of the heavenly city. There it bears twelve kinds of fruit every month, and its leaves are for the healing of the nations (Rev 22:2).

It is not difficult to see in these references a literary figure of powerful and persistent imagery. What should we then conclude about the tree of life in the Garden of Eden? Is it to be seen as a mere literary allusion without genuine existence, or is it rather a literal reality while in all other literature it is manifestly symbolic? There is really no way to tell from the text alone. It is possible that all the literary symbolism did, in fact, derive from a prototype which really existed. But it is sufficient for the theological message of the story for the tree to be symbolic of something more real and profound than even a tree: the Deity as the source of life. According to the principles indicated here, the Christian does not shrink from the data of modern discovery, but he affirms the view that "the God who is there" reveals, sometimes through innate and universal knowledge, frequently through established cultural motifs, but always truly.

The Scapegoat

The ritual of the scapegoat mentioned in Leviticus 16:7-10; 20-22 is a very curious and interesting one. There can be no doubt that the institution was dictated by God, for the chapter is initiated with the words, "And the Lord spake unto Moses." But in various periods the same act was also observed as a widespread rite in folk religion throughout the world.[4] Many of these instances could not have been derived from the Hebrew idea, since they antedate it or are found in indigenous new-world religions. Moreover, the practice seems to reflect a primitive conception found elsewhere, that the actual transference of the positive contamination of sin takes place, and is removed, *ex opere operato,* in a magical sense.

On the basis of these facts it is natural for questions to be raised about the integrity of the biblical claim to divine revelation. Does this type of occurrence invalidate the revelational aspect of the Hebrew rite? Is there a connection between the heathen practices and the ancient Israelite? Are we to conceive of God as utilizing evolved, pagan thought forms?

While it is possible to suppose that God uses natural themes to teach divine truths, I believe it is better to recognize that the principles of the imputation of guilt, transference of sin in a juridicial sense, and faith as an element in redemptive transactions may be aspects of the reality of the universe of which men innately possess knowledge, and therefore could be properly utilized in a revelational framework.[5]

It should be pointed out also that the moral efficacy of the atonement ritual in Leviticus was always dependent on the attitude of the penitent (see Ps 51:16-17). Perhaps an apt analogy would be that whereas we are concerned with the outward (humanly derived) part of the ritual, God puts primary emphasis on the inner (divinely oriented) aspect of the heart (See 1 Sa 16:7 and Col 2:16-17).

BLOOD SACRIFICE

Not only is blood sacrifice an element of foremost religious concern in the Old Testament, the New Testament author of the epistle to the Hebrews makes it the *sine qua non* of redemption. "Without shedding of blood is no remission" (Heb 9:22). And it is scarcely overdrawn to say that the fabric of Christian theology is woven upon the theme of the blood of the Messiah. It is little wonder, then, that the efficacy of blood sacrifice in general, and of the blood of Christ in particular, has been the point of violent attacks against Christianity and, at the same time, the proudest badge of defenders of the faith.

At precisely this point, too, Catholicism and Protestantism have divided over the method by which Christ's atoning power is communicated to believers. The Latin rites emphasize the objective nature of the sacrifice in its miraculous, perpetual re-creation in the mass, while the Protestant credo stresses the matter of faith, the subjective element. But the basic issue must revolve around the question of the supernatural character of the Messianic sacrifice. If, as Frazer and others maintain, the Christian emphasis on blood sacrifice is an unwelcome reversion to superstition, interrupting mankind's triumphal march toward reason, then the pagan blood-sacrifice comparisons are disconcerting or destructive.

It is true that primitive tribes commonly held a view of sin which associates it with a positive pollution or contamination which may be removed through a prescribed ritual action. Frequently the slaughtering of a sacrificial animal and the use of its blood in sprinkling, washing, and other direct applications was thought to release the guilt and propitiate the deity.

The sacrifice of Abel was preferred to that of Cain for precisely this reason; it was not only that his attitude was right, but the principle of blood sacrifice was affirmed clearly for the first time. The practice was further emphasized by the actions of Noah and the patriarchs, as well as by the Mosaic institutions.

Since this is so, it might be well to ask if this "primitive conception" is not in fact true. In other words, is not moral pollution something which has an objective existence in the real world, and cannot this contamination conceivably be removed by the juridicial requirements of a morally perfect Deity?

All that we know about man, his nature and his religious expressions, and all that we know about God through scriptural revelation would indicate that this is so.

The principle of blood sacrifice, then, is a reflection of the nature of things as they are, of a moral reality of the universe which is deeper and more profound than the ritual itself. Man is in fundamental disharmony with his Creator, and needs to be reconciled through propitiation. An even deeper truth is evident. Man cannot cleanse himself from his moral pollution but needs, ultimately, God's help. If God has allowed man to possess this knowledge from the earliest times, it may point to the inexcusability of man's religious contrivances and serve as a *preparatio-evangelium* for the Messianic sacrifice.

PRIMITIVE MONOTHEISM

It is fashionable in many academic circles today to assert that monotheism did not predate the Mosaic era—and that Moses himself, in fact, probably derived the idea of one God from the heretic Pharaoh Ikhnaton.[6]

This prevalent notion leaves the patriarchs outside the pale of the religion which, according to tradition, they themselves founded. Abraham, in particular, is frequently considered to have moved in a pluralistic Canaanite theological framework which was only clumsily disguised by the various editors of Genesis.

Such a predisposition has been largely governed by adherence to the positivist theory of the evolution of religion. This approach began under Auguste Comte (1798-1857). It relied on naturalistic philosophy and the scientific method. Their methodology was founded upon the premise that, "positive science explains natural phenomena in terms of verifiable laws of succession and resemblance, and they repudiated any suggestion that natural events could be understood by such theological devices as the intervention of supernatural beings in the stream of history."[7] Main stages in this theory were:

1. Animism—every object (potentially) animated by a spirit
2. Polydaemonism—the animation of numerous select and special objects or localities (e.g., springs, groves, high places) by spirits
3. Totemism—the worship of an animal or token of an animal as the particular deity of a clan or district
4. Idolatry—worship involving the use of baetyls or images
5. Monolatry—the worship of one god, while recognizing others
6. Henotheism—the fusion of gods into a great God
7. Monotheism—belief in one God

Wellhausen professed to find elements of all of these earlier stages of religion in the Old Testament, as well as ancestor worship and other primitive beliefs.

The facts of modern research, however, do not support the idea of religious development from "primitive" to "sophisticated" forms.[8] It can now be seen that the positivist theory labored under the grand delusion of the nineteenth century—that a simplistic evolutionary scheme based on a philosophy of naturalism held the answer to all the questions of science and religion.

The earliest recorded stages of religion in Mesopotamia and Egypt reflect a unitary concept of nature.[9] Thus the idea of one-ness likely predates the notion of plurality in nature and the spirit world.[10] A great and perhaps universal deity associated with the sky and its astral phenomena (as well as the origin of life itself) is presupposed in the oldest mythologies.

This indicates that the unity of nature is just as basic to primitive religious conceptions as is diversity. In fact, the evidence from the civilized areas of the Near East points to a fundamental conception of the "great god," which may be called incipient or primitive monotheism. "Such a conception of deity," says James, "is a religious response to the notion of Providence more fundamental than any gradual development from plurality to unity. It is rather a spontaneous purposive functioning of an inherent type of thought and emotion; an evaluation of the ultimate moral value of the universe; an awareness of the *mysterium tremendum* transcending all things."[11]

The idea of one God, profound and sublime though it may be, is nevertheless quite a simple one. It is not necessary to suppose that mankind progressed through thousands of years before the idea occurred to anyone. In fact, there is abundant scriptural evidence that the idea is innate (see Ps 14:1; 53:1; Ro 1:19-20; Ac 17: 22-24; Heb 11:6). It was only by the prolonged and perverse application of men's minds to the particularism of nature that the ancient world came to be peopled with a multitude of deities. In a similar way, the Soviet Union today makes a studied and vigorous effort to root out the idea of God through the educational process—with dubious success.

THE WILDERNESS AND SOLOMONIC SANCTUARIES

In Exodus 25 a specific commandment is given to Moses by God. It is the command to build the Tabernacle, and God's revelatory activity is very clear:

> And the Lord spake unto Moses saying, Speak unto the children
> of Israel. . . . And let them make me a sanctuary; that I may dwell
> among them. According to all that I shew thee, after the pattern
> of the tabernacle, and the pattern of all the instruments thereof,
> even so shall ye make it. . . . And look that thou make them after
> their pattern, which was shewed thee in the mount (Ex 25:1-2,
> 8-9, 40) .

It has posed a problem for devout students of the Bible to realize
that ancient Near Eastern art and architecture provide numerous
comparisons with the tabernacle construction. In particular, the
roughly contemporaneous furnishings of the famous Tutankha-
men's tomb show striking similarities to the tabernacle. The
wood with gold overlay forming a portable sanctuary, the use of
carrying-poles for small, boxlike shrines, the use of a cloth covering
for the sanctuary with metal or gilt rosettes affixed, the presence
of winged figures with wings touching, are all elements of apparent
Egyptian derivation. Some of these elements can be traced back to
Old Kingdom times, so it is obvious that the cultural parallels an-
tedated the biblical material.

It is little wonder that, faced with the choice of divine inspiration or cultural origin, scholarship has largely taken the naturalistic approach. The matter does not have to be seen in such an
antithetical fashion, however, if the principle of revelation through
culture is acknowledged. An insistence on revelation *de novo* in
opposition to the culture is contrary to the facts. It is true, of
course, that in the spiritual realm, God frequently reveals new
things which human wisdom could never achieve. But in the material realm, it is evident that the mechanics of human culture are
used to reveal the truth.

A similar situation is encountered in the Solomonic Temple.

> Then David gave to Solomon his son the pattern of the porch, and
> of the houses thereof, and of the treasuries thereof, and of the
> upper chambers thereof, and of the inner parlours thereof, and
> of the place of the mercy seat, and the pattern of all that he had
> by the spirit. . . . All this . . . the Lord made me understand in
> writing by his hand upon me, even all the works of this pattern
> (1 Ch 28:11-12a, 19) .

David said God gave him the pattern for the Temple, which he passed on to Solomon. The basic structure would seem to be based on the Tabernacle. Whereas earlier scholars had held that the design was purely Israelite, the Wellhausen school claimed that they detected early Hellenic influence and cited a postexilic date for the Temple descriptions. Today the influence is seen to be admittedly Phoenician, as virtually all scholars agree. The vigorous Phoenician culture was in fact a source of both Semitic and Greek architectural inspiration.

The sanctuary of Tell Tainat, found in 1936 by the University of Chicago in North Syria, dates from approximately the same period as the Temple in Jerusalem and has many features in common with the biblical description. For example, it was rectangular, had a porch, *Hekal* (holy place) and *Debir* (holy of holies, or oracle), and was close to the size of the Solomonic structure. Other Syro-Phoenician elements in the Israelite Temple include the carving of lilies, palmettes, cherubim, etc. Inasmuch as the Syrian alliance was the most concrete accomplishment of Solomon in foreign relations, this affinity is perhaps not surprising. Scripture also speaks explicitly of the Phoenician craftsmen sent by Hiram to assist the builders (2 Ch 2:13-14).

The question still remains, What part did divine revelation play in the Temple planning? Where does one draw the line between Davidic (and therefore revealed) plans and Phoenician (and therefore evolved, or humanly derived) contributions?[12] No line needs to be drawn if we interpret the revelation both to Moses and to David as coming through their previously acquired cultural sensitivities, not through some mystical vision of a new order with no cultural parallels or antecedents.

How then were the Tabernacle and Temple plans revealed? In the same way that the Scriptures were revealed. By the gentle, subtle, and almost imperceptible breathing of God's Spirit upon a man so that his background, training, intelligence, personality, and acquired characteristics were utilized in doing the thing that God wanted done. Yet there was the awareness on the part of the instrument that the process was divine. "The Spirit of the LORD spake by me, and his word was in my tongue" (2 Sa 23:2). The

results of revelatory activity and the concurrence of others in seeing God's hand, add objective elements which guard against subjectivity. But the principle of God's use of culture is clear in these
instances.

THE CULT OF THE QUEEN OF HEAVEN

The instance of the Queen of Heaven cult in Israel is not a theological problem per se, but it does provide an example of the
effect of human depravity in the defilement of spiritual truth. The
primary gods of the Canaanites were El, the supreme deity; Baal,
the young storm-god who paralleled the Mesopotamian Dumuzi-
Tammuz; and the three female divinities, Asherah, Anat, and
Astarte. These latter shared certain attributes but nevertheless
were separate personalities. Originally they were all earth god-
desses associated with a corn cultus, and the vegetation theme was
dominant in their ritual. They also embodied various attributes of
the great-mother theme. Each of these three possessed in some way
the attributes of Ishtar, and survived in the conception of Hera,
Aphrodite, and Artemis among the Greeks, portraying the three
aspects of womanhood as wife and mother, as mistress and lover,
and as a chaste virgin.

The myths are known in some detail from the Ras Shamra tablets (1400-1350 B.C.) found at ancient Ugarit. Anat was the sister
and consort of Aleyan Baal. Astarte stands as the symbol of sexual
love, but is also the goddess who patronizes war, and as such has a
harsh, cruel streak. Asherah was the original consort of El, the
chief god.[13]

The fact that *El* is the name frequently used for God in the
Bible has caused some scholars to assume the evolution of Israel's
religion from the older Canaanite one. The fact is, however, that
the term *El* is the generic name for God in Semitic languages, so
that one could hardly discuss any concept of the deity in Hebrew
without using it. Since the monotheistic idea did exist previously,
as has been demonstrated above, there can be no question of the
derivation of biblical theology from Canaanite religion. But the
question of religious and cultural syncretism is another matter.
Scripture reports that it did occur, and numerous references make
this abundantly clear.

The deeply ingrained Canaanite religion survived in Israel and Judah until after the exile. It was always condemned by the prophets, but its existence was undeniable. A terrific and protracted struggle can be traced in the pages of the Bible.

Elijah's contest with Baal on Mt. Carmel (Jezebel being a devotee of Baal and Asherah) was perhaps the dramatic high point of this rivalry. Amos and Hosea were strong in their denunciation of the cults of Bethel, Gilgal, and Beersheba (Amos 5:5). Jeremiah saw the children gathering wood for fires to the Queen of Heaven (Asherah) and women kneading meal-cakes marked with her image. Solomon had introduced heterodoxy; Ahab in the Northern Kingdom, and Athaliah, Manasseh, as well as others in the Southern, followed the Canaanite religion.

The evidence from the excavations shows that, during the Late Bronze and Early Iron ages, the Astarte plaques occur with considerable frequency in Palestine, at Gezer, Bethshan, Megiddo, Shechem, Dothan, Tell Beit Mirsim, and elsewhere. But the fact that they do occur at Israelite sites, together with the clear biblical evidence, makes it obvious that religious amalgamation did, in fact, take place throughout this period. Two temples found at Tell en-Nasbe (c. 850 B.C.) have been somewhat dubiously interpreted as sanctuaries to El and Asherah.[14] A more likely example is the apostate shrine of Isaiah's time found by Miss Kenyon in the Ophel excavations.

We must keep in mind that not everything reported or described in Scripture has divine sanction. Ritual prostitution was a factor of the fertility cult which was practiced from Babylon to Corinth through three millennia. The *zonah* (prostitutes) and *qadesha* (holy, sacred ones, i.e., ritual prostitutes) are mentioned in the Bible. But the copying of pagan elements in context was rejected because it promoted a dangerous syncretism. Ahaz "saw an altar that was at Damascus" (2 Ki 16:10). He liked it and ordered one for the Temple in Jerusalem. "The altar shall be for me to inquire by" (v. 15), in other words, an oracle. But the divine attitude toward all this was made clear in 2 Chronicles 28:25: "He provoked to anger the God of his fathers." Jeroboam's golden calves are another example of a cultic practice which, although probably well-intentioned, received strong prophetic denunciation.

The lesson in approaching the comparative study of religions is quite apparent from these examples. We must neither deny the possibility of God's revealing Himself by means of a previously known (and non-Israelite) cultic ritual, nor jump to the conclusion that biblical religion is not unique—and is therefore evolved—merely because syncretism was practiced by the Israelites. Some of the rulers may have made an attempt to link Asherah as the consort of Yahweh, but the strong and uncompromising monotheism of Israel was no new faith or weak shadow of a purified Canaanite religion. It was an ancient religion in its own right, and one which made claims to universal significance.

THE CONCEPT OF REVEALED RELIGION

Judaism, Christianity, and Islam share the concept of revealed religion. This concept posits a transcendent Deity who is personal and is interested in mankind to the extent of communicating with men by means of: (1) nature (Ro 1:19-20), apparent to all who possess sensory perception; (2) the prophets (Heb 1:1), which is a verbal technique applicable to hearers only; and (3) the writings (Mt 5:17-18; 23:34-36; 2 Pe 3:15-16), which serve for the benefit of those who can read and to whom a copy of the Scriptures is available. Beyond nature, the prophets, and the inscripturated Word is the living Word, the ultimate revelation, God Himself in the human form of the Messiah (Heb 1:2).

In contradistinction to the revealed religions there stand the evolved religions, the complex and multitudinous mythic patterns familiar to the pagan world, whether ancient or modern. It is demonstrably true that they did evolve amid the general cultural developments which mark the flowering of civilization. St. Paul makes it clear that, in a spiritual sense at least, this was not progress but degeneration (Ro 1:18-23). But the biblical faith came into the world of human culture and human religion.

It should not be surprising, therefore, that revealed religion has many points of contact with the evolved religions, in vocabulary, motifs, and rites. There is no inherent conflict here with the fact of the evolution of human religion, if we understand that God communicates with man at the level of his thought processes *at the time* and uses the language and imagery which reflect man's intellectual and religious understanding at that point in history. But the unique and inexplicable features of biblical religion serve to show that the substance is divine even when the vehicle is man-made. God is again accommodating Himself to humanity, an accommodation seen in its ultimate dimension in the incarnation. Scripture contains both human and divine elements, and even we ourselves are subject to the divine-human dichotomy: "We have this treasure in earthen vessels" (2 Co 4:7). The forms may be human, but the message for us is divine.

We must be careful, however, to make the distinction between natural or evolved religion and supernatural or revealed religion. The final test of the supernatural character of a religion is historical actuality, not its real (or supposed) analogies with natural religion. The only question is, Did it really happen? Did God really reveal His will, for example, through the process of casting lots using the Urim and Thummim? (Cf. Ex 28:30; Num 27:21; 1 Sa 28:6.) If He did, then any parallels with the culturally acquired technique of casting lots are theologically meaningless, although perhaps of historical interest. But the perspective endorsed in Proverbs 16:33 is helpful: "The lot is cast into the lap; but the whole disposing thereof is of the LORD." This shows how firmly committed some of the Israelites were to theism and suggests the principle which should guide us.

The importance of one's philosophical approach can be seen here. If we approach the study of mythology and religion with the prior conclusion that all are alike in origin, function, and manifestation, then there can be for us no such thing as a radically unique, supernatural or revealed religion. Christianity becomes simply one of many mythic and cultic systems which man has devised, and any effort to make it otherwise is futile.

CONCLUSION

It is possible to read the Scriptures, compare the numerous religious practices reflected there with ancient Near Eastern mythol-

ogy, and interpret each occurrence naturalistically. But a stream
can never rise higher than its source. The theistic world view demands an openness to historical revelation. The cardinal truth of
the incarnation, that "God was in Christ" (2 Co 5:19) is concep-
tually analogous to other instances of divine intervention in history—in the Abrahamic era, in the religion of Israel, in the institution of prophetism, and even in the kerygma of the apostolic age.
All of these partook fully of the human situation and have counterparts in nonrevelational systems. But the transcendent character
of the biblical message points beyond the elements, beyond the
trappings, beyond the evolved (and therefore human) aspects of
religion to the fundamental reality of the Revealer. Without
awareness of this, any interpretation of biblical religion can only
be sub-Christian and destructive. With it, knowledge of ancient
religion aids our understanding of the self-existent One who reveals Himself.

2

Archaeology and the Christian Mind

by Alfred J. Hoerth

AN ADVERTISEMENT for the Anchor Bible asks in large letters, "How much of what you want to know about the Bible is still underground?" In smaller print it makes several references to archaeological excavations and leading Near Eastern archaeologists. This prominent display of archaeology in connection with one of the newest Bible translation-commentaries points up the importance of the discipline to modern biblical interpretation. Since archaeology has become such an integral part of biblical studies, it is necessary for the serious student of the Bible to understand exactly what the discipline is and is not, and to understand a bit of the evolvement of biblical archaeology to its present station of importance.

I

Any archaeologist doing much speaking in churches soon finds that he is a misunderstood soul. Rock hounds befriend him in the mistaken belief that they have stones in common, and amateur paleontologists try to take him to their fossil collections. But the archaeologist need not be professionally attuned to either pursuit. Normally, he is attracted to a stone only if it has been anciently used by man. Expedition field registers often have entries like "red stone" or "dark gray stone." This is sufficient identification for the archaeologist until he prepares his final report. Then, for the sake of accuracy, he seeks out a geologist willing to supply the technical descriptions.

Fossil collections are even further removed from the discipline of archaeology. If there are archaeologists fascinated with paleontology, their interest is at best only peripheral to their profession.

What is archaeology if it is not paleontology or geology? Incredibly, *The American College Dictionary* has called it, "the scientific study of any prehistoric culture by excavation and description of its remains."[1] This definition confines archaeology to preliterate studies and leaves classical archaeology and much of Near Eastern archaeology homeless. But other definitions contain a limitation which archaeologists resist—namely, that the archaeologist is only a scientific collector of antiques who does no more than identify and classify his findings.* Not many archaeologists are so shortsighted.

Encyclopedia Britannica's definition is better than many:

> Archaeology is that science or art—it can be maintained that it is both—which is concerned with the material remains of man's past. There are two aspects to the archaeologist's concern. The first of these is the discovery and reclamation of the ancient remains; this usually involves field excavation or at least surface collecting. The second concern is the analysis, interpretation, and publication of the findings.[2]

This definition was written by an archaeologist. It does not limit the archaeologist to a certain portion of time. It does not leave him standing romantically beneath his pith helmet under some distant sun. It points out that an archaeologist's time is also—and it might be added, is mostly—spent trying to interpret what he has excavated; trying to answer, "What mean these stones?" (Jos 4:21).

Because an archaeologist is more than a digger, he usually must limit himself to one subfield within archaeology. For instance, too much is being found in and written about Palestine for anyone to keep abreast of both that field and, say, Mesopotamian archaeol-

---

*E.g., *Webster's Unabridged Dictionary*, 2d ed. (Springfield, Mass.: Merriam, 1935) where the fullest definition says that archaeology is "the scientific study of the material remains of past human life and human activities, such as fossil human relics, artifacts, implements, inscriptions, interments, monuments, etc., especially from prehistoric or ancient . . . times." The third edition of this work broadens the function of the archaeologist, but is deficient on other grounds.

ogy. Today, few archaeologists publish in more than a single subfield. Palestinian archaeologists probably know no more about Micronesian archaeology than anyone else who reads *National Geographic* magazine. Here, too, the archaeologist is misunderstood; most people believe that his knowledge and interests have no geographical bounds.

There is also a misconception peculiar to the Christian mind, i.e., the notion that the Bible is the foremost subject of archaeological studies. Actually, biblical archaeology is but one of the many subfields in archaeology. Consequently, most archaeological work going on today has no relation to the Bible. Near Eastern archaeology has obvious connections but, unless you are a Mormon, Mesoamerican archaeology has none. The majority of archaeological journal articles published each year have nothing to do with the Bible. Few archaeological books are Bible-oriented. The Christian should realize that not all archaeology is biblical and, therefore, that the bulk of archaeological research is of little biblical relevance.

II

While the historian of the nineteenth century was rejoicing over the wealth of information Near Eastern archaeology was bringing in, the Christian was asking what all this data meant to him and his Bible. Biblical archaeology arose in response to that question.

Some responses upset Christians. In 1872, when George Smith found a Mesopotamian flood story with numerous strong parallels to the biblical flood, critics interpreted the similarities to mean that the Genesis account was plagiarized rather than inspired.† When no Hittites were found by the archaeologists, critics solemnly concluded they were an imaginary people.

---

†See D. Winton Thomas, ed., *Documents from Old Testament Times* (London: Thos. Nelson, 1958) pp. 17-26, for a balanced appraisal of the Mesopotamian texts. In brief, it can be argued that the similarities are due to common inheritance. Both accounts go back to a common source—the event. There was a flood, both record it. After the flood, when men began falling into polytheism, they began recasting the flood account to fit their altered world views. We can trace some of what must have been a long parade of human corruptions and polytheistic incrustations on the original and actual events. The similarities which remain are those facets which were not erased during the various recensions.

Christians had no ready ripostes to some of these attacks on the reliability of the Bible. So, toward the end of the nineteenth century, when archaeologists finally did find the Hittites, evangelicals were a bit relieved.[3] Then, when biblical archaeology caused many other excesses of higher criticism to be retracted, evangelicals began to feel that their faith had been vindicated.

Archaeology did such a good job of refuting the grosser criticisms that by 1896 J. F. McCurdy pleaded, "It is now in place to use the word 'illustrate' almost exclusively instead of 'confirm' in describing the biblical function of the monuments. The stadium of needed vindication of the historical accuracy of the Old Testament is now as good as past in our progress towards the final goal of truth and knowledge."[4]

Eleven years later A. T. Clay wrote, "It must be a source of gratification to many to know that the ruin-hills of the past have yielded so many things to prove that much which the skeptic and the negative critic have declared to be fiction is veritable history. Archaeology must ever be given the greatest credit for having come to the rescue."[5]

Both men put the apologetic benefits of archaeology in the past tense. Not many scholars of their day would have agreed to the *total* historicity of the Bible, but archaeology had taught them to be more wary when making critical statements. They accepted archaeology's corrective and turned to what they recognized as a rich and positive function for the discipline. Most liberal scholars began in those days, and over the succeeding years have continued, to look upon archaeology as an ever-expanding source of illumination (echoing McCurdy's "illustrate"). They have used archaeology to search out fuller and correct meanings for the verses and passages of the Bible.

While most liberal Christian scholars were busy seeking out illuminations of our Bible, few evangelicals noted that a shift from *prove* to *illuminate* had taken place. One sentence from a book published in the same year as Clay's work illustrates the view most evangelicals had of archaeology. "Time and time again further researches and discoveries, geographical, historical and archaeological, have vindicated the Bible and put to shame its critics."[6]

Similar sentiments could be quoted from books spanning every decade of the twentieth century. Although A. Berkeley Mickelsen includes archaeology among his tools for the interpreter,[7] many evangelicals continue to see it solely as a tool for the apologist. One still popular evangelical study aid makes much of the way archaeology has confirmed the Bible. Sadly, almost all the archaeological entries are extremely old and most need major revision. Except for a tacked-on summary of the Dead Sea Scrolls, the archaeological content of the book itself is out of the past.

III

Informed students of the Bible should understand what archaeology is and what it is not; they should have some knowledge of the way biblical archaeology emerged and eventually split into illumination emphases and proof emphases. The student should also understand that, today, most evangelical archaeologists are committed to illuminating-interpreting the Bible. The reasons for their move away from proof need to be made clear.

First, after engaging in archaeological apologetics for even a short time, one realizes that his antagonist is not really interested in whether some historical objection can be explained; rather the concern is to nimbly pile fresh objection atop fresh objection to protect a citadel of unbelief. Very few people have been born again on the basis of archaeological findings.

Further, even supposing that every single historical statement in the Bible could be proved true, there would still be no proof that the theological message is true. If the biblical writers could be proved to have been infallible historians, this would increase the *probability* that their spiritual message was true—but no more. It can be proved, for instance, that world conditions were such that Solomon could be as powerful a king as the Bible says he was,[8] but this does not prove that God gave Solomon wisdom. It can be proved that first-century Palestinian tombs did have rolling stones,[9] but this hardly proves Jesus' resurrection. And no archaeological evidence will ever prove the atonement.

A point usually overlooked by evangelicals is that archaeology sometimes complicates matters. For instance, enough is now known

about the Hittites for scholars to question how they could have
been in Palestine during the time of Abraham. There was no problem until scholars knew "too much." Likewise, scholars had no
difficulty with Joshua bringing the twelve tribes peacefully to
Shechem until archaeologists discovered that the city was populated with Canaanites during the conquest.‡

The separation between historical and theological proof is clearly shown by the way archaeology altered the thinking of one scholar. William F. Albright, long the patriarch of Near Eastern archaeology, readily admitted that archaeology continually increased his
respect for the Scriptures. In an interview published a few years
ago Albright remarked, "I am still growing more conservative on
questions of date and authorship, historical background, and so
forth, having moved considerably farther to the right."[10] Such a
shift is legitimately applauded, but archaeology brought Albright
only so far. When he was asked whether he doubted the factuality
and historicity of the birth and resurrection of Jesus, Albright
replied that an empirical historian cannot answer that question.
He further skirted the issue with the statement, "Theological
truth is no less true because it is not the kind of truth that an archaeologist can validate."[11] Additionally, as he became selectively
more conservative, Albright frankly admitted that he was becoming
"even more strongly 'liberal' on general problems of the history of
theology, the use of evidence, the impossibility of man's being able
to formulate ultimate theological doctrines in human language."[12]
It seems fair, then, to say that archaeology worked apologetically in
Albright's life, but not in the realm of doctrine. Albright's final
article in *Christianity Today* showed no real change from the above
positions.[13]

While on this matter of distinction between historical and theological proof, something should be said about the danger of
using archaeological proofs to support faith. An archaeologist dis-
likes admitting it, but such supports might be resting on sandy
soil. Archaeology, as all sciences, finds some of its "facts" shifting

---

‡Abraham's Hittites could represent an isolated southern settlement, or we could
be wrong in equating them with the Hittites of Anatolia. The Amarna Letters speak
of the leaders of Shechem allying themselves with the Habiru; some equate Habiru
with Hebrew.

with the years. For example, in the thirties Jericho was excavated by John Garstang. He found what he believed were remains of the wall brought down by Joshua. Both liberal and evangelical scholars accepted Garstang's findings. The evangelicals were elated that archaeology proved the destruction of Jericho occurred just as the Bible said it had.[14] Garstang's conclusions were used by evangelicals as one more proof for the faith and for the faithful to use when dealing with the unbeliever.

Then, in the fifties, another archaeologist visited Jericho and applied better excavation techniques to the site. This second archaeolgist found that Garstang had misdated "Joshua's wall" by roughly a millennium![15] Moreover, it is now realized that peculiarities of the site make it unlikely that Joshua's wall will ever be found.§ Exit one proof.

In conclusion, archaeological apologetics was a very important corrective in earlier years, and it will continue to be needed as long as critics persist. It will continue to help those whose faith has been shaken by critical attack. But most evangelical archaeologists feel that archaeological apologetics has been blown out of all proportion to its need, comparative worth, and capability, and that evangelicals also should benefit from the immense contributions archaeology makes toward correct biblical interpretation.

IV

Archaeology primarily aids in biblical illumination and interpretation, and does so in a variety of ways. John A. Thompson's *The Bible and Archaeology* is probably the best introductory book on biblical archaeology. For Thompson, archaeology has several benefits; "in the first place, it provides the general background of the history of the Bible."[16]

Archaeology reveals the world situation at various periods. Abraham was in the world at a certain time, and it is essential to know the world of his time. Otherwise, like the early commen-

---

§Natural erosion has been heavy at Jericho, generations of villagers have been using soil from the mound to fertilize their fields, and Garstang's excavation removed most if not all the levels that could have contained the Jericho of the conquest.

tators, we run the risk of completely missing the point to several of Abraham's actions. With the background in place, Abraham and the other patriarchs can be seen as living people whose actions were not illogical but often conditioned by the historical events of their time and by the social culture in which they moved.

For someone interested in a better understanding of the patriarchs, or of any other biblical period, Thompson's book provides a beginning. One valuable feature of his book is that each chapter has a handy bibliography which points the reader toward more extensive treatments of the various topics.

When a historical framework has been provided by Thompson or some other up-to-date study, the student can then turn to works on Egypt, Mesopotamia, or others, and mesh histories into biblical timelines. Some of the historical vacuum between Noah and Abraham can be filled in this way. Bernard Ramm correctly argues in *Protestant Biblical Interpretation,* "Historical knowledge is indispensable to the best exegesis."[17] It is through such knowledge that various portions of the Bible become more fully alive, and there will be less risk of misinterpretation.

Another way archaeology aids in understanding our Bible is by supplementing our knowledge of its people, places, things, and events. Omri has been found to have been far more important extra-biblically than biblically. Ahab turned up as a key figure in one of the greatest battles in antiquity.[18] Excavation at several of Herod the Great's palace-fortresses has revealed much about Herod the man.[19] Archaeology has added to the biography of dozens of Bible characters and enabled us to more fully see the players in the biblical drama. To keep fairly abreast of these expanding biographies one must make use of the latest Bible dictionaries.

Until recent decades the locations of many biblical sites were unknown. Then, slowly, archaeologists and philologists began filling in the maps and determining what the cities and landscapes were like in biblical times. Today, almost all major sites have been located, and much of the ancient ecology can be visualized. The sheer size of Hazor is enough to add to our appreciation of the account of that city, "the head of all those kingdoms," (Jos 11:10) gathering a confederation against Joshua. Just the identification of the New Testament cities in Asia Minor makes the journeys of Paul more meaningful than they could be otherwise.[20] The locating of biblical sites has added to our understanding of the logistics and time factors involved in many biblical passages. To hike through Palestine from one biblical site to another is to find fresh meaning in Isaiah 40:3-4, where the prophet dreamed of a country easier to navigate.

The several good Bible atlases available generally fail to point out how, by surrounding the dots on the map with historical-cultural information, it becomes possible to recreate what it meant to move about in the biblical world. It is all too easy to say that some biblical figure went from one place to another without fully realizing what was entailed. In New Testament times the movement would not separate the traveler from a Greco-Roman setting; but those in the Old Testament ran the risk of culture shock. We can only surmise the extent of this possible trauma when we know the particulars of the various cultural areas.

Time and time again archaeology helps us see past the word pictures of the Bible to the reality behind. Until archaeologists began excavating horned altars (see Ex 29:12; 1 Ki 1:50) and putting them in museums, artists' reconstructions often looked disturbingly Texan. We now know what the word picture meant and the actual has been found to be quite different from the imagined form.[21] Today much of the material culture of both the Old and New Testaments has been recovered; and daily life of the various biblical periods, with its dress, implements, housing, and the like, can be faithfully reassembled. *The Ancient Near East in Pictures Relating to the Old Testament*[22] is a basic source for Old Testament illustrations. There is no comparable reference for New Testament times, but such journals as *Biblical Archaeologist* and *Israel Exploration Journal* keep one informed of the latest visuals for both testaments.

Thanks to biblical archaeology, many biblical events now are better understood and amplified. For example, the confrontation between David and Goliath can be seen in more than two-dimensional flannelgraph. Slingers were a regular component of ancient Near Eastern armies. Slingers worked closely with archers and needed a great deal of training to achieve accuracy. Slingstones can still be picked up at many ancient sites; they are not to be regarded as children's toys. Both contestants in the valley of Elah were deadly serious, and each knew the other was lethally armed.[23]

Through archaeological findings it is even possible sometimes to view a biblical event from a context other than the Bible. For instance, one Moabite king set up a large inscription to boast that he had put an end to Israelite domination. Some years later, Sennacherib recorded his version of Assyria's march into Judah. At Lachish, excavators found very poignant dispatches that were written as Judah's army crumbled in 586 B.C. For those interested in using such writings to breathe added meaning into various of the biblical passages, *Ancient Near Eastern Texts Relating to the Old Testament* is a primary tool.[24]

This archaeological amplification of biblical material could stretch into additional illustrations and source references. Perhaps one further aid with its illustrations will be sufficient to show the versatility of archaeology as a tool for the interpreter.

Archaeology has helped in the translation and explanation of many Bible words and passages. KJV translators saw no sense in cities standing still on "their tells" (Jos 11:13). The word *tell* meant nothing to them, and a mistranslation of the verse resulted. Today, the word is fully understood and is a basic designation for an ancient city mound in the Near East.[25] In the KJV, Proverbs 26:23 mentions "a potsherd covered with silver dross," an image out of balance with the remainder of the verse. Thanks to both Ugaritic and Hittite, the difficulty is removed, and the whole verse can be rendered, "Like glaze over an earthen vessel are smooth lips covering an evil heart." Now the verse has both good parallelism and beautiful imagery.[26]

The preceding examples give a taste of what biblical archaeology has been able to do, and of the kinds of helps one may expect from it. Archaeology is a never finished commentary on the Bible, and the serious student needs to know of the major discoveries as they are made.

V

As mentioned above, archaeological data provides a general background for biblical history, and it has added to the biography of dozens of Bible characters. Some years ago an entire baccalaureate address was given on the life of Shamgar! The address was a classic example of how one can surround a biblical character with the data available on his period in history. Perhaps not too many could get so enthused over Shamgar, but certainly Abraham should awaken sufficient interest. When it comes to Abraham most books will employ the Nuzi texts to explain certain of his Palestinian actions and attitudes. But what of Abraham's pre-Canaan days, what is inside those few verses which so quickly skip over fully half of the patriarch's life? No more than three sourcebooks are necessary to make those preparatory years come alive.[27]

As we place Abraham a little this side of 2000 B.C. we find that Ur's empire has splintered into many small kingdoms, each jockeying for power. When Abraham was born, the city of Ur was controlled by another city, Isin. By the time Abraham was a young man, Isin had begun losing its control over Ur. Then Ur was ruled by nomads, who would in turn be supplanted by one of the first Assyrian kings. Before Abraham was fifty the city of Larsa had taken control of Ur. Still more intrusions kept Ur an unsettled place, and this political instability would have made anyone glad to migrate northward.

The thousands of clay tablets from this period show that southern Mesopotamia had recently transferred from a state/temple-controlled economy to one encouraging private enterprise. Abraham's father experienced a very basic change in economic lifestyle.

These thousands of clay tablets include copies of law codes which predate the well-known Code of Hammurabi. These law codes contemporary to Abraham let us glimpse facets of his life. For example, the laws of Eshnunna permit us to draw a partial list of occupations: teamster, sailor, mule skinner, various kinds of farmhands. Other texts tell us of scribes, priests, fishermen, and many more. One fascinating aspect of these laws is that they let us work out the relative pay scales for the peoples mentioned. We find, for instance, that a mule skinner worked five days to earn the same amount of money a teamster made in one day. A man harvesting in the field earned twice as much as someone employed at the threshing floor. These are not earthshaking insights, but they are necessary details if one wants to create a true picture of Abraham's life.

The laws tell us much more. They tell us what could be bought with a given wage and the relative worths of the different commodities. In the days of Abraham a shekel of silver would buy nine bushels of barley or nineteen bushels of salt, three gallons of sesame oil or over three gallons of lard, six pounds of wool or two pounds of refined copper.

As we glimpse the society through these laws we see that money-lenders were charging 20 percent interest a year on silver, and $33\frac{1}{3}$ percent on grain. We find that a creditor could seize someone from a debtor's house to ensure full payment. Slaves had certain freedoms but were required to wear slave collars or identifying tags fastened by a chain to their body.

The laws enable us to see what formalities Abraham must have gone through before marrying Sarah. We find that in Abraham's society a husband could rather easily divorce his wife—but not if the marriage had produced children. This last insight, in light of Sarah's barrenness, adds another dimension to our appreciation of Abraham's faithfulness.

We have insight into the society Abraham knew. From the excavations at Ur we can also get an idea of the structure of the city he knew. In his day, Ur's city wall had a circumference of two and a half miles, and the center of the city was dominated by a religious complex. We find that town planning was haphazard at best, and that streets meandered and could suddenly terminate in a dead end.

Although there were no city planners, there was a preferred basic home plan. This model home had two stories and was built around an open central court. The main floor was used for storage or workspace. Ascending the staircase, one found the sitting rooms and bedrooms. Artists' reconstructions look rather attractive. We know that the mud-brick construction kept the inhabitants cool even in the scorching summer heat. It should have been a rather agreeable style of living. The repeated textual references to the possibility of snakes and scorpions dropping on people from the ceilings seem to show the only negative aspect.

The temple complex dominated the city of Ur, but one must distinguish between the official religion and that actually practiced by the common man. From what has been discovered in the area of religion, we know what the common man thought about the gods and his responsibilities to them. We must assume that the common man in Abraham's day believed in a world swarming with gods, demons ready to do one in, and neighbors capable of witchcraft.

We could go on and on in our re-creation of Abraham's early years. We could deal with dress, food, and the various types of literature then available. Hopefully, though, the point has been made. One can utilize books which prepackage the insights into various biblical passages, or one can enjoy the excitement of discovering firsthand fresh insights into the Bible. So when we read, for example, that Abraham's father was a polytheist (Jos 24:2) and that Abraham came from Ur (Gen 11:26-29) we can supply from archaeological evidence an incredible amount of meaning to those few biblical words. It is this kind of research and utilization of archaeology that can, and has, brought the people and events of the Bible closer and more fully into focus.

VI

The argument thus far has been for a proper appreciation and utilization of archaeology by evangelicals. Archaeology should be used largely as a tool for biblical interpretation, not biblical apologetics. Two final considerations are needed to round out the picture. One is that many good insights can be found in works by liberal archaeologists. Their contributions should not be ignored. We must see past their prejudices to the equally logical conclusion that will support an evangelical position. Somehow liberal scholars have convinced themselves that prejudice exists only in the evangelical mind. Albright, for example, denied that "the scientific quality of Palestinian archaeology has been seriously impaired by

the religious preconceptions of scholars."[28] He firmly believed that
archaeologists have been able to keep their conclusions "almost
uniformly independent of their critical views."[29] Albright thought
that it is the evangelical who violates the rule, and he cited the
excesses of Sir Charles Marston to illustrate his point.[30]

One needs to keep in mind the naiveté of the above position.
Whatever world view one holds, whatever view of Scriptures one
believes, these preconceptions are definitely going to influence the
interpretations one draws from archaeological or any other data.

The city of Ai certainly demonstrates how theology conditions
liberal archaeological conclusions. Et-Tell, one of the suggested
locations for that biblical city, was excavated early in the thirties,
and was found to have been unoccupied between 2200 and 1200-
1000 B.C. As all possible dates for the Exodus fit within this one-
thousand- to twelve-hundred-year period, liberal scholars began
amending the biblical text in order to harmonize Joshua's victory
over a city that "did not exist." The Bethel/Ai theory—that Joshua
really defeated Bethel, but the victory was transferred to Ai to
explain the ruins there—found its way into book after book. Several other ingenious solutions were propounded and argued, all
because the scholars debating the problem thought the error would
most likely be found in the received text. What few seemed to
question was the correctness of the excavation, but this is where an
evangelical would have begun to look for error. Only recently has
it been argued that the problem is not in the biblical text, but in
the designation of the mound dug as biblical Ai. Liberal religious
preconceptions caused the obvious possibility to be ignored for
years. Therefore, one need not be disturbed by apparently damaging conclusions; they may be seen as resulting from incomplete
data or faulty interpretation of the evidence.

Anyone interested in biblical archaeology must read at least the
final chapter in Edwin Yamauchi's *The Stones and the Scriptures*.[31]
In the few pages of this chapter Yamauchi graphically explains how
the biblical text is supported again and again by extrabiblical evidence. He contends that it is a mistake to demand—as liberals often
do—that in every instance the biblical text have external support
before it can be believed. Yamauchi spells out the magnitude of

the mistake by discussing the fragmentary nature of extrabiblical evidences.

VII

God's Word is exciting. Archaeology can heighten that excitement. What archaeology has done is exciting. "One of the most important benefits of archaeological studies is that they have given the *Sitz im Leben des Volkes* approach a dimension which could scarcely have been imagined in the days of Gunkel."[32] Archaeology will continue to be an indispensable adjunct to any serious study of the Bible. How much of what you want to know about the Bible is still underground? Much, but archaeology has already helped to make the Bible and its meaning surface to a degree not otherwise possible.

We are no longer limited as were Breughel and others to painting our real or mental pictures within some fanciful or contemporary landscape. We can see and touch the same things as did the patriarchs; we can see the armament used by Joshua as his forces moved out for holy war; we can catch a glimpse of the Jerusalem of Jesus, the Corinth of Paul; we can sense the tensions as they swirled about in that not so still "little town of Bethlehem."

An Israeli folksong proclaims, "David melech Yisrael, chai v'ka-yam"—"David, king of Israel, lives and lives on." A veritable host lives on for those who will equip their eyes to see.

3

Old Testament Prophets in Today's World

by S. J. Schultz

THE LANGUAGE AND VOCABULARY of the Old Testament prophets is basically the same as the Hebrew currently spoken in Israel. Should the prophet Isaiah speak in his native Hebrew to twentieth century Israelis, he would be understood more readily than Shakespeare speaking in seventeenth century English to a London audience today.

What about the message of the prophets? Would Amos, Isaiah, Jeremiah, or any other prophets preach the same, basic content to a modern audience? To what extent would they modify their approach to current social, political, economic, and religious problems?

The concept of the prophets and their messages comes to the modern scholar from the literature known as the Old Testament, primarily the Pentateuch, the historical accounts, and the books bearing the names of the prophets. Due to the wide difference of opinion among modern scholars as to when this literature was written, the prophets and their messages are interpreted from contrasting viewpoints.

The basic thesis that the Pentateuch was composed centuries later than Moses—usually dated c. 950-450 B.C.—is still widely assumed as the framework, or the most plausible theory, for interpreting the Old Testament. Representative of this position is G. Larue who asserts, "Because the documentary hypothesis is the most widely accepted of all theories of Pentateuchal analysis, this book will utilize in principle, the conclusions reached by this meth-

46

od of research."[1] J. Lindblom consequently asserts that we know nothing of the beginning of prophecy in Israel and that the first appearance of ecstatic prophets "in the reliable records of Israel" is in the time of Saul.[2] In evaluating the narrative about the early prophets of Israel as given in the accounts of Samuel, Kings, and Chronicles, Lindblom observes that these are "so filled with legendary material that it is very difficult to reconstruct with certainty the historical facts." Consequently, concerning any prophets "we can say nothing or very little with any certainty."[3]

As to the classical prophets beginning with Amos, the ideas of these men have been preserved in the books bearing their names. While some modern scholars insist that the prophets wrote down their words, others believe that the disciples of the prophets were largely responsible for writing down the messages of the prophets, supplementing them as the changing times required in subsequent generations.

Exemplary of this general viewpoint is the analysis of the book of Amos by H. Keith Beebe. He considers the book of Amos to be a homogeneous literary unit. Among the later supposed editorial additions are 1:1-2; 2:4-5; 3:3-8; 4:13; 5:8-9, 14-15; 7:10-17; 9:5-6; 11-15. Consequently, when the books bearing the names of the prophets are evaluated with critical care of modern scholarship, relatively little in these books can be claimed with assurance to be the words of the prophets in the literature bearing their names.

The book of Isaiah is considered to be an anthology composed during a period of about four centuries. The prophet Isaiah is recognized as a preacher and poet who proclaimed his oracles as messages of God. As the disciples or schools of disciples remembered these oracles, they would arrange them in writing and would "add to them biographical material, editorial glosses, and perhaps new prophecies of their own."[4]

Whatever may be attributed to the prophet Isaiah is limited to chapters 1-39. Chapters 40-55 are ascribed to a writer or an inspired follower of Isaiah during the Babylonian exile, and "still later, the prophet's spirit was reborn in the oracles with which the collection concludes, chapters 56-66," according to J. K. West.[5] Whereas West credits Isaiah with most of chapters 1-23 and 28-32, other scholars like Robert Pfeiffer would ascribe to Isaiah less than six chapters, primarily recorded in chapters 1-12.[6]

In contrast, there are scholars who take the literature of the Old Testament seriously. Moses is recognized as the great prophet through whom came the divine revelation as recorded in the Pentateuch. The historical and prophetical books are regarded as reliable and trustworthy accounts that provide the basis for considering the messages of the prophets. Representative of this viewpoint is R. K. Harrison who writes, "Prophetism as such among the Hebrews can legitimately be said to have begun with the historical Moses, who later became a standard of comparison for all subsequent personages (Deut. 18:15ff.; 34:10)."[7]

It was through Moses that the religion of Israel was revealed at Mount Sinai after the Israelis were delivered out of Egypt and established as an independent nation.[8] It was through Moses that God and Israel entered into a treaty relationship which was renewed on the plains of Moab before Moses died.[9] It was through Moses that the Old Testament canon was born after the Exodus victory and the renewal of this covenant as given in Deuteronomy.[10] As a written document the Pentateuch constitutes one-fourth of the entire Old Testament and more than three times the volume of literature attributed to any other contributor to the Old Testament canon.[11]

Prophetism in Israel is first and foremost associated with Moses, who was the mediator and recipient of revelation when Israel's spiritual vassal-union with God the great King was established. It was under Moses as prophet-priest that Israel's faith assumed its characteristic form, so that each prophet in subsequent times was to be recognized as a true prophet only if his message was in basic agreement with the Mosaic revelation, Deuteronomy 13:1-6.

Each prophet, however, had a direct and vital relationship with God in the immediacy of his experience and was inescapably constrained to proclaim what was divinely revealed to him in addition to the written message beginning with Moses. It was more than a subjective conviction. Speaking in the name of the Ruler of history, a prophet discerned the life of people in the light of divine revelation, challenging his hearers to respond to God's message.

Consequently, a prophet was a vehicle of divine revelation—not merely a news analyst with keen intellectual insight nor an ecstatic, dervish-kind of instrument possessed by a higher power.

Proclamations by the prophets often were expositions of the Pentateuch and, in the language of the common people, expressed reproof, correction, judgment, admonition, comfort, or encouragement; and often included eschatological, or predictive, elements. Predictions concerning the future usually were secondary to the historical and contemporary elements. Prophets normally made a practical appeal speaking to the problems of individuals as well as the nation, warning the wicked about future judgment, and encouraging the God-fearing people by assuring them of restoration.

THE ESSENCE OF PROPHETIC PREACHING

What constituted the core of prophetic preaching in Old Testament times? What was common to all the prophets throughout the centuries before Jesus Christ, the greatest Prophet, appeared? Are the basic ideas they proclaimed to their audiences relevant to our twentieth-century religious and political life?

Extensive and vast is the modern bibliography discussing the messages of the prophets. Much has been written to focus upon the political and social concerns of the prophets and how they apply to our current situations.

Among the Jews there was an abundance of literature interpreting and expounding the Mosaic revelation and the subsequent prophetic writings. In the wake of the prophetic era, talmuds and tractates have preserved for generations the interpretations of rabbis and other learned men since the beginnings of Judaism.

The simplest and most profound analysis of the messages of the prophets is provided for us in the conversation between Jesus and the religious leaders, the Pharisees and lawyers (Mt 22:35-40; Mk 12:28-34; Lk 10:25-28). The undisputed conclusion was that the entire body of literature—"law and prophets," which constitute the entire Old Testament—can be reduced to two simple statements: (1) love God wholeheartedly, and (2) love your neighbor as yourself. These two commandments express the essence of the Old Testament. Obedience to them is more important than sacrifice or any other ritualistic observance. All other considerations are secondary to the love relationship between man and God and the love relationship between man and his neighbor. These two statements summarize most briefly all that is written in the Law and the prophets concerning man's basic duty and responsibility Godward and manward. All other laws, requirements, and instructions are secondary to these two.[12]

THE BASIC CONCERN

The foundation stone in the ministry and message of each true prophet in Israel was the man-God relationship. Love for God or the lack of it was the starting point as a prophet began to address himself to his fellowmen. This was of primary importance and essential in making the proper adjustments to the total pattern of living. At the heart of all problems—social, political, religious, and national—was the individual's attitude toward and relationship with God. This was fundamental to everything else the prophets had to say to the people to whom they ministered.

Samuel, next to Moses, the most influential prophet in Israel, was called to prophetic ministry when the religion of Israel had declined into a state of apostasy under Eli. The people, under the leadership of Eli's sons, believed that the ark representing the presence of God would bring them victory if brought to the field of battle; but they found that they could not force God to serve them. They were defeated, and the ark was captured by the Philistines. Religion had become a matter of ritualism and external performance of rites and ceremonies. Idols interfered with devotion to God.

Recognizing that the national problem was Philistine oppression, Samuel publicly confronted his people with the challenging words, "If you return to the LORD" (1 Sa 7:3). When they brought God into focus, the Israelites experienced victory over the enemy.

Nathan had the crucial responsibility of making King David conscious of his relationship with God (2 Sa 12). Being in the foremost position as king of Israel, David acknowledged that he had tried to live excluding God from consideration in his daily life (Ps 32). The abundance of sacrifices and offerings he could supply in religious rituals (Ps 51:16) did not relieve the terrible conviction that gripped him. Only in an attitude of repentance (Ps 32:5) and contrition (51:17) was David enabled to restore his personal relationship to God. The natural sequence to this wholesome attitude toward God was the offering of sacrifices and service to his fellowmen.

Solomon began his reign by wholeheartedly seeking God in an attitude of humility and dependence. But in the course of time, Solomon permitted polygamy and idolatry to affect his Godward relationship, and the great kingdom of Israel was divided as a result of his apostasy (1 Ki 11). Prophet after prophet came to warn the kings in both the Northern and Southern Kingdoms from the time of Solomon's death to the destruction of Samaria in 722 B.C. and the fall of Jerusalem in 586 B.C. Kingship in Israel represented a trust, or endowment, of power in which the king was accountable to God as he ruled over God's chosen people (1 Sa 10:1). Toleration and promotion of idolatry was an offense of prime importance, and prophets, as messengers of God, did not hesitate to warn the kings that judgment awaited them unless they turned back to God. Consider how men like Ahijah, Shemaiah, Azariah, Hanani, Jehu, Elijah, Elisha, Oded, and other prophets boldly confronted the kings, as recorded in the books of Kings and Chronicles.[13]

Amos, who emerged on the scene when the Northern Kingdom was enjoying unprecedented economic and political prosperity, appropriately reminded his hearers that it was God who had redeemed the Israelites out of Egyptian bondage and had given them possession of the land of Canaan (2:9-10). God had sent them prophets, whom they had silenced (2:11-12). Because Israel was God's people and God's family, therefore she was to prepare to meet God lest the judgment of God's wrath overtake them (4:12). This meeting with God would be a day of darkness and gloom, because they had not maintained a wholesome relationship with God.

Hosea incisively charged Israel with breaking their love relationship with God. He spoke of it in marital terms. In an outstanding use of metaphor, he asserted, "The land commits flagrant harlotry, forsaking the LORD" (1:2, NASB). More than any other prophet, Hosea portrayed in his opening chapters the intimate personal relationship between God and Israel. Even as Gomer abandoned Hosea, so Israel had forsaken their God.

Isaiah explicitly accused his people that they had "revolted against Me" (1:2, NASB), "abandoned the LORD . . . despised the Holy One of Israel . . . turned away from Him" (1:4, NASB). The basic relationship with God had been broken, and the evils manifested in their pattern of living were the result of this absence of acknowledging God. Repeatedly throughout his book Isaiah charged his people with apostasy.

The core of Israel's problem, asserted Jeremiah, was cultic apostasy—they had forsaken God (2:13). Again and again Jeremiah confronted his people with the charge that they had broken their relationship with God as he warned them of impending doom. G. von Rad observes that Jeremiah gave much less space to "reproof for breaking legal enactments than to complaints against Israel's cultic apostasy."[14] Idolatry had been substituted for worship of God in the total pattern of living. The priests in their rituals, the prophets in their proclamations, and the rulers by their example, lacked reverence and respect for God by participating in and promoting idolatry. Fearlessly the prophet charged his people with harlotry and fornication in their relationship with God. Although they professed to be God's people, worshiped in the Temple, prided themselves in being custodians of the Law, and felt secure in being God's covenant people, Jeremiah pointedly faced them with the fact that they did not have a vital, meaningful relationship with God. Their religion was merely an outward profession.

Ezekiel, who spoke to the Israelites in the environs of Babylon, provides the most vivid portrayal of the broken relationship between God and Israel. Being exiled with thousands of Israelites in 597 B.C., Ezekiel was keenly conscious of their prevailing hope to return to Jerusalem in the near future. They did not believe Jeremiah's warning that Jerusalem was doomed to destruction by the Babylonians and that the captivity would last seventy years (Jer 27-29). In the year 593 B.C. Ezekiel responded to a divine call to be a watchman to the Israelites (1-3). After his incisive analysis of their apostasy (4-7) Ezekiel, through a vision, was given a message that realistically conveyed God's abandonment of Jerusalem to destruction (8-11). The leaders of Israel were guilty of religious practice that reflected their lack of exclusive devotion to God. Assembled in the Temple, the elders tolerated, approved of, and participated in idolatry. The women were publicly weeping for Tammuz in the gate of the Lord's house. Twenty-five men were worshiping the sun with their backs to the Temple. Consequently God's presence was being withdrawn from the Temple eastward to the Mount of Olives. Jerusalem was being abandoned to destruction because Israel had forsaken God.

Should the prophets address the religious people of the twentieth century, their messages would express in similar terms concern about prevailing conditions. People profess to be in a vital relationship with God, but in their pattern of living exhibit devotion primarily to materialistic gain. Participation in worship services and rituals, devotion to their church organizations, and bibliolatry often obscure a genuine love for God.

THE SECOND COMMANDMENT

Next to love for God, the prophets emphasized the responsibility man has toward his fellowman. Said Moses, "Love thy neighbor as thyself" (Lev 19:18, 34) ; "Love ye therefore the stranger" (Deu 10:19). The Israelites were to manifest toward the strangers among them the love that God had demonstrated in delivering them out of Egyptian bondage. Out of this experience of being loved came the ability, or capacity, to love their neighbors. In this sense the Israelites were to represent God to their fellowmen.

In the context of this command in Leviticus are the instructions for justice and equity in human relations. Consider Moses' teaching in Deuteronomy as he epitomized that which was important for their pattern of living.[15] In chapters 5-11 he focused attention upon a wholehearted commitment to and love for God. Chapters 12-26 provided instructions for the Israelites to live as individuals and as a nation so that justice and righteousness would permeate their total culture. This is the way they were to live as God's chosen and liberated people. These elaborate instructions provided guidance for them to exemplify love for neighbor in daily life.

It was the failure to exemplify these standards of justice and equity as outlined by Moses that came in for examination as the prophets assessed the problems prevailing in their times. Social injustice could easily be observed in daily practice, whereas the question of a vital, personal relationship with God was often obscured by religious rites and ceremonies. Consequently when the prophets attacked the social evils of their fellow citizens they could be much more specific and direct.

Consider the injustice when Ahab and Jezebel acquired the Jezreelite vineyard through the murder of its owner, Naboth. In denunciation of this use of royal power Elijah spoke out boldly, confronting Ahab with a sobering message of impending judgment (1 Ki 21).

Amos delineated the mistreatment of fellowmen on both a national and an individual basis. Surrounding nations were charged with deeds of oppression, slavery, cruel warfare, and invasion (1: 3—2:5). For these acts of injustice toward others, divine judgment awaited these nations.

The Israelites were in for greater punishment. God had delivered them from Egyptian oppression (Amos 2:10; 3:1-2) and had given them the land of Canaan as their possession (2:9-10). Repeatedly God warned them through prophets, crop failure, plagues, and warfare (2:11-12; 4:6-11). To these acts of mercy divinely intended to cause them to repent and return to God, the Israelites had reacted negatively.

Lacking a love for and a wholehearted devotion to God, the Israelites had become engrossed in idolatry and social evils that offered clear evidence that they failed to show love for their neighbors. The standard of righteousness and equity prescribed by God (Lev 19:35-36; Deu 1:16-17; 10:17-19; 16:18-20; 29:14-21) was ignored by them in daily life. On the basis of their own standards, they considered it permissible for those in power to accept bribes and sell a widow's son into slavery to collect the money for a pair of shoes (Amos 2:6-7; 4:1; 8:4-6). Injustice and evil abounded

(5:10-12), and cheating was considered an acceptable business practice (8:5).

Besides these inequities the Israelites hated honest judges (5: 10), silenced the prophets, and enticed the Nazirites to break their vows by drinking wine (2:12). Even Amos himself was rebuked by a priest from Bethel and reported to the king (7:10-17).

The Israelites failed to realize that man was an extension of God, created in His image. To hurt man was to stab God's integrity. God loves all men everywhere. Consequently judgment awaits the man who mistreats his fellowmen, whom God loves.

Hosea, a contemporary of Amos, indicted the people for similar inequities. As he looked at prevailing practices he observed lying, stealing, perjury, murder, debauchery, and bloodshed as accepted ways of life (4:1-2; 6:8; 7:1, 5-7; 10:4; 12:7-8). He pointed his finger at the priests and rulers, holding them responsible for ensnaring and deluding the people in the ways of idolatry (5:1). Throughout his messages he reminded them that they had failed to manifest God's love to their fellowmen. Because of this, judgment awaited them.

Micah asserted that justice had decayed. The poor were exploited, judges in the courts abused their power, and bribery was a common practice. Greediness and lust for money permeated culture so that prophets and priests browbeat the poor and favored the rich. Because of this, the hill of Zion, which was the seat of power and government, would be plowed as a field.

As God's messenger, Micah reminded the people that these were sins against God. God, who had extended His love and mercy to Israel by redeeming them, expected them to practice love, mercy, and justice toward their fellowmen (6:1-10).

Isaiah saw evidence all about him that the Israelites failed to show love to their neighbors. The poor, the widows, and the orphans were neglected and mistreated. As long as these maladjustments prevailed, God would not look with favor upon their offerings and ritualistic observances or even hear their prayers (1:1-28). Social and business relations were permeated with greed, self-indulgence, intemperance, cynical materialism, false standards of morality, intellectual pride, and a lack of integrity (5:8-23). As Isaiah analyzed their pattern of living, in which they oppressed the poor, lacked a compassion for the righteous who were oppressed, and even participated in idolatry and idolatrous rites, he concluded that they lacked respect and reverence for God (56:9—57:21). Fasting, a religious ritual, could not substitute for the inequity and injustice that prevailed in the people's daily relationships (58: 1-14). Social evils manifested toward each other had separated the people from God and made their prayers ineffective (59:1-8). Religious rites and ceremonies were futile and useless Godward when justice and equity were lacking manward.

Jeremiah, living in the final decades of Israel's first commonwealth, was divinely informed that Jerusalem and the Temple would be reduced to ruins in his lifetime (chap. 6). Incisively he analyzed the sins of the people, pointing out that they lacked neighborly love (9:2-6). Observing their daily conversation, Jeremiah was aware of their crafty cunning, deceitfulness, lying, and slander. Through cheating and trickery they took advantage of one another. Oppression was common. Injustice, greediness, immorality, murder, and theft were so common that offenders felt no sense of shame (chaps. 2-6).

At the same time Jeremiah was aware of the attitude of the people. They thought that through their religious rites and ceremonies they would avert the day of judgment. Priests and prophets, claiming to prophesy in God's name (14:13-16), misinterpreted the Law (8:8-12) and assured the people of peace (6:13-14). The people believed that God would not let the Temple be destroyed since it was His dwelling place (see 1 Ki 6-7; 2 Ch 7-8). Since they were custodians of the Law, or Mosaic revelation, nothing would happen to them. They thought that since they were God's covenant people, they were indispensable to the long-range plan of God. Jeremiah warned them that this was false security.

Jeremiah himself was deeply concerned and prayed for his people. His soul was crushed by the realization that God's judgment was about to be released upon his fellow Israelites (9:1). As Jeremiah interceded for his people, God informed him three times that his prayer was futile (7:16; 11:14; 14:11). The destruction of the Temple and Jerusalem and the termination of the kingdom was near.

Ezekiel, who spoke to the Jerusalem exiles in Babylon, portrayed the impending destruction of Jerusalem repeatedly and vividly to his fellow Israelites. His emphasis was upon the gross idolatry prevailing throughout the city of Jerusalem as well as in the Temple area. This idolatry was evidence that they had broken their relationship with God. Rites, ceremonies, worship in the Temple were but outward acts of piety. Love and reverence for God were lacking. It was because of this idolatry, and not primarily because of the social evils, that God was abandoning the Temple and Jerusalem to destruction.

In this manner each generation throughout the First Commonwealth of Israel (c. 1050-586 B.C.) was warned about their relationship Godward and then about their relationship manward. Although the former always had priority in the prophets' preaching, the latter often received the most extended analysis and denunciation.

CONCLUSION

Were these prophets to speak in our times, would they proclaim essentially the same message? Do their concerns, as expressed in Old Testament times, have any bearing on our individual and national problems? As modern scholars summarize the conditions prevailing in the days of the prophets, the similarity to twentieth-century situations seems quite apparent.

Consider how John Bright describes the situation in Israel.[16] The monarchy created a change in social structure producing a society of class distinction; few were privileged, and many were poor. As tribal identity and structure disappeared, the controversies once subject to covenant law became a concern for biased judges. The rich had lost even nominal respect for the Law. Vivid examples are given in Hosea and Amos.

F. F. Bruce analyzes the problems in a similar manner.[17] The greed of the wealthy drove them to use unfair business practices to extract money from the poor. When the poor could not meet their mortgage payments because of crop failures foreclosures enriched the greedy and made the poor more destitute. While the peasant lost his tribal inheritance and became a serf, the rich enjoyed more luxury.

Speaking about the times in which Isaiah and Hezekiah lived, Jacques Ellul describes the situation as reflected in Micah:

> At this very time Micah was vigorously denouncing injustice, hoarding, and the exploitation of the poor. Women were being driven out of their homes, the poor were being stripped of their very skin, and the princes of the house of Israel were perverting the law. They were building Jerusalem with wrong, while the prophets were prophesying for money (Micah 3-4). Thus moral collapse and social injustice characterized Jerusalem and the chosen people.[18]

Currently corruption and iniquity are erupting at all levels of society and government. The public and private breakdown of morals is apparent all about us. The new morality condones some law breaking in the name of love or compassion. Man is a law unto himself; he has no consciousness of God in his daily life. Without God in focus, there is no absolute moral law to govern the behavior of man in government or society.

The messages of the prophets are as appropriate for modern times as they were when originally given. The basic need for man to acknowledge God is as great as ever. Very timely is the charge of the prophets, "You have forsaken God." It is only as man acknowledges God that he will become genuinely conscious of the need to love his neighbor and treat him justly; a genuine love for God will ultimately be expressed toward one's neighbor.

The prophets' priorities need to be emphasized as their message is applied to modern times. It is not a question of evangelism *or* social action. Both must be considered important, but the order is significant. Man's Godward relationship must come first. Only in relationship to God can man gain a proper relationship with his fellowman.

In our concern to make the message of the prophets relevant to our modern situations, may we heed the appropriate words of Charles H. Troutman: "A gospel that rightly insists on the priority of man's relation to God may run the risk of implying that man's relationship to his fellowmen as individuals and society is unimportant . . . we must show the courage of former generations of evangelicals but refuse to follow their strategy. Too much was lost."[19]

4

Entrée to the Pentateuch Through the
Prophets: A Hermeneutics of History

by C. Hassell Bullock

WHEN HISTORIANS PROBE into the past, they attempt to come as
close as they can to a historical event through those who stood
nearest to it. While we cannot, of course, assume that these ob-
servers or recorders fully understood the event, we are still compelled to transcend the elusive element of time, which continues
to move us away from a historical event. Time removes us farther
and farther from that element of history which is vital to our understanding—the impact which the event had upon those most immediately and directly affected. This is of primary importance
if we are to discern the influence of events on later history. Thus
we are obliged first to ask how those immediately affected interpreted the event, and next we must seek to discover how those outside this immediacy have understood it and interpreted its influence upon themselves, their contemporaries, and posterity.

To cite an example outside the concern of this chapter, when
we attempt to interpret a passage from the Old Testament prophets, we should first examine the passage contextually and determine
what it meant to the prophet and his addressees. This level of understanding is basic and extremely vital to our hermeneutics. Then
we must take another step and ask if there are in the Old Testament parallels outside the text at hand. If so, they must be considered in relation to it. Then we must seek to discover whether or
not the New Testament deals at all with it; and if it does, we are

under exegetical obligation to give serious attention to that treatment. We are compelled to admit that there is a hermeneutical development in the Bible itself which cannot be avoided if we are to interpret the Scriptures properly.

We have already spoken of the New Testament treatment of the Old Testament. When we examine the prophets, we find that there is not a great deal of interaction among the writing prophets. In fact, in only one instance does the book of a writing prophet quote another by name. The elders in Jeremiah cite the words of Micah regarding the destruction of Jerusalem (Jer 26:17-18).* So the prophets were not concerned with interpreting each other. Rather, their messages paralleled one another, although there is much evidence of interdependence (e.g., Is 2:2-4 and Mi 4:1-3, to cite one of the most obvious).

We do have, however, in the Old Testament prophets the process which may be seen as the conscious or unconscious formulation of a hermeneutics for Scripture, namely the prophetic use of the history recorded in the Pentateuch. This may be called the prophetic hermeneutics of history. (Another area could be profitably examined, that of legal prescription in the Mosaic Law as cited and interpreted by the prophets. But this would require another study all its own, and has been far more the object of investigation.) We will attempt to look only at certain historical persons and episodes of Israelite history recorded in the Pentateuch as the prophets knew about them.

Chronological Relationship of the Prophets to the Pentateuch

While Jewish tradition subordinated the prophets to the Law of Moses and considered them subsequent to the Pentateuch,[1] Wellhausen, in the nineteenth century, posited the hypothesis that the so-called priestly document and Deuteronomy both largely postdated the prophets, although he saw Jeremiah as the prophetic proponent of Deuteronomy.[2] This position has been modified by

---

*Daniel 9:2 mentions Jeremiah's seventy years, but in the Hebrew canon Daniel is included among the writings and not among the prophets, although he was called a prophet by Jesus (Mt 24:15).

many scholars since Wellhausen (Alt, Mowinckel, Zimmerli, Kaufmann, et al.) .

At the other end of the spectrum stand those who believe the
Pentateuch in whole or in large part predates the prophets. This
position involves a serious treatment of Israelite history as recorded in the Mosaic books and to which the prophets bore witness. The contention of this view is that those historical episodes
recorded there were the primary source of the prophetic knowledge
of Israel's history up to the period of the settlement of Canaan, or
at least the two records have a common source.

The purpose of this essay, however, is not to demonstrate that.
Rather, the aim is to demonstrate that the prophets already exhibited a hermeneutical development in regard to Pentateuchal history. Further, an understanding of this interpretative stage is indispensable to a proper hermeneutics for the Pentateuch and for
subsequent exposition which bears any relationship to Israelite history. Thus, when we approach the prophetic view of Israel's past,
the appropriate question is not, Do we agree with the prophet? but
rather, Do we understand him?

HISTORY AND THEOLOGY

When we use the term *history,* normally the modern connota-
tion is assumed—that history is an objective record of events. The
problem with this assumption is that rarely is history written with
such objectivity. An interpretative element often creeps into the
best of objective attempts. In fact, the question should be asked
whether or not objective history is really possible.

However that may be, we can be sure that the aim of biblical
history was never merely to record events. The prophetic view of
history was unquestionably that events had two perspectives—a horizontal (as it relates to other events, things, and people) , and a ver-
tical (as it relates to God, who stands over history) . The prophets
did not conceive of history merely as events along a horizontal
continuum, but of events along such a continuum in relation to
the Lord of history, Israel's God. The contention of some, then,
is that in the prophets, history (in the modern sense) became the
handmaid of theology and is thus less reliable as a record of events.

Certainly the prophets had no scientific eye for details; but to purport that they would subject details to serve the purpose of their theology, at the expense of historical accuracy, seems quite unfair to them.

On the other hand, to react against this point of view and make the prophets twentieth-century historians is quite as unsatisfactory. They could not be objective, in our understanding of the term. They preached and worked within a God-consciousness which is not characteristic of the modern approach to history. Events outside the pale of divine interaction were simply inconceivable to them.

Thus, the position demanded by a study of the Old Testament prophets is neither of the above, but one which sees historical event and divine interaction as inseparable, parts of a whole, neither of which could exist by itself. History and theology cannot be conceptualized in compartments. The historical narrative "and it came to pass" was no less theological than the prophetic formula "and the word of the Lord was to me." Nor was the latter any less historical than the former. History and theology were not distinct concepts. One of our problems in understanding the prophetic message is that to us these terms have become far too distinct.

This statement does not mean that historical detail cannot be extracted from the prophetic message. On the contrary, it was important to the prophets, because it was bound up with God's interaction. Therefore, to understand the latter, attention to the former is required. Because of this interlacing relationship, historical event (and to the extent that the message required it, historical detail) and religious meaning require review on the same level. That is, the prophet could never put his theology above event and make it serve his theological purpose at the cost of historical accuracy. To misrepresent event was to misconstrue theological meaning.

We are compelled to conclude that, in the prophets, history and theology are not separate categories that would permit subsuming one under the other. Rather, they are like two parts of one circle, and the circle is the thing we seek finally to conceptualize.

Therefore, we seek to move toward an understanding of Pentateuchal history by entering through the door of the prophets. Our thesis is that the prophetic view is the first level of historico-theological understanding, outside the immediacy of the Pentateuch itself, which can lay claim to a clearly formulated historical consciousness. Without doubt the Pentateuch reveals a definite historical consciousness, but the prophets reveal another stage in its development. We can with validity consider the prophets a key to Israel's history as revealed in the Mosaic books. As we will attempt to demonstrate, they were familiar with their historical content, which they interpreted. They captured the historical consciousness already present and developed it further. These spokesmen propagated the spirit of the Pentateuch, preached its message, and called Israel back to her God. They gathered their people around the events recorded and maintained that these events were central to Israel's sense of national identity and an implicit part of their God-consciousness.

For purposes of illustration, we will draw upon prophetic references to the historical episodes of Israelite history prominent in the Pentateuch. Such a study as this cannot be exhaustive. Therefore, we propose to consider only the patriarchal period, the Egyptian bondage, the Exodus, and the wilderness experience.

THE PATRIARCHAL PERIOD

The prophets knew and spoke of the three great patriarchs, progenitors of the nation, Abraham, Isaac, and Jacob. They stood at the roots of national history, and the prophets utilized the personal episodes of their lives in a manner which bore out their significance for later history.

Two major schools of interpretation may be identified in relation to the patriarchal history in the Pentateuch. Those who follow in the train of Hermann Gunkel and Albrecht Alt and may be placed within the form-critical arena, identify the patriarchs with a certain quasi-historical effort of the ancient Hebrews to explain religious truth. The other school, which may claim W. F. Albright as its chief spokesman, has looked to archaeological research for data to confirm or discount the plausibility of the patriarchal period.

Each school has varying degrees of adherence among its exponents. The prophets, fortunately, did not belong to either. For them the patriarchs were real people whose existence they never questioned. To question their existence would have been tantamount to questioning the meaning and significance which their lives bore. Let us then turn to their consideration of the patriarchs.

ABRAHAM

We observe that Abraham received treatment in the prophetic hands of Isaiah and Ezekiel. In fact, Isaiah may have been alluding to that patriarch's immigration from Mesopotamia when he identified the Lord who tendered restoration to Israel as "the LORD, who redeemed Abraham" (Is 29:22). Abraham and Sarah together were mentioned as the source of hope for Israel, as the prophet recalled how the Lord had kept His promise to multiply his descendants (Is 51:2). We should probably understand this as a general reference to the covenant with Abraham (Gen 12:1-3 and 17:1-21; 22:16-18), which was actualized in his son Isaac. His unique relationship to the Lord is further suggested when he is called "my friend" by the Lord (Is 41:8). The divine relationship to Israel in Micah's prophecy was shown to have its origin and base in Abraham and Jacob: "Thou wilt give truth to Jacob and unchanging love to Abraham, which Thou didst swear to our forefathers from the days of old" (Mic 7:20, NASB). The prophet knew of the sealing of this covenant by an oath as recorded in Genesis 22:16, a detail also cited by the writer to the Hebrews (6:13, 17). In Ezekiel's day the people were drawing courage from Abraham's possession of the land (false though their courage was, the historical source they chose to cite was valid enough): "Son of man, they who live in these waste places in the land of Israel are saying, 'Abraham was only one, yet he possessed the land; so to us who are many the land has been given as a possession' " (Eze 33:24, NASB).

ISAAC

To reinforce our thesis that the prophets gathered around Pentateuchal history as the treasury of divine activity among men, their treatment of Isaac revealed his historical significance to have had the same proportions in their historical consciousness as he assumed in the Pentateuch. Even a cursory reading of Genesis reveals that Isaac, the long-awaited son born under unnatural circumstances, fades into the historical background of Genesis while Abraham and Jacob (along with Joseph) occupy the center stage. Interesting in this regard is that the prophets obviously knew and observed the patriarchal balance that we see in the Pentateuch. Only once is Isaac acknowledged in company with Abraham and Jacob (Jer 33:26), and twice in Amos his name is a term for the national identity of Israel (Amos 7:9, 16).

JACOB

We would correctly expect that this name or its subsequent form, Israel, should be found most frequently in prophetic writings, if for no other reason than that he contributed to Israel their name. However, the prophet Hosea was the only one at all interested in the biography of this patriarch. Indeed, Hosea 12 includes a brief record of several events in his life: his taking Esau by the heel at birth (Ho 12:3; cf. Gen 25:26); his struggle with the angel (12:3-4; cf. Gen 32:24-31); the flight to Aram to secure a wife and his service there as a shepherd (12:12; cf. Gen 29:20-21); and his encounter with God at Bethel (12:4; cf. Gen 28:11-17). The purpose of these citations is not easy to determine. However, if we understand Jacob's flight in Genesis to be a consequence of his deceiving his father, and his subsequent encounter with Esau as a kind of punishment for his transgression against his brother, we may also see this patriarchal person as an example of what Israel should not have done but did. The juxtaposition of the story with 12:2 would suggest this: "The LORD also has a dispute with Judah, and will punish Jacob according to his ways; He will repay him according to his deeds" (NASB).

In view of the instances when Jacob encountered God and angels (Gen 28:11-22; 32:1, 22-32; 35:9-15), the titles for God which are related to Jacob's name are worth consideration. The difficulty, of course, is whether they are consciously related to the patriarch or to the national entity. Since the use of the name *Jacob* rather than *Israel* in reference to the nation may be a conscious or unconscious usage to conjure up the historical relation of the nation to the patriarch, we may understand these apellations for God to serve a similar purpose. He is called the God of Jacob (Is 2:3; Mic 4:2),

Holy One of Jacob (Is 29:23), King of Jacob (Is 41:21), Mighty One of Jacob (Is 49:26; 60:16), and Portion of Jacob (Jer 10:16; 51:19). The phrase "God of Abraham, Isaac, and Jacob," identifying the Deity in the Pentateuch and other nonprophetic writings, does not occur in the prophets. Once the three patriarchs are mentioned in the same phrase, but there they are the national progenitors (Jer 33:26). So I submit that at least some of the prophets traced God's special relationship to the nation back to the ancestral father Jacob. Further, in view of the Genesis account of Jacob's encounters with angels and the Deity, this tradition may be seen as consonant with his biography as recorded in Pentateuchal records.

EGYPTIAN BONDAGE

To demonstrate further that the prophets represented a stage in the development of a hermeneutics of history, let us look at their reminiscences of Egyptian enslavement of the Israelites.

Only three prophets had an interest in this era of history. One of them, Amos, mentioned by way of example the pestilence of Egypt: "I sent a plague among you after the manner of Egypt" (Amos 4:10, NASB). Obviously the story of the plagues was common knowledge during this prophet's time. Hosea, with a somewhat similar motivation, drew upon that period and described the imminent captivity by the Assyrians as a return to Egypt with Assyria as the oppressing king (Ho 11:5). He was not alone in the use of this figure of speech, for Deuteronomy 28:68 also describes a return trip to Egypt as a consequence for disobedience to the Mosaic Law. And there, said Moses, the Israelites would offer themselves for sale in the slave market but no one would buy them.

Ezekiel's interest in this period was broader than that of either Amos or Hosea. For him the Egyptian period was the formative stage of Israel's life, the time when God revealed Himself to them: "On the day when I chose Israel and swore to the descendants of the house of Jacob and made Myself known to them in the land of Egypt, when I swore to them, saying, I am the Lord your God" (Eze 20:5, NASB). And this was also God's revelation of Himself to Israel at Sinai (Ex 20:2); on the mountaintop He revealed Himself to Moses and instructed him to convey the word to Israel:

"Say, therefore, to the sons of Israel, 'I am the Lord, and I will bring you out from under the burdens of the Egyptians. . . . Then I will take you for My people, and I will be your God; and you shall know that I am the Lord your God" (Ex 6:6-7, NASB). Very interesting is Ezekiel's own use of the formula, "you shall know that I am the Lord," a knowledge which would result from God's action among and in relation to His people. That was the historical point, for this sixth-century B.C. prophet, when God entered into a particular revelatory relationship with Israel.

On the other hand, the Egyptian period was the soil for another organic development in the nation's life, the origin of their idolatrous inclination (Eze 20:7-8; 23:3, 8, 19-20, 27). The two sisters, Oholah and Oholibah, had practiced idolatry since their days in Egypt. The readiness with which the Israelites requested and accepted gods to lead them in Moses' absence certainly inclines in that direction (Ex 32:1, 4, 8, 23). The tension regarding the golden calf episode in identifying the divine deliverer from Egypt as the Lord or other gods implies that this was a problem which Moses faced at the outset of the wilderness experience. We can understand, then, Ezekiel's identification of the origin of idolatry; not that it originated there in toto, but its roots were anchored in Egypt, and Israel had never lived down that formative experience.

Therefore, Ezekiel saw both the legitimate religion and the illegitimate anchored fast in the Egyptian period of history. God's action in the ancient period was designed to prove that He was the Lord, and His action in the sixth century B.C. was called forth from the same divine motivation.

The Exodus

If the Egyptian bondage was the formative period of the national life, the Exodus was the historical event that solidified this entity as a nation, the point at which the Lord established formal diplomatic relations with Israel, recognizing their national existence. Amos, Isaiah, Hosea, Micah, Jeremiah, and Ezekiel all knew of and mentioned this historical episode. Even Micah and Jeremiah employed the same derogatory term for Egypt, "house of slavery," as occurs in Exodus (13:3, 14; 20:2, NASB) and Deuteronomy

(5:6; 6:12; 7:8; 13:5, 10, NASB). Micah, in pleading with Israel for internal fidelity to the Lord, reminded them: "Indeed, I brought you up from the land of Egypt and ransomed you from the house of slavery, and I sent before you Moses, Aaron, and Miriam" (Mic 6:4, NASB). This was God's primary act to demonstrate His love, power, and identity to the nation. Amos recalled it with similar intent. The Exodus was the one event which bound Israel to responsible existence before her God: "Hear this word which the Lord has spoken against you, sons of Israel, against the entire family which He brought up from the land of Egypt, 'You only have Me among all the families of the earth; therefore, I will punish you for all your iniquities' " (Amos 3:1-2, NASB). Further, the Exodus was one of the divine feats that should have elicited a response of gratitude from Israel, but it did not (Amos 2:10).

Amos' successor, Hosea, understood the Exodus in precisely the same way—the Exodus was an act of God's love for Israel, but the response was disappointingly negative: "When Israel was a youth I loved him, and out of Egypt I called My son. The more they [God's prophets] called them, the more they went from them; they kept sacrificing to the Baals and burning incense to idols" (Ho 11:1-2, NASB).

The moral and religious climate of the nation was not a recent development. Its tendrils extended historically to the great events in national history, which events became the poles for the prophets' religio-historical consciousness.

The prophets Isaiah and Jeremiah, however, recalled the Exodus not as a reason for moral obedience or the point of reference for religious fidelity, but as a historical event which was a prototype of a yet greater event in the future, the new exodus. It became for these prophets an occasion for eschatological prediction of regathering from the dispersion under more joyful and less treacherous circumstances (Is 35:8-10). Moreover, Isaiah and Jeremiah envisioned the future return as far more glorious and miraculous than the first Exodus: "Do not call to mind the former things, or ponder things of the past. Behold, I will do something new, now it will spring forth; will you not be aware of it? I will even make a roadway in the wilderness, rivers in the desert" (Is 43:18-19,

NASB). Isaiah 51:10-11 revealed the same motivation for reminiscing about the historical Exodus—it served as an occasion for predicting the future exodus, that is, the return from exile.

Jeremiah too understood the first Exodus to be a signpost pointing to a greater one: " 'Therefore behold, the days are coming,' declares the LORD, 'when they will no longer say, "As the LORD lives, who brought up the sons of Israel from the land of Egypt," but, "As the LORD lives, who brought up and led back the descendants of the household of Israel from the north land and from all the countries where I had driven them." Then they will live on their own soil' " (Jer 23:7-8, NASB). Both Jeremiah and Isaiah represent a new level in the historical consciousness of Israel. They foresaw a new landmark to be established in the historical life of the nation. This certainly is illustrative of the hermeneutics of history which developed in prophetic thought; the method is clearly delineated in this example.

As we have already seen, the past was the arena in which the prophets saw the formative stages of national history. In fact, their message made little sense if divorced from it. The anteroom was a significant and integral part of the architectural design of Israel's history. So much so was this true, that not only the times contemporaneous with the prophets but also the rest of history must be understood in relation to it. The Egyptian slavery, as already noted, became the photographic negative from which the image of the Assyrian captivity was envisioned in Hosea's thinking (Ho 11:5). In the same way, the Exodus from Egypt was the negative from which Isaiah and Jeremiah developed their beautiful picture of the return. Hosea even had a keen interest in the prophetic nature of that deliverance, a fact which he saw as lending validity and credibility to his own activity: "But by a prophet the LORD brought Israel from Egypt, and by a prophet he was kept" (Ho 12:13, NASB).

The prophets saw the coming of a new age. They projected into the future their hopes which had not been fully realized in the past and present eras. As one commentator has observed, it was not basically out of a dissatisfaction with the present that the prophets predicted a new age, but rather the recognition that only that age could completely usher in what they had already tasted as reality.[3]

Wilderness Period

We have yet another illustration to offer of the prophets' hermeneutics of history—their treatment of the wilderness experience. As with the Exodus, we begin with Amos, whose historical memory included the wilderness period also. He knew of the forty years' wandering (Amos 2:10; 5:25), yet the wilderness was only preparatory for Israel's possession of Canaan: "And it was I who brought you up from the land of Egypt, and I led you in the wilderness forty years that you might take possession of the land of the Amorite" (Amos 2:10, NASB). This prophet made no particular moral pronouncements about the wilderness period, except to say that God's leadership there was worthy of an appropriate response of gratitude from Israel. So he was rather positive toward that historical period.

Even more explicit in his attitude was Jeremiah, who saw the wilderness wandering as a rather ideal time in the national records: "I remember concerning you the devotion of your youth, the love of your betrothals, your following after Me in the wilderness, through a land not sown" (Jer 2:2, NASB). Yet he was not so enamored by the honeymoon that he wished Israel could make a geographical and chronological backtrack. He did, however, desire a spiritual return to the "devotion of your youth" and "the love of your betrothals." That is, the relationship between Israel and the Lord during the wilderness period was for Jeremiah the ideal point of their historical love affair.

Ezekiel obviously understood it in the same way, as the time of youth and love. He was more explicit even than Jeremiah in regard to what had made it so—the Lord had entered into a covenant with the nation: " 'Then I passed by you and saw you, and behold, you were at the time for love; . . . I also swore to you and entered into a covenant with you so that you became Mine,' declares the Lord God" (Eze 16:8, NASB). He made the Sinai experience central again in 20:10-12.

Hosea too saw the wilderness as a time of obedience (2:15). It has been suggested that he expected a geographical return to the wilderness,[4] for after the list of punishments which the Lord had purposed to execute on Israel (Ho 2:6-13), he added: "Therefore, behold, I will allure her, bring her into the wilderness, and speak kindly to her" (Ho 2:14, NASB).

Upon an examination of Hosea alone, we might be inclined to go along with this suggestion. But when we look at the language of Isaiah and Ezekiel, we discover that they thought of the exile as a wilderness experience. Isaiah viewed the purpose of the exile to be to bring Israel to a recognition that the Lord is God. In the final analysis, both the exile and return were aimed toward the confession, "that you may know and believe Me, and understand that I am He. Before Me there was no God formed, and there will be none after Me. I, even I, am the LORD; and there is no savior besides Me" (Is 43:10-11, NASB). While the imagery of the wilderness is absent here, it may be present in Isaiah 1:26: "Then I will restore your judges as at the first, and your counselors as at the beginning; after that you will be called the city of righteousness, a faithful city."

The language descriptive of the wilderness is unequivocally present in Ezekiel's prophecy. After relating the spiritual failure of both generations in the wilderness (20:13-26), he promised that the Lord would bring Israel into "the wilderness of the peoples, and there I shall enter into judgment with you face to face" (Eze 20:35, NASB). It would be a time of spiritual purge, as in the first wilderness (Num 14:13-25).

Both Hosea and Micah recalled the negative quality of the wilderness—the former, the divine care, followed by the ungrateful reaction of the people (Ho 13:5-6; cf. Deu 8:15; 31:20; 32:15); and the latter, the apostasy provoked by Balaam and Balak (Mic 6:5; cf. Num 22-24).

Now we may look more specifically at what the wilderness period became in the prophets' hermeneutics of history. Isaiah evidently viewed this time as one of suffering and physical hardship, because when he envisioned the return from exile he described the wilderness through which the people passed as transformed into an oasis (Is 35:1-10). Through it would run no mere trade route for merchants but "a highway will be there, a roadway, and it will be called 'the highway of holiness.' The unclean will not travel on it, but it will be for him who walks that way, and fools will not wander on it" (Is 35:8, NASB). Again he did what he did so well with the Exodus. He made it a photographic negative from which he developed his picture of a more glorious future event. This seems to be the approximate intent of Hosea 12:9, where the Lord says He will make them "live in tents again, as in the days of the appointed festival" (NASB).

Ezekiel performed this same kind of interpretative maneuver with the wilderness, as we have already observed in 20:35-36. While in 16:60 no mention of the wilderness occurs, the covenant is spoken of, and it concerns the youth of Israel's life. This prophet used the occasion of the covenant at Sinai to speak of the everlasting covenant which the Lord would establish with Israel.

It is quite understandable that the wilderness could represent two things to the prophets. The covenant was given there, and the judgment of the Lord dispensed because of the people's sins and disobedience. Unquestionably it came to represent both an ideal time—a kind of spiritual axis—and an unromantic place where disobedience marred the historical conscience.

A Principle of Hermeneutics

Having observed the prophetic treatment of such historical events as the Exodus and wilderness, we may formulate a basic principle for interpreting the prophets. The description of the new exodus by Isaiah (52:1-12) can hardly be removed from its historical connections and made merely an eschatological event. When the prophets spoke of the new exodus, they had two historical events clearly in mind: the Exodus from Egyptian slavery and the return from exilic slavery. Old Testament prophecy cannot be spiritualized to the extent of depriving it of its historical meaning. To do this is a contempt of history itself and a blatant disregard for the realm in which theological truth is incarnated in historical event, the world of God's own creation. The prophetic message was never a helium-filled balloon that hovered above the earth without touching it. The prophets rooted their message in the

world of people, things, and events. The roots would always remain there. So prophetic eschatology grew out of the soil of history
and was dependent upon that source for sustenance, for meaning.

The analogy may be developed further by saying that prophecy
is like a tree that has its roots anchored in history, and the foliage
and flowers of the plant must always be considered and admired
in relation to the roots and soil by which they are sustained. That
is, historical event and eschatology are organically one. We would
certainly not contend that the two are indistinguishable, but they
are definitely interrelated and interdependent. Therefore, to deny
to a passage such as Isaiah 52:1-12 a historical interpretation is to
deprive it of vital meaning. Yet if we deny the universal tenor
(52:10) and the ultimate establishment of the Kingdom of God
(52:6-7) which are suggested by the prophet, we have committed
an injustice in the other direction. The prophecy then predicts the
historical return from exile and suggests that even that event will
not exhaust the good which the Lord intends to do for His people.

Therefore, our principle may be expressed thus: prophecy is *one*,
a unity, and its meaning is a unity. That unity may bear the nature
of "the whole equals the sum of the parts," but the parts must be
viewed with reference to the whole. Both historical event and
eschatological event may be included in the whole. We should not,
however, force every prophecy to have such a dual nature. If we
can interpret a passage historically, sound exegetical principles
and the gravity of the meaning of history in the Bible obligate us
to interpret historically. However, on the basis of the language of
a passage we may confront difficulty in following a strictly historical
interpretation. Then we may consider whether or not the language
(such as eschatological expressions, concepts of universal salvation
and judgment, symbolism, and New Testament interpretations of
the passage if there are any) would incline toward eschatological
considerations.

If we may digress from our consideration of the new exodus in
Isaiah 52, a passage in the prophecy of Zephaniah beautifully illustrates this hermeneutical principle that prophecy is a unity, and
the whole must be viewed in terms of the sum of its parts. Zephaniah 1:2-3 and 3:8 form an inclusion dealing with universal judg-

ment. That is the whole, the main thrust of the prophecy. The language of 1:2-3 describes an eschatological event when God will deal with all of mankind: " 'I will completely remove all things from the face of the earth,' declares the LORD. 'I will remove man and beast; I will remove the birds of the sky and the fish of the sea, and the ruins along with the wicked; and I will cut off man from the face of the earth,' declares the LORD." And 3:8 ends the section on the same note of universal judgment: " 'Therefore, wait for Me,' declares the LORD, 'for the day when I rise up to the prey. Indeed, My decision is to gather nations, to assemble kingdoms, to pour out on them My indignation, all My burning anger; for all the earth will be devoured by the fire of My zeal.' "

However, in 1:4, Zephaniah began delineating that judgment in terms of historical entities, with a universal passage breaking in again at 1:14-18. That is, universal judgment can be understood only in terms of history, but even the historical entities of the prophet's time could not exhaust its meaning. The judgment obviously began in the seventh and sixth centuries B.C., but it will not end or be completely dispensed until all of mankind has tasted its bitterness. This is a telescopic way of viewing time, to be sure, but as one commentator has remarked, biblical prophecy has height and breadth but not much concern with depth.[5] It is this eschatological judgment that the Revelation of John and other New Testament passages vividly describe. Thus we might diagram the inclusion as follows:

UNIVERSAL JUDGMENT = U

(1:2-3)   (1:14-18)   3:8

A = Judah (1:4-13)	B = Philistines (2:4-7)	C = Moab and Ammon (2:8-11)
A$_1$ = Judah (2:1-3)		D = Ethiopians (2:12)
A$_2$ = Jerusalem and Judah (3:1-7)		E = Assyria (2:13-15)

Thus, U = A + A$_1$ + A$_2$ + B + C + D + E.

To return to Isaiah, now, and look briefly at 52:1-12 again: we may understand the fulfillment to have begun at the historical return from exile and to continue into the eschatological age which the New Testament generally indicates to have been initiated by the first advent of Christ and to be completed only at the second advent.

CONCLUSION

We may reiterate our thesis that in regard to the nation's history, the prophets represent a level of thought that was highly developed and may be called a hermeneutics of history. They viewed the historical process in stages, and those different phases were pivotal points for their understanding of contemporary events and their foretelling future episodes of history. Indeed, the prophetic acumen for reading the past clearly and interpreting its meaning for their present time was a validation of their prophetic office. No prophet who did not know the past could predict the future, for it was only from that source that the Lord's relations with His people could be discerned and His present and future actions be understood and validated.

Of course, from the foregoing discussion it is clear that the main source of prophetic history was those eras represented by Pentateuchal history. Israel's historical consciousness was rooted in those events which we know through the Pentateuch. Further, the level of development in the method of interpreting that history was advanced significantly enough to set it largely apart from the historical consciousness of the Pentateuch. While we do have eschatological concerns there, in the prophets these have assumed a form that clearly demonstrates a sense of history that is a product of the historical process we observe in the patriarchal, slavery, Exodus, and wilderness periods. Both the Exodus and wilderness, and in a lesser sense the Egyptian slavery, have become not only pivotal historical episodes but the photographic negatives from which the prophets, by the inspiration of their God, developed the beautiful eschatological pictures of the future. This kind of history represented an advanced stage of a hermeneutics of history in the Old

Testament prophets. The same method was used by the New Testament writers, but they were indebted to the prophets, whose historical consciousness was unsurpassed by any other Old Testament group of spokesmen.

5

The Old Testament in the New Testament

by Donald A. Hagner

EVERY READER of the New Testament is aware of the frequency of Old Testament quotation in the New Testament writings. There are, in fact, somewhere between two and three hundred actual quotations of the Old Testament in the New Testament. Beyond this, of course, there is a great amount of allusive material, some of which is deliberate, and some of which is unconscious, though nonetheless real.

The New Testament writers were thoroughly immersed in the Holy Scriptures which had been handed down to them by their forefathers. They lived and breathed the content of these writings, particularly the recital of God's saving activity in behalf of Israel and the covenant promises concerning the future of God's people. When they were confronted with the ministry of Jesus—its proclamation by word and deed of the presence of the Kingdom—they were, as we would say, "programmed" to understand it as the consummation of God's saving activity and the fulfillment of the covenant promises. Thus, when they came to narrate the story of Christ in the gospels and the meaning of that story in the epistles, these writers continually made use of the Old Testament to show that what had so recently taken place in their midst was in fact the goal of Old Testament anticipation. In perceiving the unity of the Bible thus evidenced, the Christian Church rightly affirms, following St. Augustine, that the New Testament lies hidden in the Old, and the Old becomes manifest in the New.

But the way in which the Old Testament is made manifest in

78

the New has often caused difficulty for Christian readers of the Bible. We have all had the experience of encountering an Old Testament quotation in the New Testament which, when we looked it up in the Old Testament, was found to differ in wording quite considerably from its occurrence in the New Testament, or which seemed to violate the sense of the Old Testament passage in its larger context, or which in some other way seemed to be arbitrary and unjustifiable. Our purpose here is to look into the subject of Old Testament quotations in order to suggest lines along which the solutions to these difficulties may lie. This will involve us in questions of text, hermeneutics, and apologetics; and in the process we shall hope to discover more of the mind of the New Testament writers in terms of their perception of the relationship between the two Testaments.

In any attempt to understand the writers of the New Testament (or the Old Testament, for that matter) it must be insisted upon that we make every effort to enter their world, to stand in their shoes, and to perceive, think, and feel as they did. This is true not only as the foundational principle of exegesis, but also with respect to our present concerns.

FREEDOM OF QUOTATION

Exact, verbatim quotation was generally foreign to the spirit of the Graeco-Roman world of the first century A.D. In our modern world, we are constantly confronted not only with the accuracy of scientific measurement, but also with the exactness of the printed word, and the precise use of quotation marks delimiting material borrowed verbatim from a writer's sources. These things were either unknown or of no actual consequence in the ancient world. Careful and accurate copying of the Scriptures was known, but did not carry over into the use of the Scriptures. The copies of Torah were a special matter of sacrosanctity. Direct discourse was sometimes indicated by the recitative *hoti,* but this served only to point out the beginning of a quotation, not its end.[1]

Today we attach very great importance to word-for-word accuracy in quotation. It is quite evident that this was not a real concern in the New Testament period. One need only remember the difficulty of passages in the synoptic gospels where the words of Jesus occur in two or three parallel accounts but with considerable variations. It is true that some of the variations may be explained as alternative translations of the same underlying Aramaic. However, not all the variations are thus accountable, and unless one takes the route of harmonizing every such instance (i.e., arguing that very similar things were spoken or done on different occasions), one is left with some freedom on the part of the Gospel writers in presenting the words of Jesus.

In the gospel of John there is the well-known problem of where the words of Jesus leave off, and where the words of John begin (John 3:10ff.). The RSV closes the quotation at the end of verse 15; NASB and NEB close it at verse 21. The KJV skirts such problems by simply avoiding quotation marks (its usual practice). In 1 Thessalonians 4:15ff., it is not clear how much of Paul's declaration is to be understood as "the word of the Lord." Nothing was more authoritative in the early Church than the words of Jesus, and yet even in our New Testament there is little concern for verbatim reporting of those words. There is a vital concern for accurate representation of the message of Jesus, but this was not understood to demand the *ipsissima verba* of Jesus. It is not our purpose to deny that verbatim or very nearly verbatim reports of the words of Jesus are ever found in the gospel narratives. Our main point is that a verbatim account was not considered *necessary* to an accurate representation of what Jesus said. This is also reflected by the popularity of oral tradition even after written gospels were available. Oral tradition containing the sayings of Jesus, although it varied from place to place, was reasonably stable and some preferred it over the written gospels. Papias is reported as saying (at the beginning of the second century), "I did not suppose that information from books would help me so much as the word of a living and surviving voice."[2] The early apostolic Fathers similarly cited oral tradition rather than the written gospels when they quoted the sayings of Jesus.[3]

If the Church exhibited little concern for the verbatim words of Jesus when it treasured His authority above all others, we may expect that the early Christians in their use of the Old Testament, which they also treasured as the Word of God, may similarly have been unconcerned with verbatim quotation. This is in fact what we find as we look at the quotations in the New Testament. What was regarded as important was not the precise wording of a passage, but rather the sense of the passage.[4] Here too, as with the words of Jesus, citation from memory seems to have been the rule.

Man's capacity for memory was considerably more practiced in the ancient world than it is today.[5] The unavailability of the written word, because of the high cost of hand-copied manuscripts, made the use of memory a necessity. Even when copies of Old Testament writings were available, they would have consisted of scrolls which had to be unwound and rewound as they were read or consulted, thus making reference a very demanding task. Added to this difficulty was the fact that the text itself was without chapter or verse divisions. All of this contributed to the acceptability, if not desirability, of memory citation.

Now, despite the fact that the memory was more developed in that era, it was by no means flawless in the sense that it could consistently come up with verbatim reproduction of an Old Testament passage. On occasion it may well have been able to do so. But for the most part, memory produced a fair representation of the passage not dissimilar to what our less practiced memories today will provide. Very often when we quote from memory, the sense of the passage is clear enough, but we should not like to be held responsible for its exact wording.

The point which must be stressed, however, is that verbatim citation, a procedure so familiar and important to us today, was no matter of concern in the New Testament period. There are instances, to be sure, when a particular single word in an Old Testament passage may be of crucial importance for the argument of a New Testament writer. For example, Paul's argument in Galatians 3:16 depends not only upon the meaning of the word *seed* (*zera,* Heb.; *sperma,* Gk.) as found in Genesis, but also upon the singular form of the word (despite the fact that the singular is here a collective). Similarly, Matthew's application of Isaiah 7:14 to the birth of Jesus (1:23) may be said to depend upon the Septuagint's word *parthenos,* "virgin." But these are the exceptions rather than the rule. A precise word or phrase may at times have been of central importance; but much more often than not, the importance lay in the sense of the passage as effectively conveyed by free quotation.

As we shall see, however, the freedom of quotation as it conveyed the sense of the Old Testament passage was neither haphazard nor capricious. It was carefully informed and guided by the Church's understanding of the events and the significance of the events that on the one hand were the fulfillment of the Old Testament promise, and on the other hand that now constituted the basis of the kerygma which it was the Church's mission to proclaim.

THE TEXT OF THE QUOTATIONS

Although free rather than exact quotation is common in the Old Testament quotations found in the New Testament, it is often possible to discover the underlying text form which served as the writer's source. Three main possibilities present themselves as sources of these quotations: (1) a Hebrew text, whether non-Masoretic or proto-Masoretic;* (2) a Greek text from the Septuagint tradition or parallel to that tradition;† and (3) an Aramaic targum text (whether oral or written) reflecting the interpretive, paraphrastic translations in use during the New Testament period.‡ As materials for the comparison of texts, we have (1) the standard Masoretic Hebrew text, and now, thanks to the discoveries beside the Dead Sea at Qumran, portions of the Hebrew

---

*Before the Dead Sea Scrolls were discovered in 1947, the earliest manuscripts of the Hebrew Bible dated from the tenth century A.D. They were produced by Jewish scholars (Masoretes) who added the vowel signs to the consonantal text during the seventh century. They were also responsible for the careful transmission of the text into the Middle Ages. The Hebrew text of the first century A.D. is often called the proto-Masoretic text insofar as it resembles the later text. See E. Würthwein, *The Text of the Old Testament* (Oxford: Blackwell, 1957).

†The Septuagint is the Greek translation of the Hebrew Bible. According to tradition (*The Letter of Aristeas*), it was begun in the third century B.C. and was completed before the New Testament era. There has been much debate on its early history, and the possibility of Greek translations other than what has come down to us must be reckoned with. See S. Jellicoe, *The Septuagint and Modern Study* (Oxford: Clarendon, 1968).

‡Aramaic targums (translations) came into existence in the centuries prior to the New Testament era when the Aramaic-speaking populace began to forget the Hebrew language. The influence of Aramaic began with the settlement of the Northern Kingdom after 721 B.C. and grew during the following centuries. By the first century A.D., Hebrew was apparently used only in liturgy and rabbinic scholarship.

Scriptures, both in proto-Masoretic text form and in the text form reflected in the Septuagint; (2) our manuscripts of the Septuagint which in complete form date from the fourth century A.D.; and (3) manuscripts of targums of the Pentateuch and the prophets, which in complete form date from the fifteenth and sixteenth centuries A.D., but which in various ways are attested in the Middle Ages and earlier.[6]

As we seek to understand the writers of our New Testament and their use of the Scriptures, we must remind ourselves of the varied and complex textual traditions that were available to them. The message of the Scriptures was available not only in three different languages, but often in variant forms in each language. Today we are used to a relatively stable textual tradition for both Testaments (i.e., the eclectic, critical texts represented for example by Kittel's Hebrew edition and Nestle's Greek edition), and it is difficult to appreciate the situation of the first century. We may, however, catch at least a glimmer of that complex situation by thinking of the diversity reflected in our English translations of the Bible, especially if we consider the more paraphrastic translations of, say, J. B. Phillips, or Kenneth Taylor in the *Living Bible,* alongside the free *New English Bible* and the literalistic *American Standard Version* of 1901. But the parallel is only a partial one since these are all English translations and are all essentially based on the same relatively stable textual substratum. With the consideration of translations in different languages and the lack of a fully stable substratum for any of them, the situation immediately becomes much more complex.

It would be wrong to imagine the New Testament writers at every point carefully reviewing the available Hebrew, Greek, and Aramaic sources and then specifically choosing which to make use of in a particular quotation. Quite the contrary. Not only is this out of sympathy with the mood of the times, as we have seen, but it fails to appreciate the importance of a primary datum—that Greek was the *lingua franca* of the Mediterranean world and the language used in the writing of the New Testament. Now, when one is writing in Greek and desires to quote the Scriptures in Greek, it is only natural that existing Greek translations currently used

by the Jews of the Dispersion should come to mind. Thus it does
not come as a great surprise to discover that a very high percentage
of Old Testament quotations in the New Testament reflect dependence upon the septuagintal tradition. Quotations in Luke-
Acts and Hebrews follow the Septuagintal tradition very closely.
Other writers, such as Paul and Mark, do not adhere to it quite
as faithfully, although they often depend on it. The influence of
the Hebrew Scriptures and the Aramaic targums, where it can be
detected, is clearly exceptional rather than normal, and we are
justified in looking for particular reasons for the preference of such
textual traditions over the Septuagintal tradition.

We have already referred to the fact that the Aramaic targums
are interpretive translations. This is particularly the case with the
Palestinian Targum of the Pentateuch as compared with the more
literal Targum of the same material by Onkelos. What we have
not yet mentioned is the relationship between our Septuagintal
tradition and the Hebrew Masoretic tradition. The relationship
is complex for the simple reason that the translations which make
up our Septuagint were evidently made by a number of persons
of varying ability and over a lengthy period of time.

In comparing the Septuagint translations with the Masoretic
Hebrew text (and supposing that something like the Masoretic
text constituted the Hebrew text being translated), it has been
noted that while the Pentateuch has been translated very carefully
(this is probably explained by its preeminence in the Hebrew
canon), the translations of certain prophetical and historical books
were relatively poor, and the translations of the wisdom writings
of Job and Proverbs were markedly free and paraphrastic. Particularly puzzling were those translations which were for the most part
carefully literal, yet here and there departed radically from our
Masoretic Hebrew text form. The Septuagint translation of Jeremiah, for example, not only drastically differs in the order of the
contents of the Masoretic text, but also lacks material to the extent
that it is one-eighth shorter than the Masoretic text.

Wherever the Septuagint translation diverged significantly from
the proto-Masoretic text, the divergence was in the past attributed
to the industry of the translators despite the obscurity of their pos-

sible motivations. All this changed suddenly when among the discoveries at Qumran were found fragmentary manuscripts of such books as Samuel and Jeremiah in Hebrew which agreed closely with the Septuagint both in text-type and abridgment or alteration of order. The conclusion which has been drawn from the discovery of these manuscripts is that the Septuagintal text, where it differs from the proto-Masoretic text, is not the result of the caprice of the translators, but depends on an early non-Masoretic Hebrew recension which existed alongside the proto-Masoretic recension.[7] Thus the Septuagint, with the authority of an identifiable Hebrew substratum, has gained a new respectability.[8]

As already indicated, it was normal for the authors of the New Testament, who were writing in Greek, to employ the Septuagint translation when they quoted the Old Testament. The Septuagint translation was, after all, a Jewish product, having been completed about a century before the time of Christ, and enjoying a widespread popularity among Jews who knew the language of Alexander better than that of Moses. Only after the Christians had made such effective use of the Septuagint in arguing the truth of their faith did the Jews become disillusioned with the Septuagint, ban it from Jewish use,§ and set about producing alternative Greek translations of the proto-Masoretic text which purposely avoided possible Christian interpretations.||

This use of the Septuagint by New Testament writers will often account for our puzzlement at the lack of agreement in wording between a quotation in the New Testament and its Old Testament source as we study our English Bible. Our Old Testament is invariably an English translation of the Hebrew Masoretic text; in

§This was a radical departure from the earlier glowing approbation of the Septuagint (referring to the Pentateuch only) in the legend contained in the *Letter of Aristeas*, according to which the seventy-two translators (six from each tribe of Israel) worked exactly seventy-two days to produce a divinely superintended translation.

||The second century A.D. versions thus produced are: (1) Aquila, characterized by extreme literalness; (2) Theodotion, whose work was perhaps more revisional than original (and whose translation of Daniel was accepted by the Church over against the Old Septuagint translation, which was markedly inferior); (3) Symmachus, an Ebionite, who attempted to produce a translation of literary merit of which very little has survived. See B. J. Roberts, *The Old Testament Text and Versions* (Cardiff: U. of Wales, 1951).

most instances our quotation in the New Testament is an English translation of the Greek of the Septuagint text. This will obviously produce variation in actual wording, although we often find that the sense is substantially the same.

At times, however, the Septuagint will differ more significantly from the Masoretic text, and here our problems are more serious. A classic example of a difference between Septuagint and Masoretic texts which is reflected in a New Testament quotation is the use of Isaiah 7:14 in Matthew 1:23. There the Septuagint word *parthenos* specifically indicates that it is a *virgin* who is to conceive and bear a son, whereas the Hebrew word *'almah*, meaning "young woman" (and not *bethulah*, meaning "virgin") is used. But the fact that Jewish translators more than a century before Christ chose *parthenos* to translate *'almah* indicates not only that "virgin" is a legitimate translation, but that it was then regarded as the most appropriate word to use. #

Another example of a Septuagint reading in the New Testament which differs from the Masoretic text is to be found in the citation of James at the Jerusalem Council recorded in Acts 15:16-18. In addition to a few interesting but not very significant variations, there is the clause, "that the rest of mankind may seek the Lord" which in the Masoretic text of our Old Testament reads, "that they may possess the remnant of Edom" (Amos 9:12). There are three key differences: (1) in the Masoretic text, "remnant" is clearly the object of the clause; in the Septuagint it is the subject; (2) in the Masoretic text "Edom" qualifies "remnant"; in the Septuagint the qualifier is "men"; and (3) the verb in the Masoretic text is "may possess"; in the Septuagint it is "may seek." This is an example of the Septuagint's dependence on a Hebrew text other than the proto-Masoretic, although in any case the differences that would be required in the Hebrew are very minor: (1) omission of the objectifying particle *eth;* (2) addition of one letter changing *yireshu* (may inherit) to *yidreshu* (may seek); (3) use of different vowel points changing *edom* to *adam* (man). The Septuagint

#Although *neanis* (young woman) does not occur in the Septuagint of Isaiah, there can be no doubt that it was known to the translator(s) and thus they could have used it (cf. their relatively frequent use of *neaniskos*, "young man"). The later Jewish translations, of course, avoided the word *parthenos*.

reading quoted by James will be seen to be particularly effective in his argument that the conversion of the Gentiles is the fulfillment of Amos' prophecy.

As a final example we may refer to Hebrews 1:6: "And again, when he brings the first-born into the world, he says, 'Let all God's angels worship him'" (RSV). The last six words reflect the Septuagint text of Deuteronomy 32:43, which is considerably fuller than the Masoretic text of the same verse. Indeed, upon consulting our English Old Testament (reflecting the Masoretic text) we will be frustrated at finding no material which corresponds to our quotation in the New Testament.

The examples we have given may be regarded as representative of the impact of the Septuagint tradition upon the New Testament. (For further conspicuous examples, see Ac 2:25-28 quoting Ps 16:8-11, and 1 Co 15:54-55 quoting Ho 13:14.) Quite frequently a knowledge of that tradition will help us in difficulties posed by Old Testament quotations. The use of the Septuagint is so prevalent throughout the New Testament[9] that we would not be far off the mark in referring to the Septuagint as the Bible of the early Church. In addition to the actual quotations, the influence of the Septuagint upon the New Testament in terms of allusory language, specific vocabulary, and conceptuality is incalculable.[10]

The importance of the Septuagint in the first century is primarily due to the reality of Greek as the language which united the Mediterranean world. But the linguistic scene was nonetheless a complicated one, and most Jews were bilingual and perhaps even trilingual.[11] In this kind of situation one may expect that the quotations of the Old Testament in the New Testament would at times reveal the influence of Aramaic targums and the proto-Masoretic Hebrew textual tradition.

Although the influence of the Aramaic targums on New Testament phraseology seems to have been quite extensive,[12] the actual impact of the targums in the Old Testament quotations has often been difficult to substantiate owing to the complexity of the whole matter. However, a couple of examples will illustrate that this is a factor which must be given serious consideration.[13] The citation of Isaiah 6:9 in Mark 4:12 agrees neither with the Masoretic nor the Septuagint text. The citation has the third person pronoun "*they* may indeed perceive" for the second person "you" and also has the phrase "and it be forgiven them" for "be healed" (active, "I heal them," in the Septuagint). But the text of Isaiah 6:9 as it is found in the Targum of Jonathan agrees exactly with the text of the quotation as found in Mark.

Another instance where there is evidence of a targumic text supporting a quotation in the New Testament which differs from both the Masoretic and Septuagint traditions is to be found in the quotation of Psalm 68:18 in Ephesians 4:8. The Targum of the Psalms agrees with the New Testament in that gifts were *given* to men, whereas the Masoretic and Septuagint traditions have the gifts being *received* rather than given. These examples suggest that careful scrutiny of the Targums may well solve problems created wherever the Old Testament quotation in the New Testament differs from both the Septuagint and Masoretic traditions.

Many quotations in the New Testament agree exactly with *both* the Masoretic and Septuagint texts. In these instances, as we look up the Old Testament reference, we find the text in complete accord with our quotation and we encounter no problems. Probably we are to assume that the New Testament writer was dependent on the Septuagint text, which here coincides exactly with the Masoretic. There are, of course, numerous other instances where a quotation in the New Testament will be found to agree with the Masoretic text *against* that of the Septuagint. Since, as we have stated, we ordinarily expect the quotations in the New Testament to reflect dependence upon the Septuagint, we may here entertain the notion that our writer has used the equivalent of the Hebrew/Masoretic text directly, or at least has had some kind of indirect access to its contents. So far as formal quotations are concerned, only one strand of New Testament material rather consistently reflects what may be called a mixed text form rather than the Septuagintal text form.** This is the group of some twenty formal

---

** R. H. Gundry, in calling attention to the mixed text form of the allusive material in Mark, has argued that in the synoptic tradition it is the formal quotations in Mark that are peculiar in having a consistently septuagintal text form. See Gundry, *The Use of the Old Testament in St. Matthew's Gospel* (Leiden: Brill, 1967).

quotations peculiar to the gospel of Matthew, as contrasted with the Septuagintal nature of the quotations which are borrowed by Matthew from the Marcan tradition.

Among these formal quotations in Matthew, we may cite the following examples of the apparent influence of the Hebrew text on quotations as they exist in the Greek of Matthew: Matthew 2:6, quoting Micah 5:2; Matthew 4:15-16, quoting Isaiah 9:1-2; Matthew 8:17, quoting Isaiah 53:4; Matthew 27:9-10, quoting Zechariah 11:12-13. Examination of these examples will reveal that the text of the quotation does not agree exactly or completely with that of the Masoretic Hebrew text. The text type is a mixed one, yet at significant points it will be seen to agree with the Masoretic text against that of the Septuagint. Agreement with the Masoretic text is, of course, no concern or problem to the average reader, since after all his English Old Testament is a translation of the Masoretic text.

In summary, we have seen that the various text forms in which the Old Testament was available to writers of the New Testament often explains apparent divergences in specific Old Testament quotations. Thus to understand the textual makeup of these quotations we must be aware of the major sources, viz., the proto-Masoretic Hebrew, the Greek Septuagint, the Aramaic Targums (as well as other sources of much less importance which we have not mentioned), while remembering that our English Old Testaments invariably are translations of the Masoretic tradition. This knowledge will take us a good distance toward our goal, but we will still fall somewhat short. The fact is that we must continually reckon with the reality of paraphrase, in keeping with what we argued in the first section, both deliberate and from memory. The latter especially will often result in the combination or the conflation of different Old Testament passages thus causing us problems and sometimes making the quest for source next to impossible. For example, the quotation in 1 Corinthians 2:9 looks as though it is a free rendering of Isaiah 64:4 with some conflation of the Septuagint of Isaiah 65:16. A famous example of combination is the quotation of Malachi 3:1 and Isaiah 40:3 in Mark 1:2, with the quoted material being introduced as from Isaiah the prophet. Compare the quotation of Zechariah 11:13 in Matthew 27:9 ascribed to Jeremiah (but see Jer 18:1-3). It is possible that this phenomenon is to be explained by dependence upon early collections of prophetic passages useful to the Christian apologetic which have been named "testimony books."[14]

There is one further factor which often has a natural, if at times unpredictable, bearing on the text of a quotation—that is, the interpretation of the Old Testament material by the New Testament writer. Not only would the writer's interpretative perspective occasionally determine which of the various available text forms he would choose for his quotation, but often the New Testament writer himself did not hesitate to make creative adaptations of the quoted matter in order to heighten the effectiveness of the quotation. R. H. Gundry has convincingly argued that the process of targumizing or paraphrasing the Old Testament text, with which the Jews of the first century were very familiar, carried over into the early Church quite readily, and was used freely by Christian preachers and writers. Thus he states that Matthew's Old Testament quotations reveal the Targumic activity of Matthew himself.[15] Similarly, E. E. Ellis has shown that many of Paul's Old Testament quotations contain ad hoc renderings along the lines of what Ellis calls "midrash pesher," or paraphrastic interpretation governed by the fulfillment motif.[16]

In this type of approach to the Old Testament materials, the New Testament writers reveal that their interests lay not in the letter of the Old Testament text but in its meaning—and more particularly, its meaning as apprehended in the light of the fulfillment which has come in Jesus Christ, and as apprehended by the instrumentality of the Holy Spirit in guiding them into all truth. The interpretation of the Old Testament by New Testament writers as it is revealed in their quotations has in itself often caused problems for readers of the New Testament, and it is to this subject that we must now turn.

The Interpretation of the Old Testament

The thinking of the authors of our New Testament was dominated by the idea of fulfillment. For them Jesus Christ was the goal of the Old Testament: "For all the promises of God find their Yes in him" (2 Co 1:20). The fulfillment had come in their own day, and they therefore saw themselves as the true heirs of the Old Testament promise. Ultimately what the Old Testament had in view was the succession of events that so recently had occurred in their midst. Thus Paul could describe himself and his contemporaries as those "upon whom the end of the ages has come" (1 Co 10:11).

It follows that these men were alive to the writings of the Old Testament in a new way. Paul and the early Church believed that it was through Christ that the veil which obscured the meaning of the Old Covenant was taken away (2 Co 3:14f.). Working with the theme of promise and fulfillment, the earliest Christians saw signs pointing to the Christ event not only in obviously prophetic passages, but also in passages which to us do not seem oriented to a future expectation at all. To understand and appreciate this interpretation of the Old Testament, we must attempt to move into the mental world of the first-century Jew.

Let us begin with some examples of the more literal prophecies that are quoted in the New Testament. Often these prophecies are self-explanatory and present us with no serious problems. In Matthew 2:6 the straightforward prophecy of Micah 5:2 about the birth of a Messianic ruler in Bethlehem of Judah is quoted. Matthew's formula quotation in 4:15-16 presents a prophecy from Isaiah 9:1-2, which involves simple prediction and fulfillment. That the words of the prophecy are in the past tense is no difficulty when it is remembered that often the prophets used the Hebrew perfect (past) tense when describing future events (thus the so-called prophetic perfect).[17] The prophecy and fulfillment relating to the entry of the King of Israel into Jerusalem as recorded in Matthew 21:5 (cf. Zec 9:9) cause no difficulty to our mind.†† In Acts 2:17-21 Peter describes the Pentecost event as a fulfillment of Joel's prophecy (2:28-32) about the pouring out of the Spirit

††The question concerning the number of animals has caused considerable discussion, since Zec 9:9 should be understood as referring to a single animal (in accordance with synonymous parallelism). See Gundry, *The Use of the Old Testament in St. Matthew's Gospel*, pp. 197ff.

upon all flesh. The prediction and fulfillment here is manifestly plain, although the latter section of the passage quoted from Joel (referring to astronomical phenomena accompanying the Day of the Lord) is, as we shall see, subject to different interpretations. These prophecies and others involving this same kind of straight-line prediction and fulfillment are the easiest for us to grasp. The prophet clearly had a future event in view which can be easily identified as having happened in the New Testament and only there.

This is not the case, however, with the majority of Old Testament quotations in the New Testament. Very often fulfillment involves a new complexity in that it is ascribed to prophetic passages which must also have had some kind of fulfillment for the prophet's contemporaries. Beyond this, fulfillment is often ascribed to Old Testament passages which have no semblance of predictive intention, such as historical narrative, devotional utterances of a psalmist, or descriptive assertions of the prophets.

All of this leads us to the recognition of what has been called the *sensus plenior*, or "fuller sense," of Old Testament Scripture.[18] To be aware of *sensus plenior* is to realize that there is the possibility of more significance to an Old Testament passage than was consciously apparent to the original author, and more than can be gained by strict grammatico-historical exegesis. Such is the nature of divine inspiration that the authors of Scripture were themselves often not conscious of the fullest significance and final application of what they wrote. This fuller sense of the Old Testament can be seen only in retrospect and in the light of the New Testament fulfillment.

Sensus plenior is thus based upon and presupposes the unity of the Bible. The events recorded in the New Testament constitute the goal of the entire Old Testament. The result of this viewpoint is that the Old Testament has an immediate relevance to the message of the New Testament. God is one; there is one people of God and one plan of salvation, and thus the whole of Scripture is interrelated. This can readily be seen in the large amount of Old Testament material that is applied by the New Testament writers to the Church quite directly, whether in terms of exhortation, example, or explanation.‡‡ It is this kind of application that was in Paul's thinking when, having described the experiences of Israel in the wilderness, he wrote, "Now these things happened to them as a warning, but they were written down for our instruction, upon whom the end of the ages has come" (1 Co 10:11). The Old Testament is written for the instruction of the Church, and the interrelation is such that the large body of nonpredictive matter in the Old Testament is capable of direct application to the Church.

We must tie in with this concept of the unity of God, His people, and His work, the Jewish (and biblical) insistence on the sovereignty of God in all the affairs of history. This overarching sovereignty of God guarantees that recurring patterns in the history of salvation (God's work with Israel and the Church) are not simply fortuitous but are carefully designed according to His will. Thus events, patterns of thought, and lessons in the experience of Israel serve the purpose of anticipating God's fuller work for His people in the end-time in Jesus Christ. In this way our attention is directed to the unity of God's plan and the consistency of His saving activity on behalf of His people down to the present era of fulfillment.

This view of history and the sovereignty of God so controlled the minds of our New Testament writers that they not only were aware of the perfect applicability of Old Testament exhortation and example to the New Testament Church, but were also particularly alert to correspondences between Old Testament material and the salvation they witnessed to in Jesus Christ. The study of such correspondences has taken the name *typology*, since the Old Testament elements are referred to as types and the New Testament counterparts antitypes. The word *type* is a biblical word (*typos*, meaning "mark," "figure," or "model"). For example, in Romans 5:14 Adam is referred to as a "type of the one who was to come." In 1 Corinthians 10:6 the word occurs again (RSV translates "warnings") when referring to the experiences of Israel in the wilderness. Note also the occurrence of the adverb *typikos* (typologically) in 1 Corinthians 10:11.

‡‡For exhortation, see Heb 12:5-6 and 1 Pe 3:10-12; for example, see 1 Co 10:7 and Heb 3:7-11; for explanation, see Ro 4:3, 7 and Paul's use of the Old Testament in Ro 9-11.

The question of the extent to which such correspondences are to be detected in the Old Testament and the fulfillment of the New Testament has been much discussed with the matter of proper controls being a major concern.[19] This question is asked at two levels. First, what typology did our New Testament writers make use of? Second, to what extent can we go beyond them in the tracing of types and antitypes? Although at the second level the question is very interesting,[20] our concern here is with actual use of typological correspondences by our New Testament writers.

Given their basic understanding of salvation history, the New Testament writers freely engaged in typological thinking about the relationship between old and new. For these men typological relationships were the result of God's design so that in some sense the type "prophesied" the antitype, and the latter "fulfilled" the former. This terminology, which we tend to automatically associate with prediction and prediction alone, is applied to correspondences in the patterns of events in view. The tracing of typological correspondences is a special instance of detecting the *sensus plenior* of Old Testament material. That is, the Old Testament is seen to contain a fuller sense than immediately meets the eye and, indeed, which is discernible only in the light of its New Testament counterpart.

We must now turn to some illustrations of what we have been discussing theoretically. It is best to begin with some of the more difficult quotations in the gospel of Matthew. The key to understanding these quotations is the concept of *sensus plenior*. In Matthew 1:23 the prophecy of Isaiah 7:14 is rightly quoted as finding its fulfillment in the birth of Jesus. This is the fullest significance of the prophecy. In its context, however, the fulfillment of the Isaiah prophecy was to serve as a sign to Ahaz concerning contemporary events.[21] Since the child's name was to be Immanuel (God with us), it was natural to associate him with the great promises of Isaiah 9:6-7 and 11:1-5, and thus to see the prophecy of his birth to be ultimately fulfilled in the birth of Jesus. Thus we may well speak of "multiple fulfillment," provided we stress the continuity of promise and the underlying unity of sense or meaning that ties together the separate fulfillments.[22]

In the quotations in Matthew 2:15 and 2:18, we see *sensus plenior* in terms of typological correspondence. In both instances a historical event of the past is likened to a corresponding event in the infancy of Jesus. These events are accordingly spoken of in the language of fulfillment. Thus when Hosea 11:1 says "out of Egypt I called my son," Matthew could see in this literal reference to the Exodus of Israel from Egypt a pattern corresponding to the departure from Egypt of *the* Son of God, Jesus. In the same manner, Matthew was alive to the correspondences between the wailing of the Bethlehemites at the slaughter of their male infants and the wailing of Rachel (whose tomb is on the outskirts of Bethlehem) for the exiled captives (Jer 31:15), and thus describes the former as the fulfillment of the latter. These correspondences, to repeat, were not regarded as coincidental but were seen as divinely intended. There is not only interconnection, then, but also foreshadowing and fulfillment.

One of the notoriously difficult quotations in Matthew is where it is said that Jesus dwelt in Nazareth, "that what was spoken of by the prophets might be fulfilled. 'He shall be called a Nazarene' " (Mt 2:23). No such quotation can be found in the prophets, in the remainder of the Old Testament, or in the extracanonical literature. The quotation is evidently a creation of Matthew, again on the principle of analogy. The name *Nazareth* immediately suggested the Hebrew word for branch, *nezer*, and the passage in Isaiah 11:1 referring to the righteous branch of the line of David who was to come. (Compare the references to the branch in Jeremiah 23:5; 33:15; Zechariah 3:8; 6:12. The Hebrew word for "branch" in each passage is, however, from the Hebrew root *ṣmḥ*.) Matthew argued that this agreement was divinely intended and that Jesus of Nazareth is Jesus the promised *nezer*. Thus we have promise and fulfillment in this unfolding of God's plan under His sovereignty.

The quotation of Jonah 1:17 in Matthew 12:40, although not preceded by a formula of introduction as are the other quotations in Matthew which we have discussed, nonetheless reflects the same tracing of correspondences—this time by Jesus as He related the three days and nights Jonah was in the belly of the whale to His own future burial in the heart of the earth for the same period of time. The language of fulfillment could have been as appropriately used here as in the previous quotations. Indeed, that the similarity is not coincidental is indicated by the somewhat emphatic reference to the "sign" of Jonah which Jesus gave to the scribes and Pharisees.[23] What was about to befall Jesus was the counterpart of that sign, which was simply another way of saying its fulfillment.

A further difficult quotation occurs in Matthew 27:9-10, where Zechariah 11:13 is combined with material from Jeremiah (18:2-3; 19:2-6; cf. 32:6-9). The latter material explains the attribution of the quotation to Jeremiah in the introductory formula. The combination may be Matthew's own or a combination that came to him from the apologetic tradition of the church. The same kind of problem can be seen in Mark 1:2-3, where a combination of words from Malachi and Isaiah are simply ascribed to Isaiah. Inasmuch as Zechariah was a rich source of prophetic anticipations of the events relating to the death of Jesus, it was only natural that the reference to the thirty shekels of silver in 11:13 be understood as foreshadowing the blood money that Judas, having repented of his betrayal, cast down in the Temple. Since this money, in turn, was associated with the purchase of a field, it was easy using the pivot word "potter" in Zechariah 11:13 (the RSV takes the reading "treasury" instead of "potter," following the Syriac rather than the Hebrew) to bridge to the potter of Jeremiah 18 and 19, and thence to the purchase of the field in Jeremiah 32:6-9. While the interconnection of this material may appear at best rather tenuous to us, we may remind ourselves of the far-reaching conviction of these early Jewish Christians concerning the singleness of direction of the Old Testament and thus its unity of purpose (in always pointing to the New Testament fulfillment) as well as their ever present appreciation of the overarching sovereignty of God in the writing of Scripture and in the ordering of events. Thus, correspondence perceived by the illumination of the Spirit was justly understood in the framework of foreshadowing and fulfillment—by *sensus plenior* the latter was alluded to by the former.

In the twenty-seventh chapter of Matthew material from Psalm 69 and especially Psalm 22 is applied to the crucifixion narrative.

The offering to Jesus of wine mixed with gall to drink (27:34; cf. 27:48) corresponds to, and thus echoes the language of Psalm 69:21. When Jesus cried out from the cross "My God, my God, why hast Thou forsaken me?" (27:46) He was quoting the opening words of Psalm 22. At several points in the remainder of Psalm 22, striking similarities to specific items of the crucifixion narrative are to be found, and Matthew understandably made use of these. In Matthew 27:35 the casting of lots and the dividing up of the garments is expressed in the language of Psalm 22:18; in verse 39 the derision and wagging of heads echoes Psalm 22:7; and in verse 43 the words "He trusts in God; let God deliver him now if he delights in him" are drawn from Psalm 22:8.

This material in Psalm 22, as well as in Psalm 69, must be understood to have its own historical context and referent. That is, in the first instance it describes the experience of an Israelite centuries before Christ. However, with *sensus plenior* in view, God superintended the writing of these words in such a way that they would find a vivid application and their fullest realization in the narrative of the crucifixion. Here too, in keeping with Matthew's use of the Old Testament, the language of fulfillment could have been used in introducing these references.

This approach to the Old Testament is by no means limited to the gospel of Matthew; it is found in virtually all the New Testament writers. In John 12:38 the unbelief of the multitude in the face of the many signs performed by Jesus is described as the fulfilling of Isaiah's words (53:1) : "Lord, who has believed our report, and to whom has the arm of the Lord been revealed?" Isaiah's words refer to the unbelief of his own day, but in a fuller way—especially when the total context of chapter 53 is considered—to the unbelief of the Jews as far as Jesus Himself was concerned.

John had several of his own contributions to the application of Old Testament passages to the crucifixion narrative. Recording that the soldiers did not break Jesus' legs because He was already dead, John says in 19:36 that this happened "that the scripture might be fulfilled, 'Not a bone of him shall be broken.' " The words are from Exodus 12:46 (with possible allusion to Ps 34:20, referring to the deliverance of the righteous) where they refer to the preparation of the Passover lamb. Thus there is not only the correspondence óf the unbroken legs but, much more significant for John's Christology, the correspondence of the Passover lamb and the sacrifice of Jesus (cf. 19:14, where John indicates that Jesus was put to death at the time of the preparation of the Passover). The fuller meaning of the Passover lamb in the Old Testament points to the fulfillment in the death of Jesus. (Note Paul's words, "Christ, our paschal lamb, has been sacrificed," 1 Co 5:7 and 1 Pe 1:19.) In the next verse (19:37) John quotes from Zechariah 12:10, "They shall look on him whom they have pierced," arguing that these words were fulfilled in the soldier's spear thrust into the side of Jesus. However, in this instance, because of a number of complicated questions, it is difficult to ascertain what, if any, historical referent was originally in Zechariah's mind.[24] It is just possible that here we confront not *sensus plenior*, but rather a matter of straightforward predictive prophecy pointing from the beginning, as does Isaiah 53, to the death of Jesus.

The use of the Old Testament in Luke-Acts is both extensive and interesting. That Luke regarded it as highly significant is also underlined by his repeated reference to the teaching of Jesus concerning the true meaning of the Old Testament Scriptures (Lk 24:27, 32, 44-47). There is an insistent emphasis on the fulfillment that has occurred in Christ. This emphasis can be seen in Peter's Pentecost discourse in Acts 2:14-39, where he cited Joel 2:28-32 as prophetic anticipation of what had occurred. It is possible that the second part of the quotation, referring to "wonders in the heaven above" (2:19), was understood as in some sense already fulfilled, whether by the supernatural darkness at the time of the crucifixion or in a nonliteral manner (i.e., viewing the language as hyperbolical). More probably, however, the latter part of the quotation was understood as not yet fulfilled but as nonetheless properly belonging to this eschatological perspective. Eschatology has been inaugurated yet not completed; the blessings of the Kingdom are presently enjoyed, while the accompanying judgment is delayed. Thus, theologically the two parts of the quotation stand together; chronologically they do not.

A little further in Peter's discourse, Psalm 16:8-11 is quoted, and the key assertion, "thou wilt not abandon my soul to Hades, nor let thy Holy One see corruption," is referred to the resurrection of Christ. The Psalm can be understood historically as referring to David's confidence that God would deliver him from death at the hands of his enemies. There is, however, a much fuller sense to these words than can be satisfied by the deliverances that David enjoyed; after all, David did eventually die, as the presence of his tomb testified. Such is the nature of Scripture that David, here referred to as a prophet, "looked ahead and spoke of the resurrection of the Christ" (2:31, NASB). We have here not direct prophecy but *sensus plenior*. For although David certainly knew that God had promised him a never ending dynasty (cf. 2:30), and may have alluded to some such deeper meaning in the words of Psalm 16:10, that he was conscious of the fullest meaning of the words and their specific fulfillment in the resurrection of Jesus is very improbable.§§

This same passage (Ps 16:10) was used in Acts 13:35 by Paul, who similarly finds in it the fuller meaning of the resurrection of Christ. In the preceding verse Paul cited Isaiah 53:3, "I will give you the holy and sure blessings of David" (following the Septuagint against the Masoretic text). Here the giving of "the holy and sure blessings of David" is associated with the resurrection of Christ. Whereas in the popular mind these blessings were equated with national-political aspirations, Paul pointed to the true fulfillment of this hope in the resurrection of Christ: "And we bring you the good news that what God promised to the fathers, this he has fulfilled to us their children by raising Jesus" (13:32-33). A fuller meaning in this connection is also found in the quotation of Psalm 2:7 in Acts 13:33.

One of the most interesting quotations in Acts, so far as interpretation is concerned, is the quotation of Amos 9:11-12 in Acts 15:16-18. In Amos the passage refers to the rebuilding of the Davidic

§§One may compare Jesus' reference to Abraham who rejoiced at the prospect of seeing Jesus' day and who "saw it and was glad" (Jn 8:56). What Abraham rejoiced in was the promise that God had given him and his knowledge that God would be faithful to this promise. The ultimate meaning of that promise is what has come in Jesus Christ. Thus in the fullest sense Abraham's rejoicing was in the day of Jesus, though his specific knowledge of that day was limited by his early position in the history of salvation.

kingdom, the eschatological restoration of Israel. James, presiding at the council of Jerusalem, suggests that the deeper meaning of the passage is to be found in the establishment of the Church. The recent conversion of large numbers of Gentiles was what Amos was referring to, and thus the Church was to be understood as the process of the rebuilding of the fallen house of David‖ ‖ (which ultimately would come to its climax in the conversion of Israel to the church and the full establishment of the Kingdom of God on earth). There is therefore a *sensus plenior* involved here. Amos was not aware that he was speaking prophetically of the church and the conversion of the Gentiles begun by Peter. This was, however, the thing in view, as James and the apostles were able to see in retrospect.

In the letters of Paul, the Old Testament citations often depend upon the understanding of *sensus plenior*. By way of example, we may consider the quotation of Hosea 1:10 and 2:23 in Romans 9: 25-26. In Hosea, those who are described as "not my people" and "not pitied" are not Gentiles, but rather the unfaithful Israelites of Hosea's day. Yet the passage as used by Paul (and also in 1 Pe 2:10) is understood to refer to the Gentiles and their being made a part of the people of God. The words thus find their fullest significance not in the repentance of unfaithful Jews but in the events of the New Testament period, wherein Gentiles responded to the proclamation of the Good News. We may compare the ascription to the Christian Church of such titles as "chosen race, a royal priesthood, a holy nation, God's own people" (1 Pe 2:9), language which is here understood in its fullest sense and so in a far deeper way than had previously been true.

In Romans 10:18 Paul cited Psalm 19:4, "Their voice has gone out to all the earth, and their words to the ends of the world." The words are an answer to the question, "Have they not heard?" and

---

‖ ‖It is not accurate to interpret the prophecy of Amos as referring to the future on the basis of the beginning words, "after these things" (*meta tauta*). *Meta tauta* is merely another way of saying "in that day" (*en tē hemēra ekeinē*, the reading of the Septuagint and Masoretic text). The quotation loses its significance if it does not refer to the events of the apostles' day. The conversion of the Gentiles, moreover, is associated with the rebuilding of the house of David. Therefore it must be understood to be occurring in the church. For further discussion of the text of the quotation, see p. 86.

are meant to underline an affirmative answer. In Psalm 19 the words refer to the ubiquitous witness of nature to the glory of God. The influence of general revelation referred to here had now been matched by extensive proclamation of special revelation, i.e., in the evangelistic activity of Paul and others. The patterns are quite similar and thus the latter may be described in terms of the former. Here again is *sensus plenior* expressed by typological correspondence.

In two places Paul appears to have employed an approach to the Old Testament that comes close to allegorizing. The first is in Galatians 4:22-31, where he referred to Sarah and Hagar as two covenants and actually used the Greek verb *allegorein,* "to speak allegorically" (4:24). This, however, is not true allegory. Paul did not mean that the two women were two covenants—i.e., that the real meaning of the women is only what they symbolize. What he was really doing was drawing an extended analogy between the women and their children on the one hand, and the covenants and their "children" on the other. In both instances children are born either to slavery or freedom. There is thus a continuity in the analogy of the women and the covenants, a meaning common to both, which distinguishes it from true allegory, which on the basis of superficial similarities imports an alien meaning into the interpreted materials. Here *sensus plenior* is found in strong typological correspondence.

The second place where Paul came close to allegorizing is in 1 Corinthians 10:4, where, describing Israel's wilderness experience, he wrote, "they drank from the supernatural Rock which followed them, and the Rock was Christ." Paul does not mean to deny that the Israelites drank water from a rock in the wilderness. Here we may well have the statement of a typological correspondence between the supernatural provision afforded by the literal rock and the ultimate source of supernatural provision, Jesus Christ. Since Christ is the incarnation and thus the ultimate expression of God's provision for man, He is implicitly present in all supernatural provision. This idea is strengthened and extended, however, by the belief that the preincarnate Christ is to be found throughout the Old Testament (the name of Jesus Christ is virtually interchangeable with the name *Yahweh* in the Old Testament, cf. Ac 2:21; Ro 10:9, 13) , and especially in contexts of God's gracious provision for His people. Thus Paul argued that in the case of this supernatural provision of water in the wilderness, one is quite right in understanding that Christ, the ultimate Provider, was the underlying reality in the provision. Thus in the deepest sense, Christ is the Rock from which they drank.

For a final illustration of the interpretation of the Old Testament in the New Testament, we may look at Hebrews 2:6-8, where Psalm 8:4-6 is quoted and referred to the superiority of Jesus over the angels. In Psalm 8 the words refer to man as the handiwork of God. In 8:4 the question is asked, "What is man that thou art mindful of him and the son of man that thou dost care for him?" The words "son of man" are in synonymous parallelism with "man" in the first clause. In both clauses the question is: What is man? The words which follow provide the answer. The author of Hebrews found, of course, a fuller content in the passage by immediately associating it with *the* Son of Man, Jesus. If the words of the psalm are true with respect to man, then they are supremely true in the archetypal, or representative Man. The incarnation made Jesus "for a little while lower than the angels," (2:9) but now, following His death, He has been "crowned with glory and honor" (2:9) , though for the moment "we do not yet see everything in subjection to him" (2:8) . Thus the author was sensitive to the *sensus plenior* of the psalm and of its applicability to, and perfect realization in, Christ.

We have described the interpretive approach of the New Testament writers to the Scriptures which we call the Old Testament, and we have given a number of illustrations which reflect that approach. What remains is only to comment on the effectiveness of this approach in arguing for the truthfulness of Christianity. That is, what is the apologetic value of the use of the Old Testament in the New Testament?

The fulfillment of prophecy has long been regarded as an effective "proof" of Christianity. One occasionally encounters long lists of "prophecies" and their "fulfillments" produced for apologetic purposes by well-meaning individuals. Straight-line predic-

tive prophecy with simple fulfillment in the New Testament period does have apologetic usefulness. But such clear predictive
prophecy and fulfillment is seldom found in the New Testament;
it is the exception rather than the rule. Instead, as we have seen,
the New Testament writers looked for the meaning of the Old
Testament as contained in its *sensus plenior*. In so doing, they
found varied correspondences, analogies, and suggestive similarities—some more substantial, some less substantial—but all based on
the underlying presuppositions of the sovereignty of God in the
affairs of history; the unique character of the Scriptures as divinely
inspired; and the identity of Jesus as the *telos*, or goal, of the history of salvation.

Where these presuppositions are shared, such arguments concerning Old Testament fulfillment are cogent. Where they are
not shared, such arguments are less than convincing. One may indeed argue that the patterns of promise and fulfillment discerned
through *sensus plenior* make an impressive mosaic of confirmatory
evidence once Jesus is regarded as these writers regarded Him. But
our argument concerning the identity of Jesus does not rest primarily on these patterns of promise and fulfillment, but rather
upon the objective events of His ministry, His death and His resurrection.

Thus the true value of the arguments from the *sensus plenior*
of the Old Testament is for those who are already in the household
of faith. These patterns of fulfillment underline for them the continuity of the Old and New Testaments. The Old Testament is
their book as much as the New Testament, for the entirety of the
Old Testament points as one great arrow to the fulfillment which
the New Testament records. And with this new sense of the continuity of God's purposes will come an increased appreciation of
Jesus as the consummation of God's plan for the universe.

If the frequent quotation of the Old Testament in the New
Testament has anything to teach us, it is that our New Testament
writers were utterly filled with excitement about Jesus and what
He had brought. Jesus encouraged their excitement: "Truly, I
say to you, many prophets and righteous men longed to see what
you see, and did not see it, and to hear what you hear, and did not

hear it" (Mt 13:17). The Kingdom had come! Eschatology was beginning! The Scriptures were being fulfilled! Christianity rightly understood is the celebration of fulfillment. It may also be described as "fulfillment on the way to fulfillment," for the consumation of eschatology, the full experience of the Kingdom of God on earth, remains a future expectation of the Church. During the interim period she looks for the return of her Lord. But the focus of attention in the New Testament is on the fulfillment already experienced, and if we are to begin to understand the use of the Old Testament in the New Testament we must recapture this excitement of the early Christians. When we do recapture this excitement we will better represent the Good News of Jesus Christ here and now.

6

The Genre of New Testament Literature and Biblical Hermeneutics

by Gordon Fee

It should be an axiom of biblical hermeneutics that, as a part of valid contextual exegesis, the interpreter must take into account the literary genre of the text he is interpreting as well as the questions of text, philology, grammar, and history. Such a principle would appear to be so self-evident as not to need belaboring. Yet, except for the Apocalypse, this principle is seldom applied in the interpretation of the New Testament.* It is as if the gospels, the Acts, and the various kinds of epistles were all of a kind, and one needed only the general maxims of hermeneutics in order to interpret them; whereas the Apocalypse is of a special kind and needs further special rules. This is surely true of the Apocalypse. The burden of this paper is that the others are also special kinds and that a consideration and understanding of the literary genre of each must become a part of valid hermeneutics.

The point is that not every biblical statement is the word of God in precisely the same way. The questions must often be: Given that a historical narrative is included in the Acts, *how* is it the word of God for today? Is it merely informative? Does it establish a precedent which is in some way normative? Or are we to

---

*One generally looks in vain for such a discussion in the standard works on hermeneutics. Bernard Ramm (*Protestant Biblical Interpretation*, rev. ed. [Grand Rapids: Baker, 1956] pp. 138-39) does have a short section on "the principle of interpreting according to literary mold," in which he insists that "it is necessary for the interpreter to recognize literary forms *as necessary* to the interpretation of Scripture" (italics his). However, he gives no guiding principles for many of the molds he isolates.

elicit a "principle" from the narrative? Or in the case of the epistles: Is a statement spoken to a given historical context, in response to a specific historical problem, the word of God for us in precisely the same way it was for them? How, or when, does something that is culturally conditioned become transcultural?

It will be recognized that these questions, although seldom articulated, are indeed answered in practice. For example, many Christians consider the imperative to Timothy, "Use a little wine for the sake of your stomach" (1 Ti 5:23, NASB), to be culturally and specifically bound. Water was unsafe to drink, we are told, so Timothy was to take wine for medicinal reasons. All of which might be true; but many of the same Christians insist that men today should not have long hair, because "nature itself teaches us" (1 Co 11:14) this (although it is seldom recognized that short hair is "natural" only as the result of a *non*natural means—a haircut!). The question here is not whether such distinctions are right or wrong, but on what *principles* one comes to such conclusions.

Consider as a further example how many divisions there are in Christendom over the how of Christian experience or the mode of Christian practice, many of which are derived from the precedent of historical narratives. For example, "restoration" movements usually attempt to get back to New Testament practices on the basis of certain models found chiefly in Acts. Such practices are regarded as the "plain teaching of Scripture"; the hermeneutical problems involved are scarcely recognized. But since the same things are not "plain" to all, the whole question as to how historical narratives are the word of God *must* be raised.

By looking at each of the New Testament literary genre in turn, I hope to define some of the problems and to suggest some directions for finding answers. There is no thought of being exhaustive. Hopefully, merely having the questions asked will be a step in the direction of better hermeneutics.

THE EPISTLES

Traditionally, for most Christians the epistles seem to be the easiest portions of the New Testament to interpret. They are

looked upon as so many propositions to be believed and imperatives to be obeyed. One need not be skilled in exegesis to understand that "all have sinned" (Ro 3:23), or that "by grace are you
saved through faith" (Eph 2:8), or that "if any one is in Christ, he
is a new creation" (2 Co 5:17). The difficulty most of us have
with "Do all things without grumbling or questioning" (Phil 2:
14) is not with understanding, but with obeying. How, then, do
the epistles as epistles pose problems for interpretation?

The answer to that becomes quickly obvious when one leads a
group of Christians through 1 Corinthians. "How is Paul's opinion
(1 Co 7:25) to be taken as God's Word?" some will ask, especially
when they personally dislike some of the implications of that opinion. And the questions continue. How does the excommunication
of the brother in chapter 5 relate to the contemporary church, especially when he can simply go down the street to another church?
What is the point of chapters 12-14, if one is in a local church where
charismatic gifts are not accepted as valid for the twentieth century? How do we get around the very clear implication in chapter 11:2-16 that women should wear a head covering when praying
and prophesying?

It becomes clear that the epistles are *not* as easy to interpret as is
often thought. What principles, then, apply specifically to this
genre?

First, it is necessary to note that the epistles themselves are not
a homogeneous lot. Many years ago Adolf Deissmann, on the basis
of the vast papyrus discoveries, made a distinction between letters
and epistles.[1] The former, the "real letters," as he called them,
were nonliterary, i.e., not written for the public and posterity, but
"intended only for the person or persons to whom [they are] addressed." In contrast to the letter is the epistle, which is "an ar-
tistic literary form, a species of literature . . . intended for public-
ity." Deissmann himself considered all the Pauline epistles as well
as 2 and 3 John to be "real letters." Although W. R. Ramsay cau-
tioned us not "to reduce all the letters of the New Testament to
one or other of these categories"[2]—in some instances it seems to be
a question of more or less—the distinction is nevertheless a valid
one. Romans and Philemon differ from one another not only in

content but also in the degree to which they are occasional. And in contrast with any of Paul's letters, 1 Peter is far more an epistle.

Further distinctions must also be drawn. For example, Hebrews is, as A. M. Hunter said, "three parts tract and one part letter."[3] But it is far more than a tract; it is an eloquent homily, proclaiming the absolute superiority of Christ, interspersed with urgent words of exhortation. James, on the other hand, looks very little like a letter, but often very much like the wisdom literature of the Old Testament and Apocrypha, except that these are poetry and James is prose.

But however diverse the epistles may be, they have one thing in common. They are occasional documents of the first century, written out of the context of the author to the context of the recipients. It is precisely these factors—that they are occasional and that they belong to the first century—that make the interpretation of the epistles so difficult at times.

First, they must be taken seriously as being more letter than epistle. But that often increases our difficulties, because the author assumed so many things on the part of the recipients. We are often on one side of a telephone conversation and must piece together from this end what the other party is saying, or what his problem is. As R. P. C. Hanson said of 2 Corinthians:

> As we read it, we sometimes feel as if we had turned on the [radio] in the middle of an elaborate play: characters are making most lively speeches and events of great interest and importance are happening, but we do not know who exactly the speakers are and we are not sure exactly what is happening.[4]

Second, all of this took place in the first century. Our difficulty here is that we are removed from them not only by so many years in time, and therefore in circumstances and culture, but also very often in the world of thought.

Sound hermeneutics with regard to the epistles, therefore, seems to require three steps.

1. *To understand as much as possible the original setting.* The interpreter, if you will, must remove his twentieth-century bifocals and shed the filter of twentieth-century mentality and put himself

back into the first century. For the epistles this has a double focus:
(a) He must try at all costs to reconstruct the situation of the recipients. That is, he must ask, *How* is this letter, or this section of
the letter, an answer to their problems or a response to their needs?
In every case, a primary concern of interpretation is to try to hear
what *they* would have heard. (b) He must try to live with the author and understand his mentality and his context. Above everything else the interpreter must try to understand what the author
intended the recipients to hear.

It must be a maxim of hermeneutics for the epistles: what
neither the author could have intended nor the recipients could
have understood can be the true meaning of a passage. For example, it has often been suggested that the phrase "when the perfect
comes" (1 Co 13:10) refers to the canon of Scripture, and that
therefore it points to the end of the first century as the time when
charismatic gifts will cease. But surely that is altogether twentieth
century. Not only does the immediate context (v. 12) imply that
the Eschaton is intended, but there seems to be no way that either
Paul could have intended such a thing, or the Corinthians could
have so understood it.

It should also be candidly admitted that the distance of nineteen
centuries simply closes the probability that we will ever be able to
understand everything in the epistles. Until history or dogged research sheds more light on some aspects of the first century, the interpreter needs the integrity to admit at times, "I'm not sure what
that means."

2. *To hear the Word of God that is addressed to that situation.*
This, of course, will be very closely tied to the first principle, and
sometimes they will be one. The point here is not that some things
are inspired and others are not, but rather that the recipients' context often reflects a problem which needed correcting or a lack of
understanding that needed enlightening. Our task is to discover
(or "hear") the Word of God that was addressed to that situation,
which called for their obedience or brought understanding.

3. *To hear that same Word as it is addressed to our situation.*
Understandably enough, most of us want to go directly to this one,
that is, to have Paul speak directly out of the first century into

ours. This is not to suggest that such may not or cannot happen. But the point is that very often the words of the epistles are culturally conditioned by the first century setting.† If these words are going to be God's Word to us, then we must first of all hear what God's Word was to them. Otherwise, one of two things happens. A. Sometimes the words never leave the first century. Thus some things address us, and some do not. If we have no one struggling with whether to join his pagan neighbors at feasts in the temple or no one denying the bodily resurrection, or if our culture does not insist on women's heads being covered, or if we have no one drunk at the Lord's Table or shouting "Jesus is cursed" by the "Spirit," then the epistles have historical interest at these points, but they scarcely address us.

B. On the other hand, the epistles frequently are not allowed to speak to their first-century context. Every word comes directly to us; but sometimes that "direct" word, because it was not what was being said to them, is not God's *intended* Word to us. For example, if the intent of Paul's word about partaking of the Lord's Supper "unworthily" is to correct an abuse of the Table through divisiveness, gluttony, and drunkenness while at the Table, then our ordinary application of that text to personal piety does not seem to be God's *intended* Word. What was being said to *that* situation had to do with an attitude, or lack of it, toward the Supper itself. Their division and drunkenness were profaning the Supper, not "discerning the body," missing the whole point of it all. Surely it is *that* Word we need to hear today more than one's first getting rid of the sin in his life in order to be worthy to partake.

If we are to escape either of these errors, then we *must* discover what God said to that setting; and it is that Word which *we* must hear, even if we must hear it in a new setting or learn to recognize contemporary settings to which it should be addressed.

These three principles may perhaps be best illustrated from a passage like 1 Corinthians 3:9b-17, which has been frequently misunderstood and misapplied, and has served as a theological bat-

---

†In a certain sense, of course, every word of Scripture is culturally conditioned, in that it was first spoken in the context of the first century. The degree of "cultural conditioning" is a relative matter. See pp. 113-14 for some suggestions in this regard.

tleground for a controversy to which Paul is not speaking at all.

It takes no great expertise to recognize that the context of 3:9b-17 is party-strife in the church at Corinth. In 1:10-12 Paul said that Chloe's people had told him all about the tendency to divide into cliques over favorite leaders. On either side of the immediate context (3:4-9 and 21-23) this party-strife is obviously still in view. Unless vv. 9b-17 can be demonstrated to be a digression, then one must assume them to speak directly to this problem.

Paul's answer is twofold. His first great concern is theological—their sloganeering and dividing on the basis of human leaders reflected on their understanding of salvation, as if men (especially men with great wisdom and eloquence) had had something to do with it. So in 1:18—2:16 Paul reaffirms that salvation is God's business from start to finish; and as though deliberately to leave men out of it, God wisely chose the foolishness of the cross as His means of accomplishing it, so that their trust ("boast") would be not in men but in God.

In chapter 3 Paul then turns to the practical implications of their divisions, by showing first of all the role of the human minister in salvation. In one figure the minister plants or waters (3:5-9a); in a second figure he lays a foundation, or builds the superstructure (vv. 9b-15). Verse 11 is simply a parenthesis reiterating the point of 1:18—2:16, namely that Christ alone is the foundation. Verses 2:12-15 therefore have nothing to do with personal morality or piety, as to how one builds his own life on Christ. Rather, this was Paul's charge to those who had responsibilities of building the Church; and the point is, it is possible to build poorly! So let each one (Paul, Apollos, Cephas, elders, deacons, etc.) take care *how* he builds. To have built with emphasis on human wisdom or eloquence is not going to make it, although the minister "himself will be saved, but only as through fire."

Within the same context Paul then turned the figure slightly and addressed the "building" (2:16-17) —and this is the real point of the section. He was *not* here writing about individual Christians, and especially not about the human body (a matter which he does address in a whole new context in 6:12-20). It is the whole Church whom Paul addressed. They, especially when they are assembled, are God's temple, among whom God's Spirit dwells. If anyone destroys the temple, God will destroy him! How were they destroying the temple? By their party-strife, which inevitably would banish the Spirit.

What then was God's Word to them? First, there was a word to those who had "building" responsibilities—to build with care. Second, there was a word to the Church—not to divide over human leaders. The church in Corinth was God's alternative to that city. To be divided was to destroy the Church as God's option. Since the Church was where God was gathering His new people, and since the Church was where He was now pleased to dwell, to destroy the Church was to put oneself under the prospect of fearful judgment.

What Word does that have for us? Very much the same as it had for them, I think. There is still need for those with responsibilities in the Church to take care how they build. It appears sadly true that the Church has too often been built with wood, hay, or stubble, rather than with gold, silver, or precious stones, and such work when tried by fire has been found wanting. Furthermore, this would seem to be the place where God addresses us as to our responsibilities to the local church. It must be a place where God's Spirit is known to dwell, and which therefore stands as God's alternative to the alienation, fragmentation, and loneliness of worldly society.

If this is indeed the proper hermeneutical approach to the epistles, or at least to those sections which are clearly responses to first-century occasions, then there is one other problem which must be spoken to: How does one determine what is cultural and therefore belongs only to the first century, and what is transcultural and therefore belongs to every age?

In all candor it should be admitted that this is usually answered by our own cultural predispositions. If we have been raised in a context where women pray, or prophesy, or teach, then 1 Timothy 2:9-15 is seen as culturally conditioned. But if our context is more strictly patriarchal, then those words are seen as transcultural and as applicable to every situation.

Such distinctions are not easily made. Let us begin by noting the obvious: some things are clearly culturally conditioned while others are just as clearly transcultural. For example, for Western man the eating or noneating of food offered to idols is of no consequence. The only possible way, therefore, that 1 Corinthians 8-10 can speak to our situation is by going through the steps outlined above and "translating" their situation into the twentieth century. The stumbling block principle, which was God's Word to them, is just as surely God's Word to us. *Our problem is to recognize comparable culturally-defined contexts.*

On the other hand, there are those indicatives and imperatives which clearly transcend culture, such as, "And so, as those who have been chosen of God, holy and beloved, put on a heart of compassion, kindness, humility, gentleness and patience; bearing with one another, and forgiving each other, whoever has a complaint against any one; just as the Lord forgave you, so also should you" (Col 3: 12-13, NASB) .

With the caution that not all "obvious" things will be equally obvious to all, these guidelines are suggested at this point:

1. To determine what is culturally conditioned, one may begin by asking whether the matter is inherently moral or nonmoral, theological or nontheological. Although some may differ with my judgments here, it would appear that eating food offered to idols, women having a head-covering when praying or prophesying, women teaching in the church, and Paul's preference for celibacy are examples of issues not inherently moral; they may become so only by their use or abuse in given contexts.

2. One should further ask whether something would truly be an issue for the twentieth century if one had never encountered the issue in these first-century documents. Hence, the head-covering of women or the length of men's hair would not seem to be issues were they not raised in 1 Corinthians. At this point, of course, one might always argue that man is fallen, and that just because it is not an issue now does not mean that it should not be one.

3. One must remain alert to possible cultural differences that are sometimes not immediately obvious. For example, to determine the role of women in the twentieth-century Church, one should take into account that there were no educational opportunities for

women in the first century, whereas such education is the expected norm in our society.

4. One must exercise Christian charity at this point. Christians need to recognize the difficulties, open the lines of communication with one another, start by trying to define some principles, and finally have love for and a willingness to ask forgiveness from those with whom they differ.

THE ACTS OF THE APOSTLES

In his appreciative survey of the contribution of Martin Dibelius to the study of Acts, Ernst Haenchen notes: "For the first time the deeply-rooted tendency to regard Acts as no more than a quarry to furnish material for the reconstruction of primitive Christianity was overcome. For the first time the question could be faced of what this biblical author was trying to tell his readers."[5] What was true at the level of scholarship, however, scarcely existed for the ordinary Christian pastor or layman as he read Acts. The book served simultaneously *both* as a quarry of history *and* as a word from God.

The result of this, however, has been that the hermeneutics of Acts has generally suffered from ambiguity. On the one hand, Acts does serve as the basic source of early Christian history. At the same time, some of its sections, especially the words of the apostles, have been treated very much as the epistles, i.e., as speaking directly to our situation. On the other hand, the narratives from which we quarry history are also seen as God's word to us, as in the common expository admonition, "What this is trying to teach us is—"

It is the lack of *hermeneutical precision* as to what Acts "is trying to teach" which has led to so much division in the church. Such diverse practices as the baptism of infants or of believers only, congregational and episcopalian church polity, the necessity of taking the Lord's Supper every Sunday, the baptism of the Holy Spirit accompanied by speaking in tongues, the selling of possessions and having all things in common, and even snake handling (!) have been supported in whole or in part on the basis of Acts.

The hermeneutical problem of Acts, therefore, is a crucial one and touches many parts of Scripture which are basically historical narrative. How is the book of Acts, which *prima facie* narrates a small segment of the early spread of Christianity, to be understood as the Word of God? That is, what is its Word which not merely *describes* the primitive Church but *speaks as a norm* to the Church at all times? Indeed, do such narratives somehow establish normative precedents for succeeding generations? Or are they merely illustrative or informative? If they do have a word for us, and I think they do, how does one discover it, or set up principles in order to hear it?

Unfortunately, one looks in vain in the standard works on hermeneutics for answers, because for the most part the questions themselves are not asked. However, hermeneutical precision at this point seems to be of crucial importance. Therefore, the following suggestions are proffered, not as definitive, but as some basic guidelines for further discussion.

1. In the hermeneutics of biblical history the major task of the interpreter is to discover the author's (I would add, the Holy Spirit's) *intent* in the recording of that history. This, of course, is a general maxim of hermeneutics and applies to the other literary genres as well. But it is of special importance to the hermeneutics of the historical narratives. For it is one thing for the historian to include an event because it serves the greater purpose of his work, and yet another thing to take that incident as having didactic value apart from the historian's larger intent.

Although Luke's broader intent may be a moot point, it is a defensible hypothesis that he was trying to show how the church emerged as a chiefly Gentile, worldwide phenomenon from its origins as a Jerusalem-based, Judaism-oriented sect of Jewish believers, and that the Holy Spirit was ultimately responsible for this phenomenon.

An event such as the conversion of Cornelius serves this broader interest not simply to "represent a principle . . . or higher historical truth" (so Dibelius) [6] nor as an illustration of Christian conversion in general or the baptism in the Holy Spirit in particular (so Pentecostals). Rather Cornelius serves for Luke as the firstfruits of the Gentile mission, and he is important to Luke's purpose because his conversion is by direct intervention of the Holy Spirit through one of the Jerusalem apostles (Ac 15:7; cf. 10:19, 44; 11:12, 15). Through these combined circumstances the eyes of the church were opened to the fact that "even to the Gentiles God has granted repentance unto life" (11:18).

Whatever else one gleans from the story—whether it be the place of visions in Christian guidance, or the nature of Christian conversion, or the role of tongues in the coming of the Spirit—such gleanings are *incidental* to Luke's intent. This does not mean that what is incidental is false, nor that it has no theological value; it does mean that God's Word *for us* in that narrative is primarily related to what it was intended to teach, and the whole point of the hermeneutical task, of course, is to discover what is intended.

On the basis of this discussion the following principles emerge with regard to the hermeneutics of historical narrative:

a. The Word of God in Acts which may be regarded as normative for Christians is related to what any given narrative primarily teaches.

b. What is incidental to the primary intent of the narrative may indeed reflect an author's theology, or how he understood things; but what is incidental cannot have didactic value in the same way as the *intended* Word has. This does not negate what is incidental, nor imply that it has no word for us. What it does suggest is that what is incidental may not become primary, although it may always serve as additional support to what is unequivocally taught elsewhere.

Thus, for example, it is probably incidental to Luke's overall purpose that the early preaching in Acts reflects a strong Servant-Messiah Christology (3:26; 4:25, 30; cf. 8:30-35). This does indeed serve not merely for historical interest but further to support an understanding of Jesus found throughout the New Testament. However, what does one do when the incidental reflects ambiguity, such as the diverse attitudes toward the Temple one finds in the apostles on one hand (Ac 3:1; 21:23-26) and in Stephen and the Hellenists on the other (7:44-50)? There are several options: harmonize the attitudes, subordinate one to the other, or accept diversity at such points as within the framework of divine revelation. I prefer the latter, for such points are surely incidental to Luke and probably we ought not extract one of them as *the* biblical truth. Sometimes, of course, the ambiguity is only apparent, and a thorough exegesis of all texts involved reveals a biblical harmonization or subordination.

2. One of the purposes that Acts has often served for the church is to establish norms for its experiences and practices. But almost always such norms derive from descriptions of *what* happened, not from statements as to what *should* happen. That is, they are made normative by way of historical precedent. The question as to whether or how one is to understand God as addressing him through precedent is a thorny one, but here are some suggestions:

a. In general it is doubtful whether what is merely reported, even if a given model is repeated, is ever to be elevated to a normative level. On the basis of precedent alone it is probably not valid to say, "Therefore, one *must*." The only conceivable exception would be related to the foregoing discussion of the author's intent. If it could be demonstrated that an author included a narrative with the specific intent to establish a norm, then it would indeed be normative.

b. The use of historical precedent as an analogy by which to establish a norm is probably never valid, since it is a non sequitur and/or irrelevant. Thus to urge the necessity of water baptism on the analogy of Jesus' baptism is bad exegesis as well as irrelevant. John's baptism and Christian baptism, though the latter is probably rooted in the former, are different things, and the meaning and necessity of Christian baptism must be made of sterner stuff.

Likewise the analogy of Jesus and the apostles as having been born of the Spirit and later baptized in the Spirit may be interesting as analogies, but they are only analogies, and probably based on dubious exegesis at that. There is not the faintest hint in either case that these are to serve as patterns for subsequent Christian experience.

c. Although it may not have been the author's primary purpose, historical narratives may have illustrative, and sometimes pattern, or model, value. In fact, this is how the New Testament people use the historical precedents of the Old Testament. Paul, for example, used certain Old Testament examples as warnings to those who had a false security in their divine election (1 Co 10:6-13); and Jesus used the example of David as a historical precedent to justify His disciples' Sabbath actions (Mk 2:23-28 and parallels).

Whether we may repeat the New Testament's exegesis of the Old Testament may be a moot point,‡ and in fact is analogous to the problem we are discussing here. It should be noted, however, especially in the case where the precedent is used to justify present action, that the precedent does not establish a norm for specific action. Men are not to eat regularly of the showbread or to pluck grain on the Sabbath to show that the Sabbath was made for man. Rather the precedent illustrates a principle with regard to the Sabbath.

A warning is in order here: for a biblical precedent to justify present action, the principle of the action must be taught elsewhere, where it is the primary intent so to teach. For example, to use Jesus' cleansing of the Temple to justify selfish anger masquerading as righteous indignation is to abuse this principle.

d. In matters of Christian experience, and even more so of Christian practice, biblical models may be regarded as repeatable, even if they are not to be regarded as normative. This is especially true when the practice itself is mandatory but the mode is not. Thus the observance of the Lord's Supper would seem to be mandatory of Christians; its observance every Sunday may be regarded as a permissible, but not necessarily normative pattern.

The repeatable character of certain practices or patterns should be guided by the following considerations:

i. The strongest possible case can be made where only one model is found (although one must be careful not to make too much of silence) and when that model is repeated within the New Testament itself. To illustrate: The Pentecostals' practice of speak-

‡Richard N. Longenecker ("Can We Reproduce the Exegesis of the New Testament?" *Tyndale Bulletin* 21 [1970] pp. 3-38) has argued that because of the revelatory character of the New Testament its exegesis should be considered "once-for-all," not normative, and in some cases not even repeatable.

ing in tongues would seem to be justified on these grounds, inasmuch as glossolalia three times accompanies the gift of the Spirit in Acts (2:4, 10:44-46, 19:6; perhaps 8:17-18 as well), where the text explicitly says that someone received the Spirit (9:17-18 is the lone exception). However, one is hard-pressed to see in these passages a baptism in the Spirit as a second work of the Spirit.

ii. Where there is ambiguity of models, or when a practice is reported but once, it is repeatable only if it appears to have divine approbation or is in harmony with what is taught elsewhere in Scripture. To illustrate: It would seem that some in what is often called the Jesus movement could justify their communal life and their having all things in common on these grounds, since such life appears to have divine approval in Acts and since there is no teaching elsewhere that would seem to prohibit such a practice. But one may well question the economic viability of the practice, since Paul eventually was raising money for the poor in Jerusalem.

iii. What is simply culturally relative is either not repeatable at all, or must be translated into new or differing cultures. To illustrate: It is hard to know what one is to make of religious vows in the twentieth century. In any case, Paul's shaving his head to fulfill such a vow (Ac 18:18) is probably closely tied to his Jewish heritage and therefore is irrelevant to our day as a specific practice.

THE GOSPELS

As with the epistles and the Acts, the gospels also at first glance would seem to be easy enough to interpret. Since the materials may be divided roughly into teaching and narratives, one should be able to follow the principles for interpreting the epistles for the one and the principles for historical narratives for the other. However, it is not quite that easy. The gospels are a unique literary genre with special hermeneutical problems.

The most important thing to say at the beginning of a discussion of this genre is that Jesus did not write a gospel. In fact, had He written something, it would not have been a gospel in the sense that ours are. If Jesus had recorded His own teaching, the result would probably have been very much like the book of Amos or Jeremiah—mostly a collection of oracles (in this case, sayings) with perhaps an occasional significant narrative. But there would have been only *one* such book. It is doubtful, moreover, that it would have been followed by an official biography of some kind.

But what we have is not merely a collection of sayings of Jesus, nor the teachings of Jesus written by Himself. Furthermore, we do not have biographies as such, for four biographies could never stand side by side as of equal value. What we do have are four anonymous documents, whose earliest titles bore the insightful words, "according to Mark," etc. What this means is that the gospels have the dual nature of being both records of Jesus' life and words and witnesses to Him on the part of the evangelists. The gospels are not photographic transcriptions of the events c. A.D. 28-30; they are a transcription of those words and events as they had also lived in a continuing ministry to the Church for a thirty- to fifty-year period.

To some people this "dual nature" of the gospels may seem like a threat. Is the Jesus whose words and deeds were ministering to the Church for a long period of oral transmission the same Jesus who actually lived and taught in Galilee at a fixed point in history? Significant differences among scholars exist right at this point; but to those who believe that the Holy Spirit was given to the Church to help her recall His teaching (Jn 14:26), this process is to be seen as a part of the ongoing ministry of the Spirit. Since the Spirit did not see fit even to preserve the words of Jesus in His native tongue (with a few exceptions), but only in translation, then perhaps we should see this dual nature of the gospels also as intended by the Spirit and therefore as their greater glory. In any case, the fact that the gospels give us not only the deeds and words of Jesus Himself, but also reveal how Jesus continued to minister to needs in the Church in new settings, must be a consideration in their interpretation.

One of the most significant ways this understanding of the dual nature of the gospels will affect our interpretations has to do with the question of context. As with the epistles, so here, this is a crucial issue. But in contrast to the epistles, where the problem was related to the writer and his readers, the problem here is first of all whether the context of a given saying or narrative goes back to

Jesus or belongs to the evangelist.§ The point is that during the oral period, whole gospels were not being handed down. Rather, the stuff of the gospels, the sayings and narratives, were being handed down, often quite independently of each other, and were probably used in isolation from their original context in much the way Paul used the teaching of Jesus in 1 Corinthians 7:10-11 and 9:14.

The rather imprecise way so many of the teachings and narratives are put together ("and as they were on the road," "when the crowds were increasing he began to say," etc.) in the gospels, as well as the fact that so many are topically gathered together (as in the so-called Sermon on the Mount, or the teaching on prayer in Lk 11:1-14) also point to the fact that the gospel materials are not necessarily "blow by blow," nor in their original chronology.

What this means to the interpreter is of some consequence, for at times he will have two contexts. This does not mean that the contexts are necessarily contradictory, but that one probably is that of Jesus and the other that of the evangelist. The historian may indeed insist on either/or. The interpreter, who sees the Holy Spirit at work in both contexts, should be ready for both/and.

For example, if we may assume (and it is a fair, if not necessarily the only, assumption) that Jesus spoke the parable of the lost sheep once, then we have it in two different contexts in Luke 15 and Matthew 18. In Luke it is a parable justifying Jesus' action in receiving sinners, for "there will be more joy in heaven over one sinner who repents, than over ninety-nine righteous persons who need no repentance" (NASB). In Matthew it is a parable telling the Church what to do about a straying member, for "it is not the will of your Father who is in heaven that one of these little ones should perish." In terms of original context most scholars think Luke has the better of it, but in terms of its being the Word of

---

§This in no way suggests that the gospel writers were reading back into the life of Jesus something that did not happen. What is suggested is that the original *contexts* of sayings and narratives were not necessarily preserved along with the saying and narrative. In fact, because of the very nature of oral transmission, the original context of many sayings may not have been preserved because the saying had meaning quite apart from its original context. But when an evangelist included that saying in his gospel, he must of necessity give it a context—even if it now is only a part of a collection of similar sayings (e.g., on prayer or faith).

God, both contexts speak to us, because this is what the parable was speaking to the Church when Luke and Matthew recorded it.

In other examples the two contexts may sometimes have to be dug out. That is, the context of the evangelist will be more or less obvious, but the original context of Jesus will not necessarily be clear. In many cases such spadework is worth the doing. A case in point is J. Jeremias' excellent study of the parables.[7] Even if one may have some uneasiness about his presuppositions or the ease with which he draws some of his conclusions, he has greatly enhanced our ability to hear the parables in Jesus' own life setting.

Take, for example, the parable of the laborers in the vineyard (Mt 20:1-16). In Matthew's context this parable has been inserted into a piece of Marcan material, which he was basically following, as may be seen from any gospel parallel. The insertion was to illustrate the point that "the last shall be first and the first last." (See how this saying is repeated in 20:16 after having already been given at the beginning [19:30].) For Matthew this was probably a reflection on the Jew-Gentile situation at about the time he wrote the gospel. This would mean, then, that in its original context the parable concluded with these penetrating words: "Is it lawful for me to do what I wish with what is my own? Or is your eye envious because I am generous?" (NASB). In other words, the original parable was a defense of God's generous mercy to all, probably as it again related to Jesus' receiving sinners. Matthew's context is not in opposition to this; it is, rather, a specific application of it. It would seem that both of these words may legitimately be considered God's Word to our situation.

There is at least one other factor that must be kept in view in the interpretation of the gospels. Since there are four gospels, and since three of them are almost certainly literarily interdependent, they should not be interpreted in isolation from one another. This point, which one may already see at work in the illustrations given above, has long been recognized in the Church and probably does not need extensive belaboring. What does need to be emphasized here is that the nature or direction of those relationships will, and probably should, affect one's interpretation of many passages.

Therefore, a good, solid exercise in the synoptic problem will greatly enhance the interpreter's abilities.

Although not all scholars are agreed at this point, the best solution seems to be to see John as completely independent from the other three and Mark as a basic source of Matthew and Luke, with both of the latter having access to other sources, one (or some) of which they had in common. But the oral tradition did not cease once Mark was written down, and many of the differences among the gospels are to be attributed not to, let us say, Matthew's use of Mark, but rather to the tenacity of the oral tradition; in some cases Matthew simply preferred a form of the oral tradition, which was well known to him and his church, to the form he found in Mark.

The significance of these conclusions are several. I suggest two.

1. Many times what is obscure in one gospel will be clarified, or interpreted, in another. Thus Mark's report of the desolating sacrilege standing where it ought not (13:14) is clarified in Matthew as referring to something from Daniel and as "standing in the holy place" (Mt 24:15, NASB), and is fully interpreted in Luke as referring to Jerusalem surrounded by armies (21:20).

2. The perspective of each of the evangelists and their immediate contexts are frequently going to be revealed as they are seen in light of the others. Luke's emphasis on joy, praise, and prayer, for example, is most easily recognized when his gospel is studied alongside Mark and Matthew. We have already suggested how the understanding of this context greatly enhances the possibilities of our hearing God's Word for our context.

One final word about the gospels. Not every word must be understood in light of its literary genre. Love for one's enemies, or unlimited forgiveness, or radical obedience to God and His will do not await our understanding of the literary genre. They await our obedience. But in many cases the principles given here will help us better to hear God's will so that we may obey it.

THE APOCALYPSE

Since the Revelation has had such a profusion of words as to how it should be interpreted, it might appear the height of ambition (perhaps folly) to try to speak to that issue within a limited context. Usually discussions of the hermeneutics of the Apocalypse begin by isolating the various schools of interpretation. While it probably is not possible to find principles which will transcend such schools, I would propose a few modest suggestions related to the question of its genre.

In the first place, as with the other genre, the Apocalypse must first of all be taken seriously as a first-century document, written to a specific group of people in a specific historical context. To lift it out of its historical context, it would seem fair to say, is to doom it. As with the epistles, and even though Revelation deals with future expectations, the maxim is still valid: what neither the author could have intended nor the recipients could have understood can be the initial meaning of a passage.||

Secondly, although I agree with those who emphasize the prophetic element in the Apocalypse,[8] this must not blind one to the fact that it is first of all cast in an apocalyptic mold. After all, in contrast to an Isaiah, Amos, or Hosea, the Apocalypse was literary from the start, whereas their writings were first of all spoken oracles, which were later gathered and written down.

There is still disagreement among scholars as to what are the essential characteristics of apocalyptic literature. Nevertheless, the following items are recognizable apocalyptic features and should be kept in view at any specific point of interpretation.

1. The tendency toward various kinds of schematizations should alert one to some of the carefully designed—and significant—structural arrangements in the Apocalypse. This is especially true of the sets of seven (seals, trumpets, vials), with their consistent pattern of smaller sets of four, two, and one. To take these as literal or sequential is probably to do far more than John "saw" or intended.

2. In contrast to the figures of speech or the realistic symbolism one finds, for example, in the prophets (plumb lines, baskets of summer fruit, a cake not turned), the apocalyptists regularly used fantastic symbolism (i.e., the symbolism of fantasy). Beasts, horns,

||I mean by this that one must "take seriously" that there was a real John, who was really in exile for his faith, that he was writing to real churches known to us from history, and that these churches were really suffering the internal disorders and external pressures indicated in chapters 2-3.

heads, and diadems are recognizable realities, but not in the combination of a leopard with bear's feet and a lion's mouth, with ten
horns and seven heads and ten diadems. Even though these symbols often serve almost as allegories, one must take care not to press
all the symbols to some specific meaning. The nature of the symbolic is that it is *not* the real thing, but merely represents the real
in some way.

3. These two features of schematization and symbolism join in
the apocalyptist's use of numbers. Here, especially, one must be
careful not to press for literalism. A thousand years to an apocalyptist *may* indeed mean a thousand years, but it is equally—or
perhaps more—possible that it merely represents a long period of
time.

4. At one point guesswork is eliminated. In several instances the
symbols are specifically identified. Here, at least, one can have
reasonable certainty as to what the original recipients understood.
When the woman of chapter 17 is identified as the great city, seated
on seven hills, which has dominion over the kings of the earth, the
original recipients could *only* have understood that to be Rome,
which after all was responsible for the exile of John and the martyrdom of the Christians, which called the book forth. Rather
than to reinterpret what is certain because it fails to fit a prear-
ranged scheme, the interpreter ought to *start* with such clues and
let any scheme be subject to them.

5. It is with some insight that scholars have recognized the dramatic nature of the Apocalypse, with its varying acts and scenes.[9]
Whether intended specifically as a drama is surely debatable, but
this insight suggests that such a work is addressed to the imagina-
tion in the way that poetry is often addressed to mood and prose
to the mind. To subject such a work to overanalysis often blinds
one to the whole, a true case of missing the forest for the trees.

Finally, let all interpreters of the Apocalypse submit to the kind
of humility that admits that the first recipients had possible keys
and insights which we may never have. Berkeley Mickelsen's word
is worth hearing: "It is much better to say: 'I do not know what
this means' than to force a meaning upon the imagery which it
was not meant to carry."[10]

The foregoing suggestions are not intended to be exhaustive, nor are they contended for as certain. Hopefully they have raised sufficient questions so as to keep one from "doing the Bible in" by lack of hermeneutical precision.

However, there remains one final problem. The suggestions offered in this paper may seem so staggering to the common man, to whom the Bible was originally addressed, that interpretation becomes an affair only of the expert. Fortunately, the Spirit, as the wind, "bloweth where it listeth" (Jn 3:8), and in this instance He has a wonderful way of graciously bypassing the expert and addressing us directly.

To this problem, therefore, I would offer these suggestions:

1. Let the expert himself really be that. That is, for the one with the responsibility of teaching or proclaiming God's Word, there is no alternative to the hard work of exegesis and all that involves of the knowing of philology, grammar, history, etc. But let exegesis be the spadework of teaching, or proclamation. Do not stop to admire the framework, nor let that framework be so obvious that no one can see the house. After all, the letter and the Spirit are not opposed to one another. It is only when one has the letter alone that it kills, or only when one has the Spirit alone that the structure is sure to collapse.

2. Let the nonexpert not despair; but let him also be prepared to study, not simply to devotionalize. To study he should use these basic tools: a) More than one good contemporary translation. This should point out at times where some of the problems lie. He should be sure to use translations which recognize the differences between prose and poetry and are aware of paragraphs. b) At least one good commentary, especially one that takes into account the hermeneutical principles offered in this paper (e.g., C. K. Barrett, on 1 Corinthians; F. F. Bruce, on Hebrews; R. E. Brown, on John). Again, consulting several will usually apprise one of various options. c) His own common sense. Scripture is not filled with hidden meanings to be dug out by miners in dark caves. Try to discover what is plainly intended by the biblical author. This inten-

tion usually lies close to the surface and needs only a little insight into grammar or history to become visible. Very often it lies right on the surface and the expert misses it because he is too prone to dig first and look later. At this point the nonexpert has much to teach the expert.

Finally, proper hermeneutics demands a stance of humility. This includes not only the humility of learning from others, but more significantly the humility of coming under the judgment of the Word one is interpreting. Although the task of the interpreter requires study and judgments, his ultimate task is to let the Word he is studying address him and call him to obedience and service.

7

History and Culture in New Testament Interpretation

by Alan Johnson

IN ONE SENSE everything in Christianity hinges on interpretation.[1] The question is not, Will we interpret the Bible? but, How will we interpret it? Sound exegetical principles are absolutely mandatory to guard us from *eisegesis,* i.e., reading into the text of Scripture our twentieth-century Western-world ideas and our own personal opinions. Because the Bible is the Word of God, our ultimate concern in interpretation is rightly with the question, What does the Scripture mean *to me?* But this question, as Dr. Fee has indicated, cannot properly be answered until we have carefully considered a prior question, What did the Scripture mean *to those to whom it was first given?* The nature of the Bible requires us to answer both questions with a sound methodology. While historical and cultural considerations are not the only concerns in answering these questions, they provide the interpreter with the basis for rigorously developing the point of view of those to whom Scripture was given.

In the long history of the church's interpretation of the Bible, there have been periods of vigorous interest in and notable neglect of historical/cultural exegesis. Whatever the extenuating circumstances, the school of Alexandria, with Origen (d. 254) as its chief representative, epitomizes the neglect of historical/cultural exegesis. All who in succeeding ages allegorize Scripture to some extent repeat the same eisegetical fallacy.

On the other hand, the early Syrian school of Antioch opposed the allegorizing method of the Alexandrians by emphasizing the literal, historical, and normal sense of Scripture as the true sense. Its chief proponents, Theodore of Mopsuestia (d. 5th century), Chrysostom (d. 407), and Jerome (d. 420) likewise continued to influence the Church, especially the sixteenth-century reformers. In the long run this later method has become the principle, though not exclusive, exegetical approach of the Christian church.[2]

More recently, since the nineteenth-century enlightenment, historical/cultural interest has led many to reformulate orthodox Christianity into a liberal, modernistic expression. Evangelical Christians, in reaction to this trend, were suspicious of any historical-critical approach to the Bible, since such a methodology seemed to lead to theological liberalism and even finally to radical and process theology. What some evangelicals are now rightly emphasizing, however, is that what caused theological liberals to go astray was not their emphasis on a thorough understanding of the historical and cultural backgrounds of the documents but their prior humanistic assumptions.[3] They started with the belief that the Bible was not actually the Word of God written but merely a product of the human mind in its own culture. Since this is the case, the evangelical student should no longer fear utilizing extensive historical/cultural background information as an aid to carefully interpreting the message of the Word of God to the original hearers. He will not always find the engagement smooth sailing, but there is certainly no other approach to the Scriptures as fruitful and God-honoring.

Historical/cultural matters take us into a wide variety of areas and details. In the New Testament alone matters of political, economic, social, geographical, religious, and philosophical background, and a great many details of culture, such as clothing, homes, and food, clamor for attention as we assess the precise intent of the biblical materials. No one person could possibly master all the background material now available; and even if one could, he would have to admit that there are gaps which perhaps never will be filled in.

Our approach will be modest. There exist already good, short summaries of the whole subject[4] as well as excellent, more extensive works on New Testament backgrounds.[5] We will sketch only the broad features of New Testament historical/cultural materials and emphasize in this essay some recent contributions that are proving fruitful to the interpreter. Method, after all, is much more crucial in interpretation than multiplication of detail.

The Crucial Importance of the Historical/Cultural in Hermeneutics

The historical/cultural nature of divine revelation

Any method of interpreting the Bible must begin with a clear understanding of the nature of Scripture. Our view of the Bible will determine how we go about understanding its meaning. In this essay we affirm as a basic assumption that the Bible is the Word of God written in the language of men. Scripture is not a *mixture* of the words of God and the words of men (cf. 2 Pe 1:21) ; rather it is totally God's message or thoughts, expressed in and through human language. Although we cannot here show it, this affirmation is clearly supported from the evidence of the New Testament and Church history.[6] To affirm a dual nature for the Bible allows us on the one hand to take seriously the Bible's own claim to be God's Word written, and on the other, to recognize that the medium used to reveal this word is fully human as well. There is no divine speech in the sense that it is not also human speech. In the Scriptures, the human speaking turns out to be also the divine message.

When we look into the Bible to examine more closely these words of men, we discover that they are not abstract statements but words about actual human events involving all types of circumstances in people's everyday lives. It is within and inseparably related to these historical events that God revealed His Word to men. Only as we understand the specifics and how events interrelated in the biblical culture of a certain period can we hope to understand the meaning of the words of the Scripture as the original hearers would have understood them.

The twofold task of hermeneutics

For us the task of hermeneutics can never be complete until we first understand the message in its historical/cultural setting and then *translate* that message to relate to our contemporary world.

To translate the message involves much more than simply matching the original Greek or Hebrew words with their English equivalents. We must also translate cultural concepts. Modern men, for example, have no real experience in slave purchasing and redemption. Consequently, when we hear the English word *redemption*, we cannot identify the meaning with any experience in our world. But we do know about POWs being freed or liberated, and this modern cultural/historical association might do far more to convey the real understanding of *redemption* than to use a term which today has no cultural experience value.

The point is that the eternal message of God's salvation was incarnated in a specific, cultural language of an ancient, historical people and must be reincarnated in today's culture or else there can be little communication, little transformation, and little active response. At least some of the powerlessness of modern preaching and the ineffectiveness of relating faith to contemporary learning must be attributed to failure in this area. If the hermeneutical task is understood to be only one sided, a passage is likely to be studied in its historical context, then the message formulated into some general, abstract, religious, or philosophical language and offered to people as biblical preaching.

Our meanings vs. the biblical authors' meaning

It has long been recognized that the context bears an important relationship to determining the meaning of biblical words or statements. Why should this be so? Simply because it forces us to consider the author's intended meaning instead of our own. Context-concern forces us away from our private meanings back into the ideological framework of the author. But context must be understood to include more than the surrounding paragraph, chapter, and book. The careful interpreter must also consider the historical/cultural context of the world to which the New Testament writers spoke their message. Although there is a valid sense in which the New Testament is self-interpreting by a consideration of the literary contexts and references, there is also a sense in which the text is not fully self-interpreting without consideration of its historical background.

Of course, it is easy to assume that the Bible is completely self-interpreting. When we read the words of a passage of Scripture where the meaning seems clear enough to us, we assume that this must be what the author intended. We hasten to identify our interpretation with what the text is actually teaching. Each interpreter, both ancient and modern, liberal and conservative, not realizing that he is reading the New Testament from his own historical context, has tended to identify what he has drawn from the Scripture directly with the teaching of the Bible. He then attributes to his interpretation the same authority that he assigns to the text itself. When this takes place, the interpretation becomes a veil drawn over the surface of the Scripture, preventing the text from saying anything that would differ from the conventional interpretation.

In Jesus' day the Sadducees and Pharisees, each in a different way, had committed themselves to just such an identification of their traditional interpretations with the teaching of the Scriptures. This practice enabled them to validate their established beliefs and practices and leave intact the main structure of their religious community. It also allowed them to reject Jesus as the Messiah because He did not fit into their interpretative tradition. In their view, to contradict traditional interpretations in any way was to contradict God Himself. They had imprisoned the Scriptures through their traditional interpretations and failed to hear them speak concerning Jesus (Jn 5:39, 46-47).*

---

*James D. Smart (*The Strange Silence of the Bible in the Church: A Study of Hermeneutics* [Philadelphia: Westminster, 1970], pp. 53-54) states this point much more effectively than I. Smart is perceptive, although I do not share some of his theological conclusions, especially his negative comments concerning belief in the infallibility of Scripture. While belief in an infallible Bible, as he says, certainly may lead some to conclude that their interpretations are infallible, there is no logical connection between the two. Smart nowhere explains the evidence of how a great many scholars today who hold to an infallible Bible also hold to fallible interpretation, nor does he emphasize that theological liberals who reject infallibility also are as guilty of absolutizing their interpretations as the fundamentalists.

It was perhaps Jesus' fresh interpretation of the Scriptures that at least in part caused the masses to acknowledge the authority and wisdom of His teaching (Mt 7:28-29; 13:54). In fact, this wisdom may well have been what linked Jesus to the prophetic tradition in Israel and distinguished Him from the Rabbinic tradition.[7] Luther also demonstrated this quality of fresh interpretation of the text which liberated the Word of God from long medieval traditions. A new hermeneutic gave birth to a new Gospel (the apostles') which, in turn, called for a new form of worship and a new life-style.

An example of how our own ideas affect interpretation can be seen in the way we read the Bible to find support for our political affiliations and theories. If the social context we move in tends to be politically conservative, it is surprising how, when we read the Bible, it seems to support separation of church and state, decentralized government, a "no work-no food" concept, strong military, separation of the races, etc. On the other hand, others find it easy to see how concerned the Bible is with social problems, activism, poverty programs, integration of the races, demilitarism, and the general criticism of middle-America, especially when they live within a context of political leftism or liberalism. We tend to adjust the plumb-line to fit our preferences by the selective reading of Scripture and by listening only to our own traditional interpretations.

What is needed is a way out of this dilemma. We must force ourselves out of the narrow confines of our own social context by first of all seriously studying New Testament culture and history and at the same time entering into meaningful dialogue with other Christians from different church traditions and social/cultural backgrounds. We must also avoid reading and listening selectively to the Bible.[8] Finally, let me stress again that we need a serious return to and respect for the text of Scripture itself and what it is saying to us regardless of how many cherished theological interpretations or church structures and practices we must discard or modify.

All this reminds us that it is never possible to read the Bible without at the same time, though often unconsciously, interpreting it from our own context. This should not cause us to despair.

Rather, we should hold our interpretations with humility (they are never final) and deliberately attempt to get back into the context of the world of the New Testament writers to avoid as much as possible the injection of our views into the Bible's.

A BICULTURAL APPROACH TO INTERPRETATION

Recognizing, then, that the Word of God comes to us in the New Testament in the specific cultural/historical language of the first century, we need a bicultural approach to Scripture.[9] In this approach, the interpreter attempts to see the immediate historical context of the writer, revealed partly in his literary context and more completely in the broader context of his world and times. While he searches for the author's full context, he constantly keeps in mind the possibility that he is reading into the text his own culture and making the biblical statements agree with his own notions and traditions.

On the basis of what has been already indicated, we see that the message of the Word of God is expressed by the cultural forms, but the cultural specifics in themselves are not the message. For example, in John 9:6 we are told that Jesus spit and made a mud pack to put on the eyes of the blind man. Whatever message we find in the text from a careful analysis of John's purpose in recording this incident, the Word of God will not consist in using Jesus' spitting as an example to follow in our culture. That which has a very important, personal quality attached to it in Eastern cultures (i.e., spit) is in ours a nasty gesture. This same point could be applied to itinerant missionary preaching methods found in the book of Acts, or to women's wearing long hair or a veil (1 Co 11), or even to the woman's functional role in the church (1 Co 14:34-35). The simple point is that the Word of God is expressed by the specific cultural forms, but the Word for us does not consist in the transmission of those first-century cultural patterns per se.

The failure to recognize this distinction is especially noticeable today in some of the Jesus People groups. They are trying to reproduce both the message and the culture of the New Testament world in their life-styles. For example, some reject the use of music and singing to spread the Gospel because "singing was never used in the early church or by the apostles to spread the Gospel."[10]

What proves confusing is that in practice everyone already makes *some* distinctions. For example, we all recognize that Paul's command to stop eating meat if it offends a brother (1 Co 8) cannot apply specifically to our Western culture, where meat is never used as a sacrificial food. Here is a plain case of a cultural difference. Everyone quickly looks for the spiritual principle, or the underlying message of the exhortation which can be applied to our situation today. This is fine. But it is at this point where a subtle deception may enter. We are blinded in assuming that where there does not seem to be any cultural difference, the plain reading of the text which seems so clear to us is all that is necessary. In these cases we may unconsciously be reading into the text our own cultural equivalents of the related biblical terms.

For example, it seems plain enough to some that Paul says that women should have head coverings in the churches and men short hair (1 Co 11:6, 14). Since women still wear hats today they should wear them in church, and obviously short side burns and neat, short hair is more scriptural for men. But some feel uneasy about whether Paul should be understood so simply in this way. They either ignore the teaching about hats or simply follow the majority in omitting a covering in church. Yet how many ask the question, What was the significance of a head covering to the society at Corinth in the first century? Or who asks how long "long hair" was for a man in that culture and what meaning was attached to it?

My point is that the principles of interpretation we apply more or less automatically in cases where the biblical culture is considerably different than our own, we should be applying all the time, even in apparently clear cases. Only in this way can we avoid reading into the text our own cultural designations. This applies also to biblical expressions like "born again" which can unconsciously take on a modern, religious, cultural understanding (i.e., of our own group). Our understanding may imply something different than Jesus' teaching in John 3, but in our minds it is equivalent to the biblical idea. It may never occur to us that Paul, who wrote most of the New Testament, never used this term to refer to a person becoming a Christian! Our emphasis and use of the term comes from our group rather than the New Testament.

In India, recently, I was told how certain 'Hmar Christians in the Nagaland were being fined a pig for becoming a Christian. It was easy for me to assume that a pig to me was a pig to them. Such was not the case. The pig is used among the 'Hmars as a legal fine for such crimes as adultery, stealing, or burning your own or another's home. Value-wise, the pig is about equivalent to an automobile here. Pigs in Nagaland have social significance in weddings and certain initiation rites for young men. Religiously they are used for sacrifices to their gods and can be killed only at certain times. The pig is interwoven with practically every aspect of 'Hmar life. For a man to give up his pig as a fine for becoming a Christian means far more than the loss of the price of the animal, as it would to us. I had experienced a bicultural problem in communication. Even though the same English word was used, the cultural significance was vastly different.

This bicultural approach applies also to metaphorical terms, such as *head*. When Paul speaks of Christ as the "head" of the Church (Col 1:18) we naturally think of a "boss" or "president" in a corporation. While this idea is not altogether missing from the New Testament thought, it is closer to first-century ideas to see the head as that which *nourishes* the rest of the body and draws it to its goal (cf. Eph 4:13).[11] The ancients did not view the head as the seat of the intellectual faculties, or brains, as we do in our culture. While the word *head* is used metaphorically in our culture, as it was in the biblical world, the connotations are not identical. By failing to grasp this principle we either distort or sometimes even destroy the true message of the Scripture.

RELATIVITY AND INFALLIBILITY

Are there problems in this approach? Some may reason that if God reveals His Word to men in their cultures, and cultures change, then is not the Word of God relative? If God's Word is relative to each age, how can the Bible contain eternal truth or speak to successive ages and entirely different cultures? It is easier, of course, to state this problem than to give a satisfactory answer.

To begin with, it may be helpful to recognize that the Bible's primary intent, as given in numerous references, is to make known the Word of God which is a revelation of God Himself, His purposes of grace, and His will for man (Jn 10:34-36; 2 Ti 3:15-16; Jn 5:39, 46-47). Since God is unchangeable, His Word of salvation and the message about Himself is also unchangeable and eternal. This eternal Word, which first finds expression in a specific culture and time, can be heard once again in that original setting by careful exegesis. In turn this Word can also be reincarnated with transforming power in successive and different cultures precisely because it is the eternal Word of God (cf. Ps 119:89).

We must remember, then, that Scripture is not designed to be a revelation of the culturally relative features which form the sounding board for its eternal message about God Himself. This is not to suggest that the biblical writers were unconcerned about the accuracy of these relative matters. Especially would this be true of historical events which are not culturally relative. But we cannot pass judgment on the eternal message of the Scriptures, the Word of God, by accusing the culturally relative medium of imprecision or inaccuracy in the light of modern knowledge.

To take a well-known example, Jesus referred to the mustard seed as "the smallest" of all seeds (Mt 13:32). We should not, therefore, judge the Word of God as inaccurate because modern botanical information discloses that orchid seeds are yet smaller. To my knowledge, there were no orchids in first-century Palestine; so the mustard seed was the smallest seed known to Jesus' audience (culturally). Jesus' message (hence, the Word of God) was not aimed at teaching the disciples botanical information. He simply used the common, culturally designated meaning as a vehicle to express His teaching concerning the Kingdom of God. If He were addressing a modern botanical society, He might have spoken the same divine message to them but used the orchid seed. Yet, on the other hand, He might still have used a mustard seed, because the contrast between smallness and largeness in the parable might not be served well enough with an orchid analogy.

No charge of errancy or unreliability should be brought against the Scriptures as the Word of God on this account, since the infallibility of Scripture lies in its eternal message, which is transmitted in and by the relative cultural milieu. It is not the truth of seeds which is at stake but the infallible truth of the Kingdom of God. This does not mean, however, that the Bible necessarily contains factual errors or outmoded concepts which were a part of ancient cultures. In every case, the cultural vehicle for incarnating the Word of God will be found to be wholly adequate and trustworthy for God's purpose.

Once we allow for culturally relative language forms, someone may ask, what is to prevent us from seeing in the Scriptures culturally relative thought patterns of the ancient world? Do we not have in the Old Testament a picture of a flat earth resting on pillars, with waters both under and over a solid, domed firmament (Gen 1:6, 7; Ps 75:3)? In the New Testament does not Paul seem to refer to a three-story view of the universe, with God in the third heaven and demonic powers loose in the world (2 Co 12:2; Eph 4:9-10; Eph 6:12)? Does not Paul appeal several times in his letters to the Old Testament as understood through a rabbinic method of exegesis, which he learned in his early Jewish training (1 Co 9:9-10; 10:1-4; Gal 4:24)? Is it not, then, possible that the biblical writers simply assimilated the thought patterns of their surrounding cultures and taught these ideas as the Word of God?

At this point it is necessary to make an all-important distinction between what the biblical author, along with his contemporaries, may have believed about certain scientific aspects of his world and what he actually teaches. For example, a prophet may have believed, as did most of his contemporaries, in the flatness of the earth. Thus, in setting forth the revelation of God certain allusions or references to a flat earth may appear as part of the cultural fabric necessary to communicate his message. If the biblical writer was trying to teach that the earth is flat, and this is in fact the point of the passage, then this teaching becomes equivalent to the infallible Word of God.

There is, however, to my knowledge no passage in the Scripture which can be demonstrated to *teach* this as its point. On the other hand, while Paul does not *teach* a particular view of exegesis of the Old Testament, or any specific view of cosmology, he certainly teaches the reality of demonic powers in the world (Eph 6:12). Christians are bound by this teaching and must make it part of their world view. John may have believed, as did most of his contemporaries, in the flatness of the earth with its "four corners" (Rev 7:1), but he does not teach this at this point. Luther's condemnation of Copernicus' heliocentric theories on the basis that the Bible *taught* that the sun rises and sets because Joshua prayed for the sun to stand still is a classic illustration of the failure to discern between what the Bible teaches and the cultural medium in which teaching is expressed.

DISTINGUISHING THE WORD OF GOD FROM THE CULTURAL

Are we, then, to engage in a process of extracting the kernel of truth from the cultural husk? The basic problem in this approach has always been that the message and the cultural vehicle are so closely interwoven that when one begins to peel off the cultural layers, the Scriptures turn out to be more like an onion than a banana. Once the separation process is begun, it usually results in eliminating parts of the message as well as the cultural mold. Liberal and more radical approaches to Scripture, such as Bultmann's demythologizing program, clearly illustrate this and have been well documented elsewhere.

In some instances where it is quite easy for us to distinguish the message from the cultural vehicle (e.g., the injunction against eating food sacrificed to idols), we are tempted to separate the principles from the cultural vehicle. These instances allow us to see clearly that it is the nature of Scripture to incarnate the Word of God in a cultural medium. However, in other instances such separation is difficult (e.g., questions of the historicity of Adam or the Mosaic authorship of the Pentateuch).[12] The radical literal approach will absolutize both the message and the cultural specifics by atomizing the text from its full context; the radical cultural approach, on the other hand, relativizes both the cultural vehicle and the message itself. Both approaches err, though in different ways. A third approach is needed.

We are not called, then, to engage in ferreting out the revealed truth from the nonrevealed, the eternal truths from the cultural vehicle, after the manner of the neoliberal. Rather, we must simply listen to the message of each unit of Scripture. We must attempt to hear the author's intended sense in his historical/cultural context. When we discover this meaning, we have heard the Word of God and are ready to articulate that meaning in our own cultural terms. If McLuhan's thesis can be trusted—that in some sense "the medium is the message"—then we cannot successfully separate the vehicle from the truth. Rather, we must listen to each writer in his literary, historical, and cultural setting and then transfuse that meaning into our nearest modern vehicle. Such a task requires much hard work, and too few in our day are doing it.

An illustration may help to distinguish these three methods of handling the problem of culture and interpretation. Consider the case of 2 Peter 3:5-6: "By the word of God the heavens existed long ago and the earth was formed out of water and by water, through which the world at that time was destroyed, being flooded with water." Most commentators point out that Peter was alluding to the accounts of creation and the flood episodes in the book of Genesis (1:2, 6-7; 7:6-24). He seems to have reiterated the ancient cosmological perception of the world being "formed out of water." It is true that some commentators explain this statement as a reference to the earth being separated from the water (Gen 1:9). However, what if Peter was in fact referring to a view of cosmology which he shared with the ancient world but which no one today would hold as correct? How do interpreters handle this difficulty?

The *radical literalist* views the words atomistically and argues for accepting the cultural reference as the Word of God in itself. He would argue that if it is in the Bible, it must be the inspired, infallible, scientific view of how the earth originated (i.e., "out of water and by water"). Thus, by atomizing the text and not distinguishing the cultural vehicle from the message of Peter, the radical literalist absolutizes the ancient cosmology as well as the message in the passage.†

A typical *radical cultural* (liberal) handling of the verse will not only put the cosmology of Peter into an outdated, unacceptable category, but will also relativize the author's teaching concerning the second coming of Christ about which Peter is talking. Both the cultural allusions *and* the teaching are viewed as ideas which were assimilated from the contemporary culture. In this interpretation the certainty of the personal return of Christ to this world is not taken as the unambiguous Word of God but is classified as a carry over from early Jewish apocalypticism.

In the *third way* of approaching the text, the *historical-interpretive*, which we are suggesting, the whole passage (especially 3:1-10) must be interpreted in its full context and not atomized. What did the author intend to teach by the passage? Clearly he was not intending to teach some particular cosmology or cosmogony. He simply alluded in passing to the current scientific view of the origin of the world to set forth his actual point concerning the certainty of Christ's return.

In order to do this Peter appealed directly to the past acts of God in creation and in judgment through the Noahic flood. God's Word was active in creating and governing the world. It is this same Word which has announced the return of Christ to this world in judgment upon the unrepentant and with salvation for the believer. He was teaching the certainty, though delayed, of the coming of Christ back to this world in fulfillment of the Word of God's promises. God has acted directly in the history of the world, and He will also act decisively again when Christ returns.

This teaching concerning the return of Christ is what Peter intended to set forth as God's infallible Word. When he mentioned God's creative activity in forming the world, he used the commonly understood, ancient way of describing how the earth originated,

---

†In fairness to the literalist, it may be pointed out that our current cosmological views are no more than modern scientific *theories*, which may be altered and even drastically revised in coming years. Recent theories may serve our age more adequately for purposes of explanation of phenomena but are not to be viewed as the truth about the world in contrast to the ancient, "false" view.

and he ascribed the process directly to the creative Word of God. We should not, then, atomize the text and attribute absolute authority as the Word of God to that which, though it conveys the teaching, is not the point of the author.

If we historically and contextually interpret the Bible rather than atomize or identify it with the ancient culture, we will avoid two opposite but damaging approaches to the full integrity of the Scriptures as the infallible Word of God expressed in fully human terms. I believe what I have argued for the Scriptures as the Word of God in human language can also be argued for the Word of God incarnated in human flesh (Jn 1:14).

EXPERTS AND NONPROFESSIONALS

One further, more practical problem in this historical/cultural approach to Scripture should be mentioned. If the interpreter's understanding of the Bible depends so heavily on knowing the full historical/cultural context of each passage, how can a nonprofessional be sure he is understanding the Scripture at all? Does not this approach prevent all but the experts from really understanding Scripture?

In the first place, we do find in some circles a somewhat naïve view of Bible interpretation. It is readily assumed that if the Bible is read in a good, modern translation and the sense seems to be quite plain, then this is all that is needed. While certainly some measure of the Bible's message and meaning can be gained from repeated readings in a good translation, the fact remains that the Bible is still an ancient book and its expressions, images, and literary genre require an awareness of the ancient world for the most fruitful understanding. Interpreting the Bible correctly demands hard work.

But, lest the nonexpert be totally discouraged at this point, he should remember that he already has at his fingertips two of the most important resources for interpreting the New Testament correctly. He has at his right hand, first of all, the Old Testament, which forms the primary religious framework for understanding the New Testament, especially the gospels. And second, he has at his left the book of Acts, which, though limited, gives him historical background for understanding most of the New Testament letters. Furthermore, if the nonexpert reader will pay close attention to the context of a passage, he often can discern a great deal of the central teaching, even though details may present problems (e.g., what does "mammon" mean in Luke 16:9?). Nonexperts should read the Scripture neither despairingly nor naïvely.

GENERAL PRINCIPLES FOR HISTORICAL/CULTURAL INTERPRETATION OF THE NEW TESTAMENT

In conclusion a number of broad principles may be kept in mind when attempting to understand the Word of God as it comes historically and culturally incarnated in the New Testament writings.

1. Be constantly aware of the general similarities and differences between the New Testament world and our own.

2. Recognize the diversity of the historical/cultural within the scope of the New Testament writings. The gospels, generally, and Acts 1-12 are Jewish-Palestinian, while most of the epistles are Graeco-Roman in background.

3. Look for direct, internal evidence in the writings to define specific cultural terms or to identify historical events, persons, etc.

4. Familiarize yourself with any Old Testament background alluded to and understand as much as possible the relationship between the epistles and history recorded in Acts. It is in most cases more important to know the general historical situation than specific dates.

5. Seek to understand in what ways the narrative transcends the surrounding culture. This provides additional help in discerning the intent of the author. It also forces us into the world of the New Testament writers through whatever external resources may be available.

We must work hard to overcome our own biases and yet be humble enough to admit that our interpretations are always fallible and that only God and His Word are infallible.

THE WORLD OF THE FIRST CENTURY AND NEW TESTAMENT INTERPRETATION

Having surveyed the importance of the historical/cultural in interpretation, it may now be helpful to look more specifically at the major areas of New Testament background. Our plan is to trace the chief kinds of information which affect our understanding of the documents.

Historically, the literature of the New Testament falls into three principal time periods. The gospels and Acts 1-12, representing the life of Jesus and early Jewish Christianity, unfolded during the Roman emperorships of Tiberius and Caligula, and the first part of Claudius' reign, approximately A.D. 26-44. A second, or "epistle," period may be identified, during which time the events of Acts 13-28 unfolded and all the New Testament letters (except John's) were written (A.D. 47-65). Finally, we have the Johannine period. This literature unfolds most probably during the later reign of the Emperor Domitian (c. A.D. 95-97) involving the three epistles of John and the book of Revelation.

Culturally, the New Testament writings involve two environments somewhat distinct but also overlapping. In the gospels and in Acts 1-12 the setting is primarily *Jewish,* while events in the epistles and Revelation transpired in the *Graeco-Roman* world.

In each setting, or environment, it is also possible to distinguish, though not to separate, four ingredients which constituted the environment: (1) the *cultural* and *physical* environment involving geography, language, and everyday items of life; (2) the *political* environment; (3) the *economic and social* environment; and (4) the *religious, moral, and philosophical* environment.

There are numerous surveys of both the Jewish and the Graeco-Roman backgrounds to the New Testament. The following remarks, together with a few illustrations in each area, will serve merely as a guide to the kinds of materials the interpreter may employ.

THE GOSPELS AND ACTS 1-12

As we have indicated, the events in the gospels and Acts 1-12 transpired primarily within a Jewish setting. Therefore a knowledge of the Jewish literature, customs, and institutions of the first century are indispensable to a careful interpretation of our New Testament literature in these areas. Our study will focus in this area of the New Testament due to the lack of general information on Jewish background material.

We may note first of all some examples of the *general cultural and physical setting* as it may affect interpretation. We are interested, in each case, in examples which show the cruciality of the cultural dimension to the meaning and not merely its illuminating quality.

An understanding of the Hebrew and Aramaic language and their idioms provides limitless help in the gospels and early chapters of Acts. For example, understanding the expression "kingdom of heaven" in Matthew's gospel as an equivalent Hebrew idiom for the term "kingdom of God" in the other gospels enables the interpreter to avoid making artificial theological distinctions between the two.

A failure to understand Hebrew idiom is responsible for the New English Bible's paraphrase in Matthew 5:3, "How blest are those who know their need of God" for the literal, "Blessed are the poor in spirit." A careful examination reveals that rabbinic sources combine the idea of "poor" with "meek" (by connecting Is 61:1-2 with 66:2). They also understand *spirit,* when associated with poverty or meekness, as a reference to the Holy Spirit.[13]

Furthermore, the Dead Sea Scrolls not only contain the expression, "poor in spirit" as a reference to the Qumran Sect itself, but they also have the same threefold phraseology of poor (contrite), meek, and mournful which we find in Matthew 5:3-5.[14] In these scrolls the meaning of the expression "poor in spirit" means "the poor who possess the Holy Spirit." Poor here means materially poor (as it does everywhere in the New Testament) and not humble or needy of God (NEB) (cf. Lk 6:20; Mt 11:5). Could it be that most paraphrased translations miss the sense because they fail to bring the Hebrew idiom sufficiently to bear on the translation?

The more obvious "mammon" (Mt 6:24), "abba" (Mk 14:36), and "Beelzebub" (Mt 10:25) provide clear examples which illustrate the need of Hebrew backgrounds for interpretation. Not so obvious is the way that Greek words found in the gospels (and elsewhere) have been influenced by their use in the Greek Old Testament used by Christ and the apostles. The gospels' usage of the word *law* (Gk. *nomos*) conforms to the Old Testament idea of the Torah (teaching) and not to the general Greek sense of law (principle). James' use, on the other hand, is entirely Greek, while Paul uses both ideas. In John's gospel, words for the Holy Spirit such as, "the Spirit of truth" (Jn 15:26), or "the Comforter" (Jn 14:26) may be influenced in their meaning more by the Greek Old Testament than contemporary Greek usage. Thus the expression "Spirit of truth" (Gk. *alētheia*) would then refer to the Spirit of "faith," or "confidence" (Heb. *'emeth*) rather than the Spirit of "reality" or "truth" as against a lie (Greek idea). Likewise, the Hebrew Old Testament background of the Greek word for *Comforter (parakaleo)* would be the idea of cessation of sorrow through a change of heart, mind, intention (Heb. *nacham*). This would correspond to the thought of a "Convictor" rather than the usual Greek idea of comforter.[15] Examples could be multiplied considerably alerting the interpreter to the necessity of good, up-to-date historical commentaries on the gospels.[16]

Geographical sensitivity often illuminates a passage. For example, understanding that the "Decapolis" cities which Jesus visited were largely Gentile-pagan population (Mk 7:31) clarifies certain incidents. However, geographical considerations may also affect the meaning. Such may be the case in Jesus' expression, "You are the salt of the earth" (Mt 5:13). If the Sermon on the Mount took place on one of the shores of the Sea of Galilee, the most immediate association would have been that salt is used for the preservation of fish. This would tend to suggest the implication of the metaphor is "preservation from corruption" rather than "use for seasoning" (though some have seen a reference to the "salt of the covenant" in Lev 2:13). Further, salt is also used externally on sheep to kill bacteria, which further supports the idea of a preservative.

Much of the material in the gospels is rural in setting, despite the extended sections of our Lord's ministry in Jerusalem. Compared to Judea, Galilee, with its higher rainfall, was heavily populated and quite fertile. The rural areas tended to produce Christians that were conservative and agricultural in outlook, while the city dwellers were progressive and commercial. Such a distinction may well account for the early social clash in Jerusalem between

the Judean country-folk and the Hellenistic town-dwellers (Ac 6:
1-7).

Simple homelife customs, such as the "three measures of meal"
in the parable of the woman hiding the leaven (Mt 13:33), occasionally take on interpretive significance. Three *seahs* (measures)
is about fifty pounds of dough, or when baked enough to feed one
hundred persons. This would not be a normal mixing but may
indicate preparation for a special feast (marriage?) or even tribute
to a divine visitor (cf. 1 Sa 1:24; Judg 6:19).[17] An awareness of
the tremendous size of the batch must modify our interpretation
of the parable in some way.

Certainly the custom of wearing a freshly washed garment to a
wedding may explain why in Jesus' parable the man without this
clean garment was thrown out (Mt 22:11-13). He was invited
sooner than he had expected and was caught off guard, without a
newly washed garment. From rabbinic parallels, the garment
would represent repentance, or in the Old Testament, righteousness given by God (cf. Is 61:10).[18] In either case, the background
of the incident is important for its correct interpretation.

When we come to the *political* environment surrounding the
gospels, we are faced in Palestine with the dual system of (1) Roman prefects (Judea) and Herodian Tetrarchs (Galilee and elsewhere), and (2) the civil priesthood, with the semicivil court of
the Sanhedrin. This dual relationship comes to the fore especially
in the accounts of the trial of Jesus. Pilate, the Roman prefect of
Judea, had sole right to order capital punishment (*jus gladii*, cf. Jn
18:31), but the Jewish civil priest and Sanhedrin had the legal
right to hear cases and refer them in capital charges to the Roman
prefect (cf. Lk 23:1-5).

Accepting a slightly later date for the crucifixion (c. A.D. 33),
for which some argue strongly,[19] not only more adequately explains Pilate's behavior but alters the meaning of John 19:12, "If
you release this man, you are not Caesar's friend." In A.D. 31 one
of the emperor's most trusted and high officials, Sejanus, who had
strong anti-Semitic feelings, led an ill-fated revolt against Tiberius
and was executed along with many of his closest friends. The following year, the emperor inaugurated a pro-Jewish policy. Pilate

was caught between his own hatred for the Jews and his fear of giving Tiberius any reason to suspect that he was anti-Semitic and possibly allied with the subversive Sejanus. To release the Jew Jesus, who apparently was not guilty of treason as charged, would have been to Pilate's credit before the emperor, but he could not allow the Jewish leaders to report to Caesar that he had allowed a man to go free who "made himself a king." Pilate's act of washing his hands of Jesus' death while at the same time permitting His crucifixion (Mt 27:24) seems to take on new significance in the light of this historical-political situation.

Most of the new discoveries concerning *economic* and *social* conditions in first century Palestine are illuminating to the times but do not bear crucially on interpretation. More significant to the unraveling of the gospels is an understanding of *Jewish thought* in the time of Jesus and during the period of the early Church.

It has long been recognized by New Testament scholars that the Old Testament (Torah) played an important role in Jesus' teaching and that this knowledge alone is the best key to understanding His words. This, however, is to leave out a quite significant factor: throughout the history of the Jewish people there grew up an enormous body of oral law, which expanded and explained the written Law of Moses. At first only in oral form (Mishnah) and then later written down (Talmud from A.D. 100 and later), this body of teachings contained additional interpretations of the Old Testament Law, and more specifically authoritative and binding directions for the everyday life of a good Jew (Heb. *halakah*). These prescriptions were held to be as fully authoritative as the written Law of Moses.[20]

Without doubt Jesus referred to this body of information in saying, "How well you set aside the commandment of God in order to maintain your tradition!" (Mk 7:9, NEB). Some see the Mishnaic tradition behind Jesus' often repeated statements in the Sermon on the Mount, "You have learned that our forefathers were told . . . but what I tell you is this" (Mt 5:21-22, 27-28, 31-34, etc.). In this view, Jesus was both correcting the Mishnaic traditional interpretation of the Law of Moses and going beyond the Old Testament teaching itself.

More recent and not very well known is the vast amount of information yielded by the Dead Sea Scrolls. We have referred to these documents earlier in connection with the Hebrew-Aramaic language background of the gospels. The Dead Sea Scrolls shed possible new light on the above argument concerning Jesus and the Mishnaic tradition in the Sermon on the Mount. In one instance, Jesus said, "You have learned that they were told, 'Love your neighbor, hate your enemy' " (Mt 5:43). While the love of neighbor is enjoined in the Old Testament (Lev 19:18), nowhere in the Old Testament or in Judaism is there any specific injunction to hate one's enemy. There are in the Dead Sea sectarian literature, however, statements like the following: "To love all the sons of light, each according to his lot in the Council of God, and to hate all the sons of darkness, each according to his guilt in the vengeance of God" (1QS 1:9-11).[21] Jesus may have had the Qumran sect (Essenes?) in mind. (However, for an argument which understands Jesus as going against the Torah at certain points, see Harvey McArthur, *Understanding The Sermon on the Mount,* chap. 1, and J. Jeremias, *New Testament Theology,* pp. 84-85).

One of the most prominent areas where the thought of Judaism impinges on New Testament interpretation is in the *parables.* Since the time of Dodd's studies it has been fashionable in both conservative and liberal New Testament scholarly circles to understand the parables as expositions of the then inaugurated Kingdom of God.[22] If this is accepted, then the concept of the Kingdom of God in first-century Judaism provides indispensable background material for a correct interpretation of the parables.

One example must suffice. Among the many sects in Judaism of the first century was the Zealot sect. Zealots were dedicated to the violent political overthrow of Roman rule in Palestine as the means of setting up the Kingdom of God. In the parable of the seed growing secretly (Mk 4:26-29), one of the important ingredients involves the mysterious and supernatural growth of the seed of the Kingdom. This would oppose the Zealot idea of a sudden and violent coming of the Kingdom through active human force. There are many other parallels in the parables to current notions in Judaism about the Kingdom of God.

Before we leave the parables, a slightly different point can be mentioned concerning one aspect of the current form-critical approach to these stories. It is now customary for certain scholars to explain the conclusions at the endings of a number of parables as later additions and applications and not parts of the original stories of Jesus.[23] However, the presence of the same kind of concluding statements in many rabbinic parables of the period alerts us that this style was current Jewish practice and that these applications could well have been part of Jesus' own teaching.[24]

Another important area for gospel interpretation is an understanding of the *Jewish sects* in the first century. We are familiar from our New Testament with the names *Pharisee, Sadducee, Herodians,* and *Zealot.* There now exist good summary treatments[25] as well as continuing detailed studies[26] of the separate sects. Take the Pharisees as an example. It is not very well known that even though they were more numerous than the other religious sects, they were a minority of only about 1 percent of the Jewish population in Palestine in the first century.[27] Noting this fact along with observing that only a few of the rulers of the Pharisees were involved in the condemnation of Jesus, helps the student to keep the gospel references to Jewish opposition to Jesus in proper balance. The Pharisees of the gospels can be put further into perspective by recognizing from the Talmud seven different varieties of Pharisees, five of which are ridiculed in this Jewish work itself for their hypocrisy and ostentatious show.[28]

It may be possible to see the different interests of the Pharisees and scribes in contrast to the Sadducees in the accounts of the accusations brought against Jesus in His trial. Some recent writers have alleged that Jesus was put to death solely because of political considerations involving revolution.[29] Certainly the gospels bear witness to this dimension, both in the accusations (cf. Lk 23:1-5; Jn 11:47-48) and in Pilate's title put over the cross, "This is Jesus of Nazareth the King of the Jews." But the records are also clear that these charges were false, even as Pilate recognized in his repeated, "I find no fault in him." But even this is not the whole story in the gospels. Jesus was also condemned by certain of the Jewish hierarchy for religious blasphemy. This twofold charge leading to Jesus' execution can be historically credible if the Sadducees, who were the civil-priestly leaders, were primarily responsible for the political charges, because they feared revolution and the loss of their positions; and if, on the other hand, the Pharisees were active in pressing the charge of religious blasphemy. Without both forces at work the strange death of Jesus cannot be explained adequately from a historical perspective.

Finally, some mention should be made to other types of *Jewish literature* than the aforementioned Septuagint, Mishna, and Dead Sea Scrolls. Principally we have in mind a group of Jewish books written from about 200 B.C. to A.D. 100. Though there are over fifty separate pieces of literature in this category,[30] twelve to fourteen of these books, known as the Apocrypha, have received more attention. While no New Testament speaker or writer actually quoted directly from this large body of literature, they were no doubt quite familiar with its content and themes. However, they did occasionally make allusions to certain sections of the apocryphal and pseudepigraphical literature. When this is the case, our interpretations will be strengthened by considering this historical/cultural dimension.

Most of the clear illustrations of this phenomena occur in the epistles. Jude 14-16 seems to refer to 1 Enoch 1:9, and there is a very probable allusion in Hebrews 11:34-35 to 2 Maccabees 6:18—7:42, and in Hebrews 11:37 to a passage in the Martyrdom of Isaiah. Paul may have been influenced in the literary form and content of Romans 1:18-23 and 3:10-18 by certain sections in the Wisdom of Solomon.

With reference to the gospels, we may note among many cases the example of John 3:14-15, where Jesus told the Jews, "As Moses lifted up the serpent in the wilderness, even so must the Son of man be lifted up: that whosoever believes in him may have eternal life." Jewish literature in pre-Christian times had prepared the way for this teaching, as indicated in Wisdom of Solomon 16:7: "For he who turned toward it [the serpent] was healed, not by what he saw, but by thee, Saviour of all." Furthermore, the Palestinian Targum (Aramaic interpretive paraphrase of Old Testament) attributes the healing to God invoked by prayer.[31] Both references stress the saving efficacy of trust in God Himself and not in the serpent. Jesus transferred faith to Himself as the Saviour.

The possibilities here are too extensive to quote at length. One can easily consult *The Greek New Testament* (American Bible Society) , edited by Aland, Black, et. al., where in footnotes on each New Testament verse and in a cumulative appendix the more direct allusions to apocryphal and pseudepigraphical literature are indicated.

Among the documents of a recent discovery (1946) of Gnostic literature, found in the Egyptian area of Nag Hammadi and written during the early post-New Testament centuries, is the Gospel of Thomas. The document is a collection of 114 sayings of Jesus, in the form of separate statements or brief conversations and parables; some are known, and some are entirely new. A few of the new sayings could reflect authentic tradition, but they add little to the material in our canonical gospels. Whether any clear light can be thrown on our gospel texts or epistles by this document must await continuing research. Help will probably come in the form of further insight into the nature of our canonical gospel tradition and early Gnosticism rather than through specific interpretive solutions.

To see Jesus and the apostles as being linked to their Jewish world and yet speaking distinctively into that world will not diminish our confidence in the authority of Scripture or minimize the important role of these backgrounds in truly hearing the Word of God.

THE EPISTLES AND ACTS 13-28

First of all, it is important to recognize that while the gospels, for the most part, portray a single period of time around A.D. 30, the epistles and Acts 13-28 represent glimpses of a continuing history of the early Church to the end of the first century. At least three periods can be distinguished: (1) the early Gentile mission about A.D. 47-60 involving Acts 13-28, the early Pauline letters (Galatians, Thessalonians, Romans, Corinthians) , and possibly the book of James; (2) A.D. 60-61, involving the prison epistles of Paul (Ephesians, Colossians, Philemon, Philippians) ; (3) a longer period from A.D. 61-95 involving the pastoral epistles of Paul (Timothy, Titus), Peter's letters, Hebrews, Jude, and John's epistles.

Because of this changing historical situation, statements within the epistles must be understood in relation to the particular time period in which they fall. Furthermore, it is also very important to know as much as possible about the specific historical and cultural situation of the recipients of each letter, although admittedly this is not always possible.

The importance of *geographical* setting to interpretation can be illustrated in the classic problem of the epistle to the Galatian churches. If the churches addressed were in the North Galatia ethnic region referred to by Luke in Acts 16:6 and 18:23, then the letter should be dated later in Paul's ministry (after A.D. 50). If this is the case, then the issue in the churches was no longer over justification by faith; rather the emphasis in the epistle should be placed more on the problem of sanctification by faith versus sanctification by works. If, on the other hand, as Sir William Ramsay argued (*A Historical Commentary on St. Paul's Epistles to the Galatians,* 1899), the churches addressed were in the Southern region known as provincial Galatia and were founded by Paul on his first missionary journey (Ac 14), then the date of the letter could be as early as A.D. 48-49—the earliest New Testament writing! Paul's emphasis would then certainly be upon the great issue of salvation by faith apart from the works of the Law and not upon the sanctification issue. Unfortunately, the problem of geographical location for the churches is not convincingly solved by the historical/cultural data now available.

There are many instances where the *linguistic* background of the words used in the epistles becomes crucial to the interpretation. For example, Paul spoke of himself as being a "slave" of Jesus Christ (Ro 1:1). If he had the Graeco-Roman slave in mind, one set of ideas would determine the sense. On the other hand, there seems to be evidence that he may have been influenced more by the Septuagint's use of *doulos* and had in mind the Semitic concept of a slave who could be one of the highest servants of the king (cf. 2 Sa 14:22; Amos 3:7).

In Hebrews 11:1, a rare word describes faith as the "substance"

(KJV), or "assurance" (RSV, NASB), of things hoped for. Recently discovered Greek papyri of the early period use the same Greek word (*hypostasis*) to refer to legal papers of the nature of title deeds. Since our actual inheritance is future, our faith could be understood with this new light as the "certificate of ownership" of the promised inheritance. The suggestion is attractive, although it should not be pressed too far.[32]

The *political* background in the epistles figures significantly in correctly understanding the numerous references to various kinds of persecution leveled at Christians in this period. While there were scattered hostile incidents in Judea (Ac 12) and other areas (Ac 18:2), there was little political persecution until the full-scale persecution in Rome under Nero in A.D. 64. No doubt, this severe trial is reflected in statements from Peter's epistles and in Hebrews. First Peter 1:6 may reflect this historical development: "In this you greatly rejoice, even though now for a little while, if necessary, you have been distressed by various trials" (NASB). Or we might cite Hebrews 12:4, "You have not yet resisted to the point of shedding blood in your striving against sin" (NASB).

Toward the end of the emperor Domitian's reign (c. A.D. 95), another brief but intensive wave of persecution occurred. The book of Revelation may have had this outbreak as background to its many references to the persecution and suffering of the saints.[33]

While it is true that Paul's exhortation to be submissive to the civil rulers (Ro 13) occurred before any hostilities against Christians were instituted, he and Peter nevertheless had the same general admonitions after Nero's famous persecutions (see Titus 3:1; 1 Pe 2:13-15). Without this historical background, one could misconstrue the force of the exhortations and argue that they apply only under peaceful governments.

Again the references in the epistles to slaves, freed men, adoption, redemption, riches, poverty, food sacrificed to idols, and many other concepts cannot be adequately understood without reference to the social structure of the first-century world.

Less known as an aid in interpreting the epistles is the important material from the *religious* environment, especially Jewish sources. For example, we might cite Paul's statement to King Agrippa, the

Roman ruler of the northern Galilee region: "King Agrippa, do you believe the prophets? I know you do" (Ac 26:27, NIV). This Agrippa was Herod Agrippa II, who was related by blood to the Jewish Hasmonaean line and was thoroughly familiar with and patriotic to the Jewish causes.[34] Without this background information, Paul's statement would seem puzzling, to say the least.

Paul may occasionally have presented his argument after the fashion of Rabbinic exegesis. Knowledge of some of the principles of this exegesis enables the interpreter to follow his thought more clearly. Such is the case in Romans 4:6-8, where Paul appealed to David's words from Psalm 32:1-2 to support his previous argument that Abraham was justified by faith. He did this on the basis of a good, rabbinic, interpretive principle known as *gezarah shawah:* When two different passages of Scripture contain the same word ("impute," or "count"), one passage can be used to explain the other.[35]

Paul may also have followed the Jewish Targums (Aramaic paraphrases of the Old Testament) when he referred in 1 Corinthians 10:4 to "the spiritual rock that accompanied them." The Old Testament does not refer to the rock following the Israelites, but the Palestinian Targum on Deuteronomy 2:6 says, "You have no need to buy water from them for money, because the well of water comes up with you to the tops of the mountains and [goes down] with you to the depths of the valleys."[36]

Paul's great doctrine of justification by faith, in his Roman letter, needs to be understood against both its Old Testament background and the contemporary Jewish views of justification. To justify means, from the Old Testament perspective, *not* "to declare righteous" (which is the Greek concept of the word) but "to make righteous," where *righteous* means "right," "clear," or "acquitted" in God's court.[37] The Jews in Paul's day also believed in this kind of justification, but in their view it was to take place at the final judgment and was to be based on one's meritorious deeds of Law righteousness. To understand this background helps to clarify one of the central doctrines in the New Testament. Paul taught, as did Jesus, immediate justification in this life, based on faith and not works (cf. Lk 18:14).

Such illustrations can be multiplied many times. The principle should be repeated: To show that God's revelation is related to the cultural forms of the period—in this latter case, the Jewish backgrounds—in no way means that the truth being conveyed is limited to or assimilated from the surrounding religious environment. This would be radical historical criticism. On the other hand, we must understand the culture and the historical references precisely in order to more accurately hear the distinctive word of the New Testament and not confuse the transient, cultural factors with God's eternal message expressed in and by these historical specifics.

This same point can be made with reference to the Greek and Roman religious culture of the first century. While emperor worship (especially in the latter part of the century) and mystery religions seem to be in the background of some of the epistles, these cults did not influence the substance of New Testament Christianity, as Bultmann and others of the radical historical school continue to maintain. Furthermore, the evidence needed to support a pre-Christian gnosticism which could have shaped Christian thought in the New Testament is wanting, although some form of heretical teaching containing ideas with similarities to this later teaching appears to be refuted in several of the epistles (cf. Col, 1 Ti, 1 Jn).[38]

THE BOOK OF REVELATION

Finally, a few remarks about the currently popular and often abused book of Revelation may provide some general guidelines for its proper interpretation. Probably no other book in the New Testament has suffered so much at the hands of its interpreters due to a lack of historical perspective. If interpretation arises as a present necessity because our situation differs greatly from that of the first century, then Revelation probably needs more interpretation than any other New Testament book.

The original readers knew some things about the Apocalypse that we do not. For one thing, they knew who the author, John, was. We are not sure who he was, although the view that it was John the apostle, the son of Zebedee, has much going for it. The reason it would be nice to know for sure is that we might be able to tell whether his thoughts ran in symbolic or in literal veins. They also knew what the symbolism conveyed, and we are often at a loss to understand its significance. Another matter they knew that we are not sure about is the date that John wrote the book. We think it was during the reign of the emperor Domitian (c. A.D. 95), but there is no way to be certain. The date would help us to know more about the type of situation the original recipients were facing.

However, we do know some things the early Church knew. We can study the content of the book and its own explanations, as they did. We have the same Old Testament books to study and most of the noncanonical, late-Jewish, apocalyptic literature they used. Our knowledge of late first-century Roman history is scanty, but every little bit helps.

In affirming for the book of Revelation what we have stated for the rest of the New Testament, we begin by recognizing that the book is the Word of God addressed to a specific, historical situation and given in cultural terms which the original recipients would have been able to understand. The prophetic nature of the book does not change this. Prophecy was always given with both a near aspect and a more distant counterpart.

There are major areas of background materials the interpreter must consider in any attempt to recover the original meaning intended by the author of the Apocalypse. Generally, they are Graeco-Roman and Jewish materials, and fall into the following categories: (1) Old Testament prophetic-apocalyptic literature, (2) New Testament prophetic-apocalyptic discourses, (3) late-Jewish apocalyptic literature, (4) Dead Sea Scrolls, (5) Targums, (6) Roman histories of the first century.

1. The *Old Testament* prophetic books, especially Daniel, Isaiah, Ezekiel, and Zechariah, are indispensable. We may safely assume that this literature shaped our author's thinking and expression more than any other source. He may have reinterpreted these sources, but his new image grew out of the old. It is in Daniel, for instance, that we encounter visions of monstrous beasts; references to severe tribulation; the man of sin; the 1260 days, or three and a

half years; the Son of Man; and many other parallel images. To interpret Revelation using the key of Daniel is certainly the sanest approach. For example, if heads represent kingdoms and horns individual kings in Daniel, then unless John reinterpreted these differently, would not the same apply in Revelation? This might be the clue to the difficult verses in 17:9-10, "the seven heads are seven hills . . . they are also seven kings." If the heads are kingdoms (the Greek can bear this sense), it is not necessary to try to force the artificial interpretation of a succession of Roman emperors. We can more naturally see these kingdoms as successive foreign powers oppressing God's people in the past, including Rome in John's day, and also as a reference to the eschatological kingdom of Antichrist in the end time.

2. The *New Testament* itself offers some orientation to Revelation, especially in Matthew 24 (cf. Mk 13; Lk 21) and the Thessalonian epistles, which present similar prophetic-apocalyptic themes. Could any explanation of the Apocalypse which does not at the same time also correlate to and explain these passages be the correct sense?

3. The exact origin and specific contribution of the late-Jewish *Apocalyptic literature* to understanding Revelation is still not clear. Some of these books are earlier than and some contemporary with the New Testament times. Since most analyses of the general character of this type of literature, in both its literary form and its theological outlook, have included the canonical books of Daniel and Revelation, the delineations are confusing.[39] We may more profitably follow George Ladd here, who, like Zahn before him, has argued that the canonical books must be separated from the strictly late-Jewish apocalyptic literature and be recognized as prophetic-apocalyptic.[40]

The apocalyptic literature was pessimistic concerning God's present activity in the world. It provided merely tracts for times to encourage the Jews to look for future deliverance by God. In contrast, the prophetic-apocalyptic book of Revelation depicts God's work in the midst of present history as well as the prospect of the future great consummation and victory. The apocalyptic writings were ethically passive, viewing Israel's plight as arising not from their own failure but from the evil state of the world. Israel was righteous, but they were suffering because God had abandoned the world to evil. But this is not the story in the Apocalypse of John. Because it belongs instead to the prophetic literature, there are sharp tones of ethical injunctions throughout the book, for example, "Remember then from what you have fallen; repent and do the works you did at first. If not, I will come to you and remove your lampstand from its place unless you repent" (Rev 2:5).

It may well be that John has deliberately given his message against the background of some of the apocalyptic literature. On the other hand, careful investigation of the whole phenomenon may reveal, as it appears to in Paul's prophetic-apocalyptic materials, that the relationship is only superficial and no binding correspondence in either form or world-view will be found between John and the apocalyptics.[41]

4. The relation of the *Dead Sea Scroll* sectarian literature to the Apocalypse is only beginning to be noticed and employed for interpretation. There are many places where the background of biblical image or wording may be an allusion to what we find in the Qumran literature. For example, the expressions in Revelation 5:5, "the lion of the tribe of Judah" and "the root of David" are similarly combined in a small Qumran fragment referring to the Messiah (Forty Patriarchal Blessings) and evidently in no other extant literature.[42] Further support for interpreting the woman in Revelation 12 as the Messianic community comes from a Qumran hymn, "For she shall give birth to a man-child . . . a Marvelous Counsellor" (1QH 111.7-10).[43] Examples from this source could be multiplied throughout the book of Revelation.

5. As they did for the gospels and epistles, the *Targums* are providing new possibilities for interpretation of the book of Revelation. In Revelation 1:4 we find a greeting from the one "who is, and who was, and who is to come." Only in the Palestinian Targum on Deuteronomy 32:39 do we find a text which explicitly sets forth the same threefold description of God as found in the Revelation text.[44] Such references as this, if they do no more, at least point strongly to the fact that the author of Revelation was steeped

in the Palestinian synagogue tradition: he had "learned his Bible," so to speak, in a Palestinian milieu.

6. Finally, we might point out a few examples of the bearing of the history of the first-century *Roman political world* on the interpretation of the Apocalypse. The factor bearing most broadly on the situation for Christians in the last part of the first century was the growing and increasingly demanding cult of emperor worship. Most New Testament surveys and history books quote from early Roman historians such as Tacitus, Suetonius, and Pliny the Younger to document this development. It was especially under Domitian that mandatory acknowledgment of the emperor as *kyrios* (Lord) was required under threat of death or severe persecution. Many feel that in Revelation 13 the beast who demands worship is a reference to the emperor Domitian and the Roman religio-political cult of emperor worship. The asiarch was the provincial Roman official who was responsible for promoting the worship of the emperor.[45] Could this explain the references in Revelation 13 to *two* administrative rulers?

In Revelation 2:13 the Lord says, "I know where you live—where Satan has his throne." The throne of Satan becomes intelligible when we learn that the first temple to honor Augustus Caesar was built in Pergamus in A.D. 29.

The fact of Christian persecution under Rome, from the time of Nero onward, is not questioned. On the other hand, just how widespread the persecution was in the empire is debatable. Nero's persecution was limited mainly to Rome, and Domitian's persecuting measures were restricted to the more severe infractions of open rebellion.[46]

Whatever bearing the immediate historical situation had on John's materials, they certainly cannot limit his message to first-century Rome, for his work is described as prophecy (1:3; 22:18) and has its final issue in the eschatological Day of the Lord.

CONCLUSION

In this chapter we have sought to discuss the vital importance of the cultural/historical to both revelation and interpretation. We have argued for the position of serious historical criticism but not radical historical criticism. Space has permitted only the barest reference to the main areas of fruitful background materials to aid the modern interpreter of the New Testament. There is much work to be done. The student should use the footnote references as bibliography for further study.

Someone may ask if it is worth the trouble to study the Bible with this approach. In my opinion, it is worth as much as it is to have God's powerful Word rather than our own. That Word which our traditional interpretations may have bound can be freed and revive the Church of Christ once again in our day. May the Lord be pleased to raise up a generation of expositors and teachers who can bring that more precise and powerful Word to our hungry generation.

8

The Place of the Incarnation in Biblical Interpretation

by Morris Inch

WHILE ALL SCRIPTURE is equally inspired, no one weighs every portion the same for purposes of interpretation. For the Christian, the person and teaching of Jesus Christ are normative for all the rest. He is the central figure in a Divine drama, the beloved Son of God to whom we give our unreserved attention (Mt 17:5).

Granted this basic premise, the history of interpretation shows a remarkable variety. The centrality of the incarnation in hermeneutics has, like the chameleon, changed in emphasis with the times. Therefore, while our primary interest lies with the contemporary situation, a brief outline of the past seems desirable. Adolph Von Harnack accidentally supplies us with a key to the historical development when he argues: "To cast away the Old Testament in the second century was an error which the Church rightly rejected; to retain it in the sixteenth century was a fate which the Reformation had no power to avert; but for Protestantism to conserve it after the nineteenth century as a canonical document, is a sign of religious and ecclesiastical paralysis."[1] Harnack rightly discovers the pivotal significance of critical points in time: the second, sixteenth, and "after the nineteenth" centuries. While disagreeing with his conclusion per se, we may entertain Harnack's three periods as crucial to Christian thought in general, and particularly in a consideration of the role of the incarnation for biblical interpretation.

SECOND CENTURY

James Wood summarizes for us the major hermeneutical concern of the first believers:

> Like their fellow Jews, the early Christians regarded the Old Testament as sacred, and of divine origin. . . . Nevertheless there were important differences between the Jewish and Christian ways of interpreting the Bible. To begin with, when the Christian read the Bible, he saw therein prophecies about Jesus Christ and, in particular, predictions which seemed to him to refer to His suffering and death.[2]

We break into Wood's discussion at this juncture to reinforce certain statements he has made, abbreviate what follows, and apply his finding to the subject at hand.

Christians, like the faithful Jews before them, were people of the Book. Harnack's zeal to dispose of the Old Testament finds few friends in the first two centuries. Quite the reverse proves to be the case; the Church reaffirmed the contemporary regard for the Scriptures as the Word of God, as sacred, as divinely authoritative.

The parting of the ways between Judaism and Christianity came at another point. Jewish interpretation in Jesus' time was far from monolithic. The Pharisees characteristically differed from the Sadducees, and the Essenes from both. The struggle between the schools of Hillel and Shammai is well documented. But for all of the variation, Jewish hermeneutics held one thing in common: that the Scriptures should be understood in the light of the Mosaic Law. What this conclusion meant practically was that the Old Testament became a foundation on which was raised a precarious structure of religious and social codes to govern life in every conceivable connection.

One does not have to assume that the Jewish interpretation went bankrupt in order to sense inherent problems in its approach. As a case in point, Wood singles out the Sadducees as especially guilty of misrepresentation: "They emphasize the letter of the Law. This practice rendered almost impossible any hope of development in Law. . . . In the New Testament also, Jesus asserts that the strictly literal interpretation of the Sadducees results in their misunderstanding the resurrection of the dead."[3]

On the other hand, Jesus did not come to destroy but to fulfill the Law (Mt 5:17). His argument was not with the Law per se but with the place it had assumed in contemporary interpretation and application. The author of Hebrews summarized the Christian alternative to hermeneutics with the explanation: "God, after He spoke long ago to the fathers in the prophets in many portions and in many ways, in the last days has spoken to us in His Son, whom He appointed heir of all things" (Heb 1:1-2, NASB). Jesus, as the divine embodiment of the Law, became the ultimate clue to interpreting Holy Writ. All Scripture turns on Him.

From another perspective, the Christians applied to Christ, Hillel's first rule of interpretation: inference from the more takes preference over inference from the less.* Jesus took His rightful place center-stage in God's revelation, as Alan Stibbs so vividly describes: "For the written word is but the completion or reflection of the Living Word. . . . It is, so to speak, the halo round His head in which His glory finds visible or intelligible, because verbal, expression."[4] Veiled prophecies became vivid realities; varied revelations fused into one vibrant whole; multiple means gave way to one Man—Jesus.

Two things resulted from this Christian hermeneutic: the Old Testament was claimed as Christian literature, and the New Testament came into being as an extention of Jesus' teaching. Christ, it was argued, is no divine afterthought but was in the redemptive purpose of God from the foundation of the world. And the Christian's use of the Old Testament did not amount to incidental and occasional proof-texting but involved a more basic understanding of the text as such (as with its application to Christ's suffering and exaltation).

In addition to establishing title on the Old Testament, the early Church wove a new body of literature around Jesus. A. Berkeley Mickelsen abridges the result for us: "The authority of the New Testament lies in the person of Jesus Christ—his acts, his words,

---

*Hillel attempted to gather the prevailing principles of interpretation under seven guidelines, the remaining six having to do with inference by analogy, constructing groups of passages which have similar content, where only two such similar passages exist, the relation between the general and particular, exposition by means of a similar passage, and deduction from context.

and his disciples' proclamation of what God would do for men who by faith enter into a living relationship with the risen Lord."[5] As with the Old, so with the New Testament. As the Old Testament had been predictive of Christ, so the New was a faithful elaboration of His teaching. The two Testaments were held alike as Scripture, revelation of the God who spoke in times past by the prophets and in the last days through His Son.

In conclusion, the incarnation became the means for the early Church to subsume the Old Testament as Christian legacy and to justify the addition of the New Testament to the same body of authoritative teaching.

SIXTEENTH CENTURY

We make one more stop before reaching the contemporary scene. We pause at the sixteenth century, where the concern was no longer with the Messianic interpretation of Scripture as such, but the credibility of that claim in the light of subsequent developments.

What had interrupted the flow of events to shift the point of discussion? While the Church faced continuing pressure from without, it had already withstood the menacing threats of foreign forces for a millennium and a half. More critical to the recasting of the issue was the collapse of a culture with which Christianity had associated itself ever since Constantine. And coupled with this cultural failure occurred an explosion of knowledge which burst the old wineskins of scholasticism.

To back up for a moment, the memory of Christ "after the flesh" could hardly have survived the second century, if that long. In its place grew up an elaborate system of theology, employing Greek concepts for apologetic purposes, to which we give the term *scholasticism*. "A place for everything and everything in its place" seemed to be the order for each day. Life was structured downward from the throne where systematic theology reigned uncontested.

As for the Bible, it became virtually a corpus of legal precedent. Its references were everywhere, tied with endless ingenuity to support theological propositions. Out of zeal to reinforce even the

more debatable assertions, passages were given improbable spiritual interpretations, such as when Aquinas submitted the phrase,
"let there be light," to the current methodology and derived a four-
fold meaning: (1) historically—an act of creation; (2) allegorically—let Christ be love; (3) anagogically—may we be led by Christ to
glory; (4) tropologically—may we be mentally illumined by
Christ.[6] There may be observed in Aquinas' explanation a marked
emphasis on Christ but one that differs substantially from what
we would have expected from the second century. The centrality
of Jesus still persisted, but a hierarchical stress had replaced a historical one. It was no longer Jesus coming among men but Christ
reigning through His Church, which governed biblical hermeneutics.

As long as the Church could maintain its hold on culture,
through persuasion or coercion, the liberties taken with the biblical text mattered little to the average person. But with the passing of the old and the introduction of new perspectives, the credibility of this ecclesiastical hermeneutic became increasingly suspect. While the critics of the Church attacked with a ruthlessness
meant to lay waste, the Reformers attempted to pare away the
stifling traditions and promote a more defensible approach to Holy
Writ.

It therefore became necessary for the Reformers to pit Christ
against the established Church, the elevated Lord against the community confessing to be His body. Luther would say: "When I
was a monk, I was an adept in allegory. I allegorized everything.
But after lecturing on the Epistle to the Romans I came to have
some knowledge of Christ. For therein I saw that Christ is no
allegory and learned to know what Christ was."[7] Luther's ideal
was not always realized in practice (the Reformers also were prod-
ucts of their age) , but to the degree that he and others succeeded,
there came about a new sense of the importance of the incarnation
in biblical interpretation, and not simply as transmitted by Church
dogma or expressed with ecclesiastical sanction but in its own
right.

To summarize, the sixteenth century experienced severe cultural tremors which revealed the ineptness of the prevailing her-

meneutic and threatened the impressive theological structure raised upon it. The idea of incarnation had, in a manner of speaking, been extended to refer to the Church (as the body of Christ). The Church thereby felt free to exercise Christ's prerogative in support of dogma. But in so doing, something of the incarnational credibility had been lost; the body would not pass for its Head. Efforts of the churchmen (Reformers and counter-reformers) to correct the deficiency characteristically proved to be too little and too late. By allowing the Scriptures to be wed indefinitely to scholasticism, the Church lost much of its initiative and had difficulty maintaining its own direction against the prevailing winds of the time.

After the Nineteenth Century

"After the nineteenth century" is a helpful way of viewing the present status of our subject, for the contemporary scene is best understood against the background of what was and is no more, by what of the nineteenth century was purposefully purged in the twentieth century.† Ernest Renan set the stage for the former era with his portrait of Jesus as an idyllic Galilean:

> Such was the group which, on the borders of the lake of Tiberias, gathered around Jesus. The aristocracy was represented there by a customs officer and by the wife of one of Herod's stewards. The rest were fishermen and common people. Their ignorance was extreme; their intelligence was feeble; they believed in apparitions and spirits. . . . The beautiful climate of Galilee made the life of these honest fishermen a perpetual delight. They truly preluded the kingdom of God—simple, good and happy—rocked gently on their delightful sea, or at night sleeping on the shores.[8]

In striking contrast to Renan's account of Jesus and His company, Walter Rauschenbusch saw Him as a social reconstructionist.[9] What is not at first apparent is that these authors have an important hermeneutical approach in common with each other and with many of their nineteenth-century colleagues as well.

---

†For the purposes of this discussion the "twentieth century" is dated from about 1914 to the present. It marks the collapse of idealism in theology and the advent of realism.

A simplified statement of the matter is that the nineteenth century predictably gave preference to the words of Jesus over other aspects of Scripture and was inclined to accommodate them to the immediate interest of the interpreter. For instance, a wedge was driven between the God of the patriarchs and that of Jesus and the high prophets. As another example, Paul's teaching was contrasted to that of Jesus. One author's title was so bold as to require a choice: *Jesus or Paul?*

But who was this Jesus who demanded our attention? Not the Christ after the flesh of the second century nor even the Christ of the sixteenth-century Church. Harry Emerson Fosdick clarified the new viewpoint: "He was to them [the disciples] that most powerful force in human experience, an incarnation, embodying and revealing in his own person the truth he represented. When they thought of God, it was more and more in terms of Jesus; when they thought of goodness, it meant likeness to him."[10] "When they thought about God" is the key to the quotation. The idea of Jesus results from religious intuition rather than divine revelation. The Bible became man's account of his experiences with God rather than God's declaration of His will for man. The ideal of discovery substituted for disclosure.

If the place of the incarnation in hermeneutics had previously suffered from conformity to Church dogma, it now became ludicrous in the light of the various interpretations. Losing the biblical revelation of His person, Christ became hardly distinguishable from any other religious, well-meaning man. Losing the context for His teaching, Jesus' words lent themselves to any idea currently popular.

Perhaps enough has been said about the nineteenth century. What followed it? Albert Schweitzer and the twentieth century.[11] Schweitzer is credited with revoking the indulgences of the earlier quests for the historical Jesus. His criticism of the previous authors was that they saw Jesus through culturally tinted glasses and made Him conform to their personal ideals. According to Schweitzer, Jesus must be put back into the framework of His day, and be found anticipating the immediate consummation of all things. He wrested Jesus from the hands of the nineteenth-century opportunists and set Him foursquare in the Jewish apocalytic setting of a past era.

What had happened, as we entered upon the twentieth century, which supported Schweitzer's case, and what would be its effect upon our understanding of incarnational hermeneutics? Two world wars and lesser holocausts ravaged the world. Never before had man amassed such imposing armies or produced weapons so capable of wholesale destruction. Overkill became a potential. Revolution swept away ancient monarchies and, with them, social structures dating back as much as two thousand years. The influence of the West was in decline.

The optimism of the previous century gave way to a profound pessimism, corresponding with the change in events in general and the special agony of the West in particular. And the pessimism seemed all the darker for the optimism left behind. With the shift in attitude came the realization by the Church that it had too readily identified with its culture. The body of Christ had entered so uncritically into the social and political scene of the day as to leave behind its point of divine leverage. Harvey Cox admitted on behalf of the Church: "Chastised rightly by Reinhold Niebuhr for putting too much hope in mere political solutions, for being too sentimentally impressed by idealistic schemes, we learned to put great emphasis on the complexity and difficulty of all moral issues."[12] An era of realism replaced the older idealism, seemingly justifying Schweitzer's disenchantment with the efforts to accommodate Jesus to utopian aspirations.

The subsequent result of this change in attitude upon incarnational hermeneutics was considerable. Of special importance to our consideration, the emphasis then shifted from the Jesus of history to the Christ of faith, a direction forcefully illustrated by the experience and teaching of Rudolph Bultmann.[13] Following the collapse of the Third Reich, Bultmann was ministering in the wards of the hospitals which held war casualties. Driven out of concern for those who had lost hope for a meaningful life, and frustrated by the seeming inability of traditional theology to revive their spirits, he hit upon an existential (experiential) interpretation of Scripture. The Jesus of history, he concluded, is relatively unimportant, but the Christ of faith is altogether necessary. What is significant is not whether our world view coincides with that of the early church but whether our faith does.

Bultmann grasped onto the existential philosophy of Martin Heidegger, but with a crucial qualification.[14] He argued that while existentialism had come to understand the necessary conditions of life, it was unable to realize those conditions. While life is the result of man's affirmation, the ability to make this affirmation comes only by God's grace through Jesus Christ.

Much of the ambiguity in Bultmann's approach is readily cleared up by a return visit to the hospital ward. Here we see men crippled not simply by the effects of war but by their own inability to accept the handicaps with which they must now live. One does not have to read deeply into Heidegger to sense what was needed. The man lying there on white sheets, with a scarred face and mangled arms, must act; somehow he must take the initiative to bring meaning back to life. Well said, but not so easily done! True enough, not easily done and not done at all but by the grace of God.

Christ became, for Bultmann, God's call to authentic living, and the Bible was the ground of that call. He commended the nineteenth-century assertion that the Bible is myth, but castigated it for throwing out that myth. The solution is not to discard but to reinterpret myth for today. Myth, for Bultmann, is the explanation of what is other-worldly in terms of what is this-worldly. It is clothing divine truth in human garb. Find the existential truth behind the antiquated jargon of the first-century testimonial, and live by the same reality that energized those early believers.

The Bible, as reconceived, was no longer the report of religious men grappling after God, but the avenue through which God now spoke. And although it was not simply the word of insightful men, neither was it actually the Word of God as traditionally understood. Bultmann rested authority with the event, namely, with man's *response* to God's offer of forgiveness in Christ, instead of with the *content* of that offer. His tendency was either to use *the Word of God* in a more exclusive sense, as a reference to God and Christ; or to extend it indiscriminately to proclamation, which may *become* the Word of God in the encounter. In either case, the traditional stress on the written Word of God suffers as the result.

Thinking men press for substance in the revelation of which Bultmann speaks but receive little. Critics complain that he is not talking of God at all, but developing a philosophy of human existence. Say what they will, Bultmann restrains God from speaking, preserving His otherness at great cost to the message of the incarnation.

The prevailing current flowed with Bultmann, but there were contrary viewpoints as well. One such notable case was Ethelbert Stauffer.[15] Stauffer saw, as did few at such an early date, that Bultmann's solution was liable to the same subjectivity as were those of the nineteenth-century authors he criticized. We needed not a shift in emphasis from the Jesus of history to the Christ of faith but a new objectivity in investigation.

Stauffer set his course accordingly. Supported by impressive credentials in rabbinic studies and a knowledge of New Testament, he announced a *historical* approach to Christ and interpretation, as opposed to Bultmann's *religious* alternative. Our methodology, he argued, should not be unique but resemble any other investigation of the past. Such a thrust would distinguish itself both from the earlier, fanciful novels about Jesus and from the then prevailing obsession with the dynamics of faith. Reject the religious road for a historical one; the former returns only to self, while the latter leads to Jesus.

"How do you discover the event behind reports of it?" Stauffer asked. By comparing contrary accounts. So Stauffer searched the historical records, biblical and extrabiblical, for references to Jesus and His time. He found that not only did Jesus' followers attribute extraordinary acts to Him, but the opposition sought to explain away such exceptional activity on the ground of demonism or magician's skill. The historical *fact* behind these biased sources was that Jesus did perform notable and astonishing works, regardless of the explanation given for them.

Most significant of Stauffer's historical finds was the discovery of Jesus' theophany claim: "I am He." For a century and more, people had been writing about the misunderstood Jesus, somehow deified by the early Church and only recently released from that role by a more perceptive audience. But Stauffer carried the divine claim back to the mouth of Jesus Himself. So, with assistance, we heard once more the radical self-attestation which had won a handful of zealous disciples while soliciting the charges of blasphemy and the cries for crucifixion.‡

It is now suggested that we have entered into a new quest for the historical Jesus. Insofar as this may be true, we should describe this effort as a mini-quest. Hugh Anderson puts it this way:

> A biography is altogether out of the question. . . .Jesus' aim, his intention, his purpose, which constitute the ground of his existence, these are the proper subjects of enquiry. The words of Jesus (and to much lesser extent the deeds), which can be judged to be authentic, provide us with some clues from which to read off the meaning of his existence.[16]

We are no longer at the mercy of novelists, because there are some *authentic* clues from the past. On the other hand, a healthy caution is called for.

Perhaps best illustrating the most recent shift in thinking about incarnational interpretation is Günther Bornkamm, a somewhat repentant disciple of Bultmann. Both the seriousness with which he takes the biblical narrative and the freedom he feels in modifying it is reflected in this quotation:

> It is controversial in how far Jesus himself intended this entry as a demonstration that he was the Messiah. Later tradition has, at any rate, understood the entry in this sense, and endowed it with miraculous features which bestow upon it this meaning. However, even if we here take into consideration the subsequent belief of the disciples . . . even then this entry of Jesus and his followers would be inconceivable without his powerful claim that the kingdom of God is dawning in his world, and that the final decision will turn upon himself.[17]

The strongly existential leanings are still evident in Bornkamm, but he sees also a historical credibility in Jesus' claims.

The essence of the current trend and, in many ways, one of the

‡The adverse effects of Stauffer's approach were to fragment the Bible, to set compatibles in contradiction to each other, to raise unnecessary doubts, and to lose the important sense of unity which flows throughout Scripture.

more satisfactory efforts to be found is in C. H. Dodd's *The Founder of Christianity*.§ Dodd comes to this problem with his characteristic insight, piercing through the layers of discussion to establish a guideline for others to follow. His earlier skepticism has been eroded by the passing of the years. Now he looks back upon what has transpired in his own experience in some three decades (roughly equivalent to the lapse of time between the events of Jesus' ministry and the first record of it) with vivid recollection. The idea of eyewitnesses still alive and contributing to the growth of a body of literature played a critical role in Dodd's reconstruction, the result of which we will most appreciate in his own words:

> When all allowance has been made for these limiting factors—the chances of oral transmission, the effect of translation, the interest of teachers in making the sayings "contemporary," and simple human fallibility—it remains that the first three gospels offer a body of sayings on the whole so consistent, so coherent, and withal so distinctive in manner, style, content, that no reasonable critic should doubt, whatever reservations he may have about individual sayings, that we find reflected here the thought of a single, unique, teacher.[18]

Dodd allows the distinction between the Jesus of history and Christ of faith but minimizes its importance as a hermeneutical consideration. Admitting the chances involved in oral transmission and related matters, the brevity of time and significance of eyewitnesses assures us of the essential credibility of the reports. The New Testament was not only primary source material for the early Church's faith but the teaching of the Master Himself. The gospels offer so consistent, so coherent, so distinctive a style and content as to persuade all but the most unreasonable person that they do in fact reflect the unique teaching of a historical figure.

In brief, the contemporary concern is with the underlying themes of Jesus' teaching and especially that of the Kingdom of God. Lacking is the earlier confidence in Holy Writ or the later assurance in Holy Church, and in their place resides a more tenuous but never-

§I have chosen to speak in regard to individuals so far as the present situation is concerned, rather than laboring broad theological generalizations, themselves misleading, although this choice makes for a rather selective treatment and bypasses many significant contributors.

theless determined trust in the Christ. Jesus appears through a uniform testimony, distorted but not beyond recognition, obscured but not so as to destroy commitment to Him.[19]

SUMMATION AND SUGGESTION

We have come the full distance in our review of incarnational hermeneutics by following Harnack's suggestive outline. One of Harnack's precocious young students, Dietrich Bonhoeffer, when asked to eulogize his professor, commented that he had left as a prized legacy the insight that "truth is born only out of freedom." No doubt this is an important consideration, but Bonhoeffer went on to suggest in his own writing how critical it is to see that true freedom is found in Christ.[20]

It remains to draw the subject together in terms of an ideal to which Bonhoeffer introduces us but, I think, fails to develop adequately. Bonhoeffer enlarges on the centrality of Jesus: "Christ as idea is timeless truth: the idea of God embodied as accessible to any one at any time. The word as address stands in contrast to this. . . . It is not timeless, but takes place in history."[21] That is, Jesus revealed once and for all the eternal nature of God—His justice, His love, His person—but we confront Jesus where we are—in our circumstance, with our capability, facing our obligation.

The problem is how to keep these two dimensions together, in creative tension—the Jesus of history and Christ of faith. Only one course seems open to us, because of both the failure of other alternatives and the direction given us by the Saviour Himself. We have documented the pitfalls of separating historical and religious considerations for the purpose of accenting one or the other. Bultmann's Christ of faith fared no better than Renan's manufactured Jesus of history. Even Stauffer's magnificent portrayal stands without garments, stripped of the uniform robe woven by the prophets and attested to by the disciples.

Lest we feel that fate has decreed persisting failure, Jesus reminded us that He had not come to destroy (regardless of Harnack's protest) but to fulfill. The alternative to continued frustration is faith in the written Word as faithfully interpreting the meaning of the living Word. And this faith is vouchsafed to us by no less than Jesus Himself, who has assured that not the slightest consideration would be set aside, but that all would certainly be brought to pass (Mt 5:18).

We are drawn back to Stibbs's observation that the written Word is the halo for the living Word, "in which His glory finds visible or intelligible, because verbal, expression." Anything less leaves God dumb, the incarnation unlikely, and man struggling with a rising level of skepticism.

Has the Almighty spoken in times past by the prophets? This fact was not in question among those who listened to Jesus or read in Hebrews the reference to His entering into the legacy of revelation. Scripture, as "thus saith the Lord," was the context in which the early Church understood Jesus' teaching and the claim which subsequent generations must consider. The decision is not ultimately between the living Word or the written Word, but between both or neither. The force of their combined witness is strong; but given time, and without reinforcement, we search first with the Jesus of history and then with the Christ of faith, back and forth, trying to discover what is and remains lacking. But try as we will, we cannot come up with a word from the living God.

Furthermore, has the Almighty revealed Himself in the incarnation? We could hardly be so assured if it were not for the verbal testimony. As astonishing as His activity may have seemed, an ambiguity lent itself to diverse explanations. Yes, Christ taught with peculiar authority, but was it due to a Divine commission or to heretical presumption? His audiences often divided on the issue. True, the Master performed astonishing works, but was it because He applied the power of God or the Devil? Or did He simply have the skill of a professional charlatan? All three explanations come down to us from the early centuries of the Christian era. Even the report of the Lord's resurrection was treated differently by the disciples and those who explained it away as a ruse the disciples had engineered. No, you cannot establish the incarnation on acts alone; there must be a credible witness to explain their meaning.

God's voice lost and Christ's incarnation obscured, but these are not the only results of disqualifying verbal inspiration: man is plunged into the logic of agnosticism. Who can deny it? The gods we fashion when the prophets go silent are seldom persuasive. We can give them lip-service, but have difficulty taking these man-made deities seriously.

Christ intends something better for us than the eternal silence of God, an ambiguous advent, and loss of the sense of spiritual reality. He means to pull the facets of Scripture together in Himself, giving them the divine point of focus. The house was built by the prophets, and He entered into it. There is a grand consistency from patriarch, through prophet, to apostle, and they are cemented in Christ. Jesus is unintelligible without the larger framework, and it is empty without Him. God is His own best interpreter.[22]

We have already turned the corner from description to prescription, from an outline of developments to an ideal by which to steer in the future. We shall continue on the latter course a bit longer in order to spell out some of the implications for biblical interpretation.

First, and of primary importance for us, is the centrality of Christ to the hermeneutical endeavor. The ploy "I believe in the whole Bible" leaves too much unresolved; it can disregard the pre-eminence of the Lord. We do well to remember that Christ lives at the heart of the Bible. From Him pulses life, and to Him flow all the streams of truth.

No sooner have we affirmed the Christocentric nature of Scripture than we must add a word of warning. We err by setting Jesus in contradiction to the prophets or apostles. The Bible holds out to us one message, and one alone. For all of the remarkable variation, a common theme runs throughout. The unity of Holy Writ provides us with a second clue to biblical interpretation.

We should also bear in mind the personal dimension in hermeneutics. The Bible is less a code for behavior than a guide to relationship. What worth has all this knowledge *about* God if we gain no access *to* Him? The centrality of Christ is the centrality of a Person. Holy Writ includes and elaborates upon the words formerly spoken by Jesus to His contemporaries. They are invitation, promise, and judgment; invitation to fellowship, promise of the value of such, and judgment considering what use we make of that opportunity. The Bible may become the means of reconciling us to God or confirming us in an estrangement from Him. In any case, hermeneutics bears this interpersonal character.

It follows naturally from the previous point that the Scripture should be understood as the revelation of God to man, not solely or even primarily as the discovery of religiously minded persons. God takes the initiative in establishing a relationship through His self-disclosure. The implications of this fact are overwhelming! It means that the One who created and sustains the universe has taken up pen and paper to write for us. It further suggests that interpretation does not touch on some incidental matter but the very essence of life itself. We should approach Scripture with a passion reserved only for the most critical and potentially rewarding of ventures.

While we handle the timeless truth of God, the truth is still expressed in time. We have already seen how unfortunate the results when interpreters disdain the historical context in which revelation took place. A sound hermeneutic presupposes a serious grappling with the historical and grammatical aspects of the text. This conclusion further implies that we must discover the meaning of a passage rather than bring to it some prior understanding. We must read out of rather than into the text.

There may also be many applications to whatever truth we uncover. God means to say something to us in the light of our ongoing experience, and this requires that we become good students both of Holy Writ *and* of the world about us. The hermeneutical skill takes shape as we allow Scripture and daily tasks to rub together.

What seems so striking about the preceding guidelines is not their originality but how often they have been overlooked by those inquiring as to the place of the incarnation in biblical interpretation. Hopefully the realization of this danger will make us the more appreciative of their importance and careful with our own undertaking.

9

The Reformation Contribution to the Interpretation of the Bible

by Donald M. Lake

WHEN WE WERE CHILDREN, most of us probably played a childish game known as leapfrog. This game of leaping or jumping over a person in a stooped position is analogous to an attitude common among people who hold the Bible in high respect. They assume that we can jump from the twentieth century back to the first without any reference to the nineteen intervening centuries. Belief in an infallible, verbally inspired Bible has often included a rejection of history. The fallacy of this error is also analogous to our own experience. It is as if we sought to establish our own identity by denying that we had any grandparents or parents! Both assumptions are false, and we ought to reject or deny both.

If one reflects upon the history of the Church, he soon discovers how an entire generation, and in some cases several generations, have been influenced by a single commentator upon the Bible. Take, for instance, the allegorical method of interpretation used by the Alexandrian school of theology which controlled the way the Bible was read and studied for over a thousand years. The real meaning of the biblical text was often lost because the interpreter was free to read into the text any meaning his speculative genius desired.

Or look at Augustine's misinterpretation of Romans 5:12. He read the Latin *in quo* (in whom) for the Greek *eph' ho* (inasmuch as). A poor text allowed Augustine to develop his concept of immediate imputation of Adam's sin to mankind. This meant that

178

all men immediately and genetically participated in Adam's sin, so that we were not only affected by Adam's sin but we were guilty of the original act as well. This interpretation of the text became the Augustinian basis for infant baptism: baptism takes away the guilt of Adam's sin and our guilt for participation in that sin. Augustine's interpretation was generally adopted by both Luther and Calvin, and it is still the theological basis for the Roman Catholic doctrine of infant baptism.

On and on these illustrations could go. Some bad, some good! What should be obvious to all readers of the Bible is the fact that we owe our particular interpretations partially, if not wholly, to some previous expositor of God's Word.

THE TEXT AND TRANSLATION OF THE BIBLE

At least one hundred and fifty years before Martin Luther brought the issue of reform to a head, a movement to revive classical culture and classical learning had been underway. This movement, commonly called the Renaissance, spawned the printing of numerous translations of the Bible. Before the year 1500, at least ninety-two different editions of the Latin Vulgate had come from the press. When Johannes Gutenberg of Mainz developed the printing press about 1450, he provided the world with a tool that would change not only the distribution of the Bible, but its interpretation as well. The vernacular translation of the Bible followed almost immediately the development of the printing press: two Italian versions before 1471, the Spanish and French by 1478, the Bohemian by 1488, and no less than eighteen editions in German by 1521! Hand-printed copies of the Bible in English appeared more than a century earlier with the work of John Wycliffe (1328-1384).

By the time Luther had finished his translation of the Bible into the contemporary German vernacular (New Testament in 1522 and Old Testament in 1534), Roman Catholic humanist scholars Cardinal Ximenes de Cisneros (1436-1517) and Desiderius Erasmus (1466-1536) had produced Greek New Testaments, but Erasmus's work was first to appear, in 1516. The humanist scholar Johann Reuchlin (1455-1522) wrote his *De Rudimentis Hebraicus* in 1506, which helped to revive the recovery of the Hebrew text and the study of biblical Hebrew. The Renaissance humanists assisted the Protestant Reformers by providing them with a more reliable copy of the Bible, but the Reformers themselves provided the world with a more reliable interpretation of God's Word. One can safely say that each would not have happened without the other!

Even to this day, the proper interpretation of the Bible depends to a very large extent upon the reliability of the text and the accuracy of the translation with which the student or scholar works. The continuing reformation in the Church and theology is one that demands repeated stress upon the reconstruction of the original writings of the Bible. If we learn anything from the Reformation age, it ought to be the danger of taking the Bible away from the people through dependence upon an outdated translation. When the Roman Catholic church gave "divine" sanction to the Latin Vulgate, the effect was to take the Bible away from the common man, since Latin was no longer read or understood. (Ironically, one of the original motivations for Jerome's translation of the Bible into Latin from the Greek was to give the Bible back to the reading public at a time when fewer and fewer people could read Greek.) But the "sanctification" of the Latin Vulgate also served to retard the process of reform, since the continual reexamination of the original text of Scripture was stopped and the reexamination of the meaning of Scripture was assumed unnecessary. Not only had the text of Scripture assumed a fixed form, but its interpretation had likewise become crystallized.

Renaissance humanism and Reformation theology opened again the issue of the original text of the Bible and its proper interpretation. In our own day, the defense of the King James Version is analogous to the Roman Catholic church's defense and deification of the Latin Vulgate. If we expect the Church to be continually reformed by the Word of God, then we must allow the example of the sixteenth century to influence our own study of the Bible. The Church in every age can do no better than to raise anew the issue of what God originally inspired prophet and apostle to write, and to ask what that inspired text means to God's people. The work of Calvin and Luther not only inspires us by its example, but provides a principle by which the Church today can do what they did for their own time. This does not mean, as some erroneously suggest, that the Bible is changing. Hopefully, we are coming closer to the restoration and reconstruction of the original writings today than the scholars were in the sixteenth century; but the issue here is a confusion between *an inspired Bible* and *an infallible interpretation*. And unless we are, in principle, open to such a reexamination of the text, we are bound by a traditionalism that is as bad as, if not worse than, the traditionalism of the sixteenth-century Roman Catholic church.

REFORMATION THEOLOGY AND THE EVANGELICAL HERITAGE

It is both accurate and inaccurate to speak of a *Reformation theology*. We might be more correct to speak of *Reformation theologies,* but there is a sense in which the whole movement for reform in Church and theology was a unified whole. No matter how diverse the interpretation of the sacraments, the relationship of grace and works or the roles of the Church and the state, the great leaders for reform in the sixteenth century were generally united in their appeal to the Bible. It is true that there were groups (as George H. Williams has labeled them, "rationalists") who looked upon man's mental qualities as reflective of divine reason. These groups functionally replaced the authority of the Bible by an appeal either to the "inner light" associated with an immediate, inner illumination of the divine Spirit or to "reason" connected with the divine *Logos*. In any case, they represent a minor deviation and are properly associated with the fringe, or radical, Reformation. Among the mainstream currents for reform and in the theology and writings of the main leaders of the Reformation, the Bible was the sole and absolute authority. The interpretations of this document may have differed, but on the fact of its authority there was little or no disagreement.[1]

On the other hand, it would be equally misleading to assume that the interpretations of the Bible were as diverse as its representatives. In all honesty, the student of the theology of the sixteenth century must confess that there was more agreement among the leaders of the Reformation than its Roman Catholic critics recognized. The point at which there was general agreement was the *Gospel,* the *evangelion.* The differences lay in the extent to which the various groups moved beyond this common core. The followers of Zwingli, Bucer, and Calvin came to be known as *Reformed theologians* because they were not content to rediscover the Gospel without re-forming the entire Church in theology, in liturgy, and in government. In some of the radical Anabaptist groups, one finds interpretations as extreme as total nonparticipation in politics and complete communal sharing of all worldly possessions. But *it should never be forgotten that the core of Reformation theology was the Gospel.*

This Gospel was nothing more or less than a recovery of grace: the fact that man's salvation depends entirely upon God's mercy demonstrated in the death and resurrection of Jesus Christ. William C. Robinson, in his excellent study on the theology of the Reformation, shows how the various slogans—*sola gratia, sola Christo, sola fide, soli Deo gloria* and *sola scriptura*—are all variations upon this one theme. They are like different movements of one grand symphony![2]

The Bible was important because it was the only infallible source of this Gospel. Anabaptist, Calvinist, and Lutheran were all agreed that the one fundamental error of Roman Catholicism was its loss of the Gospel. But why had Christendom lost its way? The answer the Reformers gave to this basic question was that it had lost the Bible in its ecclesiastical and juridical traditions. The Reformers accused Rome of the same error of which Jesus had accused the first-century Pharisees: they had set aside the Word of God by their traditions (Mt 15). If we may learn a second lesson from the great leaders of the sixteenth century, it is that we and every generation of Christians must confront our traditions with the Word of God. Have we allowed some fetish to rob us of God's Word of grace in Jesus Christ?

The major difference in all periods of the Church is not between a liberal and a conservative theology but between an *evangelical* and *nonevangelical* theology. If we only return to the authority of the Bible without recovering the message of the Bible, we shall have failed to capture the importance of what Calvin and Luther did. (Note modern-day Jehovah's Witnesses!) This fact is all too obvious when one reads the decrees of the Council of Trent—the council that was supposed to answer the charges of the Reformers and to correct the abuses of the Church. In the fourth session of the council, held on April 8, 1546, the article on the Bible was formulated. It reads:

> The sacred and holy, ecumenical, and general Synod of Trent,— lawfully assembled in the Holy Ghost, the same three legates of the Apostolic See presiding therein,—keeping this always in view, that, errors being removed, the purity itself of the Gospel be preserved in the Church: which (Gospel), before promised through the prophets in the holy Scriptures, our Lord Jesus Christ, the Son of God, first promulgated with His own mouth, and then commanded to be preached by His Apostles to every creature, as the fountain of all, both saving truth, and moral discipline; and seeing clearly that this truth and discipline are contained in the written books, and the unwritten traditions which, received by the Apostles from the mouth of Christ himself, or from the Apostles themselves, the Holy Ghost *dictating,* have come down even unto us, transmitted as it were from hand to hand: [the Synod] following the examples of the Orthodox Fathers, receives and venerates with an equal affection of piety and reverence, all the books of both the Old and of the New Testament—seeing that one God is the author of both—as also the said traditions, as well as those appertaining to faith as to morals, as having been *dictated,* either by Christ's own word of mouth, or by the Holy Ghost, and preserved in the Catholic Church by a continuous succession.[3] [Italics mine.]

What is obvious in the quotation above is the high view of Scripture held by the Roman Church of the sixteenth century. What is not so clear in this statement, but which becomes painfully obvious in a further reading of the decrees of the Council of Trent, is the interpretation of the Gospel. The statement even goes so far as to indicate general agreement with the Reformers that the purity of the Gospel must be foremost in the Church's theology. However, that Rome perverted that Gospel into another gospel, which is not another gospel, is the striking difference between Catholicism and Protestantism (see Gal 1:6-12). So belief in an inspired Bible, even a Bible *dictated by the Holy Ghost,* is not enough; hence, the demand for a proper hermeneutic.

The Meaning of Sola Scriptura

From what has been said before, it should be clear that the inspiration of the Bible was not the central question in the sixteenth century. The more basic issue was the interpretation of the Bible, or what is technically called *hermeneutics:* who has the right and how are we to interpret the Book inspired by God Himself?

The answer to this question is not as simple as is often assumed by Protestants. The double principles of *sola scriptura* and *sola fide* are not self-explanatory. We have already seen that Rome, too, appealed to the Bible, but her hermeneutic was ecclesiastical and historical. In one sense, Rome viewed the Bible as one source of ecclesiastical law to be interpreted as one would any body of jurisprudence. The proper court for the determination of the meaning of this law was the Church, whose center was in Rome. She was the guardian of the whole body of theological literature from the time of the apostles onward. She alone could determine the precise wording and meaning of a biblical passage.

On the Reformation side, the issue of hermeneutics was tied up with the nature of the Church too. The phrase *sola scriptura* became meaningful when the issue of authority was raised. Robert M. Grant has correctly observed,

> Catholic exegesis relies strongly on the authority of the fathers. It interprets the Bible by the tradition of the Church. Protestant exegesis makes a fresh start, often overturning the accumulated decisions of centuries. . . . And the reformers were willing to insist on their understanding of the Bible no matter what previous exegetes might have said, no matter whether they contradicted even the decisions of councils. The Church was not to be the arbiter of the meaning of scripture, for scripture, the word of God, was the Church's judge.[1]

As long as the issue was only the nature of the Bible, an inspired book, there was little difference of opinion between Calvin and Luther on one side and the Roman Catholic Church on the other.

What became the divisive issue was the way in which the Bible and Church were related. For Rome, the Bible was the product of the Holy Spirit's work in the Church—that institution extending from the apostles and their successors to the sixteenth century. For rather obvious reasons, the great Reformers came to distrust Rome's claim to be the most valid, if not the exclusive expression of the Church. No doubt Luther's personal trip to Rome in the years 1510-11, when he spent the month of January in the "holy city" and witnessed the corruption of the Church firsthand, did as much as anything to raise doubts about the Church's purity and legitimacy. Rome's obvious abuse of power and her perverted sacramental practices only served to reinforce these suspicions and doubts. "It is a wicked falsehood," said Calvin, "that the scripture's credibility depends on the judgment of the Church. . . . The Church is itself grounded upon Scripture."[5]

When Rome sought to justify her ways by appealing to the great body of ecclesiastical tradition preserved "faithfully" within the Church, all Reformers began to question the relationship of history to the Word of God. The most radical departures were the Anabaptist groups who saw the decay of faith with the conversion of Constantine early in the fourth century. In a letter from Sebastian Franck to John Campanus written in 1531, Franck pushed the decay of the Church even farther back, to the postapostolic period. According to Franck, many intelligent people, i.e., Anabaptists,

> are seized with a delusive idea, holding that at the time of Constantine and Constantius, Antichrist concurrently broke into the church and that the external polity of the church was at that same time reduced to ashes, especially because the worldly power and the princes of the pagans abandoned their pagan belief, were baptized, and were reckoned with the flock of Christ. Therefore the brothers were courted, war was waged, heresies rooted out not with words but rather with swords, and the things of faith were defended with fist and force. The opinion of these people is not at all bad but they are in error nevertheless. *I, however, firmly believe that the outward church of Christ was wasted and destroyed right after the apostles. This is what the wolves, that is, the Fathers amply prove for me, although Scripture gives no testimony*

on this point. For all that they teach is surely idle child's play, if they are compared with the apostles.[6] [Italics mine.]

On the other hand, a careful reading of Calvin and Luther shows that they saw the point of departure much later, sometime after the time of Augustine (354-430). Calvin gave the following title to chapter 5 of Book 4, dealing with the doctrine of the Church: "The Ancient Form of Government was Completely Overthrown by the Tyranny of the Papacy."[7] Luther, too, saw the perversion of the Church and her doctrine as an extension of the semi-Pelagian controversies which modified Augustine's strong defense of *sola gratia.* The development of the papacy only helped to institutionalize the theological perversions and distortions of semi-Pelagianism. This fact helps to explain why both Calvin and Luther refer to Augustine more than any other writer outside of the Bible itself!

With the growing suspicion that Rome herself was corrupt, the only final court of appeal would have to be the Bible itself. But who could appeal to the Bible? Priest? Pope? Or just anyone? Calvin solemnly warned in one place that the greatest danger is to abandon Scripture. He seemed less concerned that someone would misinterpret the Bible than that someone would replace the Bible by appealing to some direct illumination or revelation of the Spirit.[8] Luther likewise admonished his students, in lectures on 2 Peter 1:20-21, to be skeptical of relying upon one's own reason and wisdom.

With these words all the fathers who interpret Scripture in their own way are refuted, and their interpretation is invalidated. It is forbidden to rely on such interpretation. If Jerome or Augustine or anyone of the fathers has given his own interpretation, we want none of it. Peter has stated the prohibition: "You shall not give your own interpretation." The Holy Spirit Himself must expound Scripture. Otherwise it must remain unexpounded. Now if anyone of the saintly fathers can show that his interpretation is based on Scriptures, and if Scripture proves that this is the way it should be interpreted, then the interpretation is right. If this is not the case, I must not believe him.[9]

Luther often stated that the believer with the Bible on his side was more powerful than the pope or the whole hierarchy without Scripture.[10]

In the statement from the decrees of Trent which was mentioned earlier, the fundamental differences between Rome and the Reformers center on two issues. One is the exclusive right of the hierarchy of the Church to interpret or determine the meaning of the biblical text. And the other is the emphasis upon tradition as a secondary source of revelation. The meaning of *sola scriptura* is, therefore, that nothing is more authoritative than the Bible. History, tradition, and even the Holy Roman Church herself must come under its scrutiny!

THE REFORMATION VIEW OF HISTORY AND THE TASK OF EXEGESIS

Theologian and biblical scholar alike are constantly forced to raise the question of history. How are the history of the Church and the history of the interpretation of the text of sacred Scripture related to the truth of God?

One answer to this question, formulated during the Reformation era, was *Restorationism: the belief that God spoke definitively and decisively only in the history of biblical revelation.* The task of the biblical scholar, theologian, and ecclesiastic was to return the Church to these primitive foundations. This distinction is supported by the research of George H. Williams, a leading authority on the "left-wing, radical Reformation." He claims that

> within this Radical Reformation there were, nevertheless two subsidiary impulses which help to mark off the Anabaptists from the Spiritualists. The former looked steadily into the *past,* finding their own image and ecclesiastical blueprints in the Bible and the martyr church of antiquity. The Spiritualists gazed mostly into the *future.*[11]

This Restorationism is clearly reflected in "The Schleitheim Confession of Faith" prepared by the Swiss Anabaptists in 1527. In this standard confession of the Anabaptist movement, seven items are specifically mentioned as reflecting this divine pattern for the Christian life: believer's baptism, the church's right or power to ban and excommunicate unfaithful members, the breaking of the bread, "separation from Abomination" i.e., Rome, the true church must have pastors whose lives are above reproach and in whom the congregation have complete confidence, the sword must be rejected and all worldly political power, and finally, the word of a Christian ought to be so trustworthy that oaths would be superfluous.[12] Thomas Müntzer in a printed sermon, "An Exposition of the Second Chapter of Daniel," writes that

> the church since its beginning has become in all places dilapidated, up to the present time of the "divided" world (Luke 21:10; Dan. 2:35; I Esdras 4:45). For Hegesippus (and Eusebius) in [*Ecclesiastical History*] IV, 22, concerning the [early] Christian church, declares that the Christian congregation did not remain a virgin any longer than up to the time of the death of the disciples of the apostles and soon thereafter became an adulteress, as had indeed already been prophesied by the beloved apostles (2 Pe 2: 12-15).[13]

One might say that all history since A.D. 95 was devilish in development. But the point that needs to be stressed is not simply a matter of ecclesiastical restorationism. We are here observing a basic hermeneutical approach to the Bible: since ecclesiastical history after the time of the apostles has been decadent, we cannot trust any commentator upon Scripture but our own. Müntzer's reference to one of the Old Testament apocryphal books illustrates his flexibility toward the canon, but his interpretation is decidedly polemical and apologetic for the position he defends.

There is, however, a significant difference discernible between the Radical Reformation and the views espoused by Luther and Calvin. This is not to suggest that Luther and Calvin always agreed in their interpretation of the Bible, but it is to assert that both agreed upon the importance of history for the right interpretation of Scripture. Luther does not write his comments upon the different passages of the Bible as if nothing had transpired since the first century. Nor does Calvin! Both are aware of a long body of literature which has contributed to their own theological understanding of the text. As one reads the writings of these two great reformers, he is impressed with their knowledge of history and the particular interpretation of a text held by the early Church Fathers as well as the later scholastics. They are not bound by the exegesis of the former periods, but their own interpretation is always in dialogue with that history. They are quick to point out the excesses as well as the accuracies of those earlier commentators. This was especially true if the authority of the Bible was juxtaposed with the teaching of the fathers. Luther states his own case as follows:

> I ask for Scriptures and Eck offers me the Fathers. I ask for the sun, and he shows me his lanterns. I ask: "Where is your Scripture proof?" and he adduces Ambrose and Cyril. . . . With all due respect to the Fathers I prefer the authority of the Scripture.[14]

Calvin and Luther express their indebtedness to Augustine constantly. He above everyone else had grasped the doctrine of grace most clearly. If any interpreter of the Bible gave witness to this doctrine, he was worth quoting and worth being approved.

One important illustration of this whole problem of history and hermeneutics concerns the problem of the canon. Too much has been made of the fact that Luther held a rather low view of the book of James.[15] Some contemporary interpreters argue that this implies that at heart Luther would have been more sympathetic toward the Neo-Orthodox view of Scripture than toward the orthodox or conservative view of verbal inspiration and biblical inerrancy. But upon closer examination it becomes more evident that Luther's problem with James concerned canonicity, not inspiration. As part of the entire controversy surrounding Luther's break with Rome, not only did ancient dogmas come under new scrutiny but even the issue of the canon itself was reopened. J. Michael Reu supports this claim in his thorough study of Luther's view of Scripture.

> Now does this evaluation of the Epistle of James endanger any of the preceding results of our investigation concerning Luther's attitude toward Scripture. By no means. One must read these quotations in their full context, then it becomes apparent that Luther did not class this epistle among the canonical writings. . . . That Hebrews, James, Jude, and Revelation were not considered canonical by Luther is also proved by the fact that in his Septem-

ber Testament he did not add numbers to them and that he put a
space beween them and the others.[16]

It is interesting, however, that Reu warns his readers not to follow Luther in this judgment, and he further documents Luther's
extremely high view of the Bible in those parts that Luther considers to be canonical. Some scholars claim that Luther modified
his views later in life. It is true that his judgment on James especially softened in later life; however, there is no real evidence, to
this writer's knowledge, that he ever regarded James on the same
level as Romans or Galatians.

Luther and Calvin are both aware that the Bible as a sacred collection is the work of many centuries and reflects the judgment of
the Church as a whole. This does not mean that the Church determined the canon, but merely that the Church came to *recognize
these writings as the Word of God.* Calvin states that "indeed,
Scripture exhibits fully as clear evidence of its own truth as white
and black things do of their color, or sweet and bitter things do of
their taste."[17] Luther likewise in his lectures on the Psalms states
that "the Scripture is the womb from which are born the divine
truth and the church."[18] Accordingly neither Calvin nor Luther
would place historical criticism or the authority of the Church
above the teaching of the Bible. But in the interpretation of this
inspired document, the history of the interpretation may assist us,
as it did Calvin and Luther, to understand it better.

LUTHER'S HERMENEUTICS: THE LAW-GOSPEL MOTIF

One does not read very far into the writings of Martin Luther
until he realizes that one principle above all others determines
Luther's approach to the Bible. This principle is the *Law-Gospel*
motif. Luther rejects any interpretation of the Bible which does
not proclaim the Gospel. None of the Reformation representatives
sets forth the theme of the Gospel more clearly than does Luther.
This does not mean that Luther ever denied that there was a literal
meaning to the text. Bernard Ramm notes six elements in Luther's
hermeneutics:

(1) *The psychological principle.* Faith and illumination were the personal and spiritual requisites for an interpreter. The believer should seek the leading of the Spirit and depend on that leading.

(2) *The authority principle.* The Bible is the supreme and final authority in theological matters, and is therefore above all ecclesiastical authority .

(3) *The literal principle.* In place of the four-fold system of the scholastics, we are to put the literal principle. . . . In the *Table Talk* he affirms that "I have grounded my preaching upon the literal word" . . . Briggs cites him as saying: "Every word should be allowed to stand in its natural meaning, and that should not be abandoned unless faith forces us to it."

(4) *The sufficiency principle.* The devout and competent Christian can understand the true meaning of the Bible and thereby does not need the official guides to interpretation offered by the Roman Catholic Church.

(5) *The Christological principle.* The literal interpretation of the Bible was not the end of interpretation. The function of all interpretation is to find Christ. . . .

(6) *The Law-Gospel principle.* The Law was God's word about human sin, human imperfection, and whose purpose was to drive us to our knees under a burden of guilt. The Gospel was God's grace and power to save. Hence we must never in interpreting the Scriptures confuse these two different activities of God or teachings of Holy Scripture.[19]

It is probably most accurate to subsume all other points under the issue of Law-Gospel. The psychological, the literal, and even the Christological have as their end the proclamation of the Law to make us aware of our sin and the Gospel to bring us the joy and peace of God's grace.

It is true that Luther did occasionally deviate from this approach, as when he rejected the Copernican view of cosmology largely upon its incompatibility with the teaching of the Bible.[20] But more frequently, he would leave questions open rather than appeal to Scripture for a pattern or a blueprint for everything from economics to eschatology. Implicit in Luther's approach is the same freedom of interpretation evident in his soteriology, in which the concept of the freedom of the believer was so strongly emphasized. This fact helps to explain why the Lutheran Reformation is referred to as the *Evangelical Reformation* in contrast to the Calvinistic movement commonly called the *Reformed Tradition*.

At least two concepts are characteristic of the distinctively Lutheran approach to hermeneutics. One is the concept of *adiaphora*. *Adiaphora* means that some items are clearly open for debate, and differences of opinion among true Christians should be allowed. The essential agreement in theology must be at the point of the Gospel. This is reflected in Luther's flexible attitude toward church government, mode of baptism, and the more open attitude toward retaining liturgical ceremonies in the worship of the Church.[21] The actual controversy within Lutheranism over the problem of *adiaphora* came in the period after Luther's death, but there can be no doubt that Luther himself made such distinctions in his own writings.

Another is the principle that whatever is not expressly forbidden in Scripture is permissible. Here the stress is on how free and open, rather than how restricted, the Church should be. As long as we do not violate any clear or explicit text of the Bible, we are free to use ceremonies and rites that may not be prescribed in it. These two principles clearly distinguish the Lutheran and the Calvinistic approaches to the interpretation of the Bible. In Calvinism, whatever is taught or practiced must be found *explicitly* in Scripture. Hence, Calvanistic churches were more austere. While Luther composed numerous contemporary hymns to be used in the worship of the churches, the Calvinists restricted congregational singing only to Old Testament psalms.

Consequently, there is less emphasis upon the Bible as a repository of knowledge for Luther and the Lutheran heritage. The Bible is indeed the cradle that brings Christ to us. What good would it do us to read the Bible to prove capitalism or communism, Luther would argue, if in the process we missed the Saviour? The contemporary church which is so often splintered on the issues of *adiaphora* would do well to recover this Lutheran theme.

Reformed Hermeneutics: Biblical Revelation and the Witness of the Spirit

In the writings of John Calvin, we encounter one of the most consistent expressions of a grammatical, historical, contextual, and soteriological approach to hermeneutics to be found anywhere in Christian theology. Fullerton claims that "Calvin may not unfittingly be called the first scientific interpreter in the history of the Christian Church."[22] There is, in Calvin's theology, a much greater emphasis upon the whole Bible as an inspired book per se. We will find his interpretation less "spiritual" than Luther's. Luther frequently interpreted figures of speech with an elasticity that stretched their literal meaning, but we rarely encounter this approach in the writings of Calvin.

John Calvin came to the Reformation via Renaissance humanism. His first published work was a *Commentary on Seneca's Treatise on Clemency.* He soon developed a critical view toward the doctrines of Rome through a critical rereading of the Bible. Consequently he is less verbose, less colorful in his exposition of the Bible than Luther, but he is often more reliable as a critical commentator. Indeed, this author would prefer Calvin's commentaries to many contemporary works for clarity, accuracy, and profoundness of insight. Luther's writings may move the heart, but Calvin challenges the mind.

Calvin's use and interpretation of Scripture led him to formulate a dogmatic theology, *The Institutes of the Christian Religion.* Luther made little or no effort to bring his own theology into a system. And in some respects, the disharmony of Luther's writings are more impressive than their consistency. Calvin, on the other hand, felt compelled to bring the writings of the Bible into a meaningful framework of interpretation. In the early editions of the *Institutes,* he followed a more unstructured outline; however, by the time this classic had reached its eighth edition in 1559, the four major articles of the Apostle's Creed had provided him with a framework for his dogmatic theology. (The term *dogmatic* here refers to the idea of a creedal basis for the organization and structure of theology.) This creedal structure and this desire for a more consistent and orderly interpretation of the Bible has always characterized Calvinism, much more so than we find in Lutheranism.

In his exegesis of Scripture, Calvin was more concerned to bring a uniformity of interpretation to the text of Scripture. He was aware of the textual and harmonization problems with the Bible, but he was consistent in his affirmations that the Bible was inerrant and inspired. He even speaks of the Bible as being *dictated by the Holy Spirit.*

> Let this be a firm principle: No other word is to be held as the Word of God, and given place as such in the church, than what is contained first in the Law and the Prophets, then in the writings of the apostles; and the only authorized way of teaching in the church is by the prescription and standard of his Word.
>
> From this also we infer that the only thing granted to the apostles was that which the prophets had had of old. They were to expound the ancient Scripture and to show that what is taught there has been fulfilled in Christ. Yet they were not to do this except from the Lord, that is, with Christ's Spirit as precursor in a certain measure *dictating the words.*[23]

And consequently the objective word of Scripture holds a high place in his theology. God has communicated His message to man, and that message is contained in the written words of the Bible. And although the soteriological emphasis is never lacking in Calvin's writings about the Bible, the message of salvation is never pushed into the text. He is willing to accept the validity of a text whose salvation theme is minimal. Calvin, for instance, never had the problem with James that Luther did. And this also means that he was more insistent on finding a divine pattern not only for theology but also for the state and the Church in Scripture. The whole of life was to be restructured and reformed according to the pattern God had given in His Word. Here we repeat that basic difference between Lutheranism and Calvinism: *whatever is not expressly commanded in Scripture is forbidden.*

What is often overlooked in analyzing Calvin's theology and especially his hermeneutics is the role of the Holy Spirit. Calvin was just as suspicious of the *Enthusiasts, Anabaptists,* and *Rationalists* as any of his contemporaries, but this did not lead him to deny the subjective role of the Holy Spirit. He writes that

> only when proper reverence and dignity are given to the word does the Holy Spirit show forth his power. . . . The word itself is not quite certain for us unless it be confirmed by the testimony of the Spirit. . . . For by a kind of mutual bond the Lord has joined together the certainty of his word and of his Spirit so that the perfect religion of the Word may abide in our minds when the Spirit shines.[24]

Scholars have called attention to the *autopistos or* self-authenticating nature of the Bible in Calvin's theology of the Word.[25] The greatest proof that the Bible is the Word of God is not rational or logical proofs, history, or even fulfilled prophecy or miracles. Rather, it is the inner witness of the Holy Spirit. This meant that the actual writing of the Bible was motivated by the Holy Spirit, but it also meant that only the Holy Spirit could unlock the meaning of the text to the reader.

Coupled with this emphasis upon the role of the Holy Spirit is Calvin's emphasis upon the importance of the pastoral teaching office. "Interpretation is not left entirely, or even primarily, to the individual. There are special men, pastors and teachers, who are given the task of interpreting for others. 'We must remember, that the Scripture is not only given us, but that interpreters and teachers are also added, to be helps to us.' "[26] On the other hand, Calvin would agree that the common layman with the Holy Spirit would be a better interpreter than a theologian with Aristotle or Occam.

Calvin's balance between the objective word of Scripture and the inner witness of the Holy Spirit has provided classical Calvinism with one of its greatest attributes. And the contemporary church too often reveals a lack of this balance. The revolt of the New Reformation theology of Karl Barth did much to correct the subjectivism of nineteenth-century liberalism, but Barth's own failure to accept Calvin's doctrine of the verbally inspired and inerrant word of Scripture did not help his successors to retain the Bible in its central importance. Calvin was, himself, not simply a theologian but also a preacher. His doctrine of Scripture and his exegetical method were all calculated to give the preacher something "to say" as he stood in the pulpit.

EVANGELICALISM, NEO-ORTHODOXY AND THE NEW HERMENEUTIC

It is always good to keep in mind the fact that no one is saved because he holds a particular view of the Bible. We find no explicit or implicit references in Scripture that "if we shall confess with our mouths and believe with our hearts that the Bible is the verbally inspired and theologically inerrant Word of God, we shall be saved!" And often the inquiring student who witnesses the infighting among ecclesiastical groups over the doctrine of Scripture, asks himself, "Well, what difference does it make anyway?" Probably none, if we are able to isolate our commitment to Jesus Christ from the inescapable result of thinking about our faith. But the minute we begin to think about our Christian commitment and begin to ask why and what, we find ourselves confronted with the nature and meaning of the Bible. Granted, we are not saved by affirming any particular view of the Bible. But every serious student must ask: how consistent is my view of the Bible with my affirmation of Jesus Christ as Lord and Saviour? Other chapters in this volume are devoted to this question and other contemporary works explore it in depth.

It is more than interesting that more than one school of theology has sought to defend its view of the Bible by appealing to Calvin and Luther, and especially their use of the Bible. The views are so divergent that it is obvious that they cannot all be right. Generally speaking, the school that is called Neo-Orthodoxy or New Reformation Theology has sought to recover the Reformation basis for faith and theology in the twentieth century. The originator of this movement was Karl Barth. In his early studies, Barth had come across the writings of Calvin and Luther, and he had noticed the great gap between that age and his own. Or more precisely, he had noticed the great similarities. Just as the Church in the sixteenth century needed desperately to hear the word of God and needed reform, so the Church at the end of the nineteenth century and the beginning of the twentieth needed to hear the Word again. But Barth and the entire school of Neo-Orthodoxy were embarrassed by the doctrine of verbal inspiration and verbal inerrancy. Some of this school have even gone so far as to claim that neither Luther nor Calvin held to these views. Emil Brunner says that "the Reformers of the first generation, Luther and Zwingli, are not favorable to the doctrine of verbal inspiration, whereas Melanchthon, Calvin and Bullinger are."[27] Wilhelm Niesel's study of Calvin claims that "first, we might point out that in the Scriptural exegesis of Calvin, there is nothing to suggest a belief in literal inerrancy."[28] Niesel later admits that Calvin speaks of this subject, but only so briefly as to have no real significance.

A careful examination of Luther and Calvin will not support the claims of Brunner, Niesel, and all who stand with them. We have already called attention to Calvin's statement about dictation, and a careful examination of the sections in Book 1 and Book 4 of the *Institutes* will clearly support the evangelicals' claim that Calvin and Luther stand with the doctrine of verbal inspiration and theological inerrancy. They are excused by the Neo-Orthodox writers as being "children" of their age. How can we claim them and deny them in the same breath? Luther states, "I have learned to do only those books that are called the Holy Scriptures the honor of believing firmly that none of their writers has erred."[29]

More recently, contemporary theology has moved farther and farther away from the conservative Barthian theology to a more radical Bultmannian position. These developments are sometimes called the "New Hermeneutic." *Hermeneutik,* the German term, stands for a school of scholars who took their directions from Martin Heidegger and Rudolf Bultmann, and who have more recently been represented by the writings of Ernst Fuchs. The issue with which this school is concerned is not what the text *meant* but what it *means now.* Paul J. Achtemeier writes that

> the real problems of interpretation do not become evident in a concrete way until the actual attempt is made to translate and interpret a specific text. The difficulty lies in the fact that in the nature of the case every translation must, to some extent at least, do violence to the original, if for no other reason than that language must be transformed into something other than it originally was, i.e., another language. But it is necessary to translate, it is

not sufficient "simply" to translate, and right there lie all the depths of the hermeneutical problem.[30]

We have come full orbit now. We have come right back to where we began this chapter: the problem of translating the Bible and the text of Scripture. The solution offered by the New Hermeneutic is to move away from the original text in the direction of the contemporary reader. We suggest a better solution: let us stress the priority of a Gospel that is rooted in history, witnessed to by inspired prophet and apostle. It is related to the concrete realities of life through the written word of Scripture which is open to investigation through grammar and history. And it is related to contemporary man by the sovereign action of God the Holy Spirit, who can make each new reader of the Bible a *new creature in Christ Jesus!*

10

Biblical Authority: A Study in History

by Robert Webber

IT HAS NEVER BEEN POSSIBLE to live in the world without being subject to some kind of authority. We first became aware of authority through our parents, and as the circle of our life becomes larger we soon learn that our lives are subject to authority in every direction.

Religious authority is not unlike the concept of authority in other areas of our life. It has to do with what the framers of the Westminster Confession of Faith called "matters of faith and practice." It is the court of final appeal, the ultimate reference point where matters of dispute and questions of differences are settled.

In this essay my concern is with the place of the Bible as an authority in the life of the Church. My persuasion is that the modern Christian substantially denies the authority of the Bible by subjecting the Bible to reason or experience. Elevating reason to the place of final authority, some modern Christians are only willing to accept as authoritative those things which have been determined to be in agreement with reason. In the same manner, others are only willing to accept as true those things which are experienced to be true. Consequently *reason* as in the former case and *experience* as in the latter case become authoritative over the Scripture. They judge the truthfulness of the Scripture or at best verify its truthfulness at a particular point, allowing it at that point at least to be authoritative. My argument is that this relationalistic and subjectivistic approach to the Scripture robs it of its authority and puts man in the position of being the source of his own authority.

I will use the historical method in developing this picture. Because the breakdown of biblical authority occurred in the seventeenth through the nineteenth centuries, I will concentrate on that period of time, showing how a rationalistic view of the Bible and an experiential view emerged and combined to set the stage for the collapse of biblical authority among modern thinkers. I will conclude by setting forth some suggestions about biblical authority which will help to guide our thinking toward a conclusion for today.

THE EMERGENCE OF A RATIONALISTIC VIEW OF AUTHORITY

Interpreters of history agree that the sixteenth century is a turning point, a watershed in the life of the Western world. The spirit of a new age emerged out of the rubble of that revolutionary century, and it began almost immediately to express itself in the unfolding of cultural forms.

Two distinct cultural forms emerged in the Renaissance and the Reformation. The Renaissance was rooted in the Greek past which reveled in the art, literature, philosophy, and spirit of a bygone era. It tried to emulate the love for life, the freedom to be "this worldly" that it found in the old Hellenic world. On the other hand, the Reformation was rooted in the biblical and patristic past which rejoiced in the truths discovered in the literature of the Bible and the early Church Fathers.

These two spirits, although closely aligned in the thinking of many (e.g., Erasmus), began during the sixteenth century, but especially thereafter, to separate into two different world views. The Renaissance spirit became more firmly rooted in humanism, while the Reformation spirit continued to elaborate its theistic stance.

The lines of both the humanistic and theistic world views began to cross over one another during the development of history in the seventeenth, eighteenth, and nineteenth centuries. Although a continuity of reformational thought did continue, an intellectual and influential line of theological thinkers gradually became sympathetic to a more humanistic way of thinking. In time, theological methodology became secularized.

The slow secularization of theological methodology ultimately

changed the shape of theology. Its assumptions about God, creation, sin, Christ, redemption, the Holy Spirit, and authority made
a sharp turn away from historic Christianity. It is this course which
we will follow paying special attention to the demise of biblical
authority.[1]

ORTHODOXY

The time immediately following the Reformation of the sixteenth century, and preceding the more rationalistic orientation
of eighteenth-century theology, is often termed the period of orthodoxy. Webster defines the term "orthodox" as "conforming to
established doctrine." This points to its major emphasis which is
correct thinking.

Although we often use the word orthodox to denote loyalty to
the teaching of the historic church (against newer interpretations
of Christianity which have been labeled liberal), we must nevertheless recognize that seventeenth century classical orthodoxy de-
notes a fresh beginning in theology. It is a step away from the
Reformation, and a movement toward the rationalism that reduced the Scripture to a mere human book by the nineteenth century.

This new orientation of orthodoxy is associated with the philosophical school of Neo-Aristotelianism. This school originated in
Europe and gained a foothold in the Protestant universities by
the end of the sixteenth century. It gave birth to a Protestant
scholasticism which provided the presuppositions for the theology
of the seventeenth century.

In the universities of the seventeenth century, philosophy was a
gateway to all the professions including the ministry. Because of
the comprehensiveness of the Aristotelian system, every student, regardless of his discipline, had an opportunity to relate it to his
chosen field. Consequently the terms and categories of Aristotelian
philosophy soon dominated the academia of the seventeenth century, including its theology. For this reason the theology of the
seventeenth century is often called "scholastic" for by that term is
meant the integration of Christian theology and Aristotelian philosophy.

The theological controversies[2] which dominate this age soon began to show a bias toward discussing Christianity through philosophical terms. Exegesis was left behind in favor of philosophy, and the theological works of the day appear more concerned about the clarification of philosophical points than the exposition of the biblical text.

The problem of biblical authority emerged in relation to the problem of certainty, which is often the key to understanding any theology, ancient or modern. Certainty among orthodox theologians was generally defined as "the intellectual assurance that what God says corresponds to what God does and what really is." Revelation is a disclosure of truth. The Holy Spirit convinces the mind of the accuracy, reliability, and ultimate infallibility of the Scriptures, creating an assurance that the Bible is the truth. The theologian, using the Scripture, reasons his way to a complete and intellectually valid system which satisfied the mind.

This scholastic approach to the question of certainty produced three results which paved the way for a biblical authority based on reason.

The first result was the creation of a harmonious and symmetrical system of thought based on Aristotelian categories of thought. This was accomplished through the acceptance of the analytical method and the scriptural principle as the foundation of theology. The analytical method, a deductive approach to theology, presupposes the use of philosophical categories of thought. It lends itself to the development of a well-rounded system of thought that contains all the answers. The foundation for this system of thought is the revelation of God which is understood through philosophical categories of thought. Consequently, reason and Scripture, combined with the Aristotelian view of reality, became the tools for knowing truth. (While this is generally true, it should be noted that there is a difference in this matter between Lutheran and Reformed orthodoxy. The Lutherans held that every rational argument must give way to the testimony of Scripture, whereas Reformed orthodoxy attempted to harmonize the content of revelation with the arguments of reason. For example, most Lutherans made no attempt to explain the Trinity philosophically or rationally, whereas the Reformed did.) What we see developing is an objective form of theology. Revelation which was codified in Scripture provided the point of departure. From it one could create a system of truth.

The second result was the need to prove the system to be true. At first, scholastic theology was readily accepted because it fit the categories of thought which had already been accepted through the university training. When these Aristotelian categories were later questioned, however, the Christian faith which had become so dependent upon them also came under question. Consequently, theologians soon found themselves becoming concerned with all manner of proofs for the existence of God, the trustworthiness of the biblical narratives, the plausibility of miracles, and the reasonableness of the Incarnation.

The third result of the scholastic approach was the creation of an authoritarian faith. Faith increasingly tended toward an assent to facts, an intellectual acceptance of a prescribed system of thought. An increasing emphasis was laid on the intellectual truths of Scripture which could be understood by a mere examination of its contents. Because of the philosophical presuppositions, theological scholarship had to recognize that truth could be known in the mind apart from any experience with it through the work of the Holy Spirit. The point of contact then between the non-Christian and the truth of the Bible was man's mind. Man could understand the faith intellectually without believing it. But he could only understand it savingly by believing it. Thus faith became an act of believing, an intellectual acceptance of the whole corpus of doctrine.[3]

Orthodox theologians had now placed their theology in a position where it was dependent upon reason for its validity. Consequently, authority shifted from the reformational Word and Spirit (the inseparable connection between the authority of the Word and the activity of the Holy Spirit) to a view which brought Word and reason together. Now the Word is authoritative because it is reasonable. It had been validated by reason—soon it was to be tested by reason. For this debate we turn to the period of rationalism.

The spirit of rationalism which has much to do with shaping the religious expression of modern man began in the late seventeenth century, reached its climax in the German enlightenment of the eighteenth century, and reverberated into the nineteenth century into what has come to be known as modernism.

Two significant revolutions occurred during the age of reason which had far-reaching consequences for the formation of theology, and which bear on the question of authority. The first is the epistemological revolution (how do we know). Formerly (and even in the age of orthodoxy), knowledge was based on revelation in the Scripture (although orthodoxy made reason the interpreter and defender of its message). But now new voices appeared on the horizon to proclaim new ways of knowing. For Francis Bacon knowledge came through science. John Locke opened up an avenue of knowledge through sense experience and René Descartes insisted that all knowledge must be based on reason. The net result of these new voices was to replace supernatural revelation with the natural method of acquiring knowledge through science, experience, and reason.

The second important shift came in the area of cosmology. Through the findings of Copernicus, Galileo, Kepler, and Newton, the old medieval moralistic view of the world gave way to a scientific world view. The new conviction was that the world was run not by divine fiat but by natural law. The world was viewed as a predictable machine capable of being understood by the mind of man. Such a law-bound cosmology contained no room for divine intervention, miracle, and mystery.

In this cultural milieu theology took two steps beyond orthodoxy. Orthodoxy (especially Reformed), as I have previously argued, insisted that theology must be reasonable. What God revealed was consistent with reason (although in some cases such as the Trinity it was above reason). The hallmark of Christian orthodoxy was that revelation was declared to be in accord with reason. John Locke steadfastly stood in the tradition. Although he gave greater place to reason than his orthodox predecessors, he nevertheless would not dispense with Revelation. In his *Reasonableness of Christianity* (1965) he sought to show that the excellence of Christianity is in its reasonableness. Revelation, he contended, did not contradict reason and experience.

The first step beyond orthodoxy is the conviction that nothing can be believed without proof. John Toland illustrated this step in his book, *Christianity not Mysterious: or, A Treatise Showing, that there is nothing in the Gospel Contrary to Reason, nor Above it: and that no Christian Doctrine can be properly called a mystery* (1696). This work provoked a controversy which produced no less than 115 responses. In the preface Toland declared that he would show that the use of reason is not dangerous in religion. He insisted that he would hold only as an article of faith what evidence persuaded him to believe. Conviction based on rational grounds, not sheer biblical or church authority, was enough for him to believe. True religion had to be reasonable and intelligent. Although Toland insisted that there was nothing in the Scriptures which was unreasonable, he nevertheless ultimately defeated his own argument by elevating reason to a position of authority. Identifying reason with revelation laid the groundwork for the rejection of revelation on the basis of reason.

Indeed the second step beyond orthodoxy was the rejection of revelation on the basis of reason. After all, what happens when revelation and reason are in conflict. If proof is the touchstone for truth, and certainty is verified by empirical credibility, then whatever is unreasonable must be untrue.

This conclusion clearly emerges in *Christianity as Old as Creation* (1730) in which Matthew Tindal set forth the thesis that natural religion is all men need. What is valuable in Christianity is not what is given in so-called revelation, but what is consistent with natural religion, that which has always been known since creation and which is evident in all the religions of the world.

In this way Tindal paved the way for the triumph of rationalism over revelation which found its most extreme articulation in deism. One of the sharpest deistic minds was Voltaire (1694-1778), a Frenchman. Voltaire has become a legend because of his bitter attacks against the Christian faith. Reason, he argued, established the existence of God and a simple ethic based on nature. But he regarded Christianity as an unreasonable fraud and spent much of his lifetime "debunking" the church, the Bible, and the creeds. His view and that of his followers tended more and more toward atheism and total disrespect for all authority, except the authority of reason.

It is significant that the most widely publicized answer given to the deists was based on a rational argumentation. It was the theory of probability set forth by Joseph Butler in his famous *Analogy of Religion* (1736). His argument was that since the objections which are raised against the course of revelation can also be raised against the course of nature, it is probable that both have the same author. His argument for revelation was that it was probable rather than improbable or impossible. While it didn't conclusively solve the problem, it did at least show that even on the ground of reason a probability for the authority of Scripture was still possible. His book became a popular answer to deism and was required reading in many universities both in England and America.[4]

THE EMERGENCE OF A SUBJECTIVE VIEW OF AUTHORITY

The age of reason is a very critical juncture in the erosion of biblical authority. It shows the extent to which a dependence on reason can ultimately become destructive of the Christian faith. The insatiable desire to harmonize all revelation with reason inevitably led to the repudiation of revelation. But subsequent history demonstrated that man was not satisfied with reason alone. Two responses to rationalism illustrate this point. The first one which I will discuss is the subjective response which finds authority in the experience of the inner man (Pietism and Revivalism). The second is the attempt to keep the best of two worlds—a subjectivistic rationalism which emerged in the movement known as modernism.

PIETISM AND REVIVALISM

The first subjective view of authority emerged among the pietists and revivalists, the conservatives of the seventeenth, eighteenth, and nineteenth centuries.

Pietism can be described in part as a reaction to orthodox formalism and creeds. It opposed the interpretation of saving faith in terms of intellectual assent. It decried the rationalistic approach to the Christian faith and in the words of William Law regarded reason as "the cause of all the disorders of our passions, the corruptions of our hearts." On the positive side it set forth the message of personal fulfillment in an experience of the spiritual presence in simple Christian living. It was dominated by a Bible-centered faith, a sense of forgiveness through the work of Jesus Christ, and a practical bent toward worship, self-discipline, Bible study, and prayer.

It would be a mistake, though, to regard pietism as a mere reaction against orthodoxy and rationalism. It was much more. Pietism represents a new theological position which was based on a new concept of reality and which carried within itself the seeds of the modern point-of-view. This is particularly true in its understanding of authority, as we will see.

The founder of Lutheran pietism and the recognized theologian of the movement is Philip Jacob Spener (1637-1705). Although he sought to remain in the orthodox view of things, he nevertheless manifested a new theological spirit in his method of presentation and in his way of thinking. The most widely read of his works, *Pia desideria* (1675), called for a general reform in the church and set forth a number of concrete proposals including the more extensive use of Scripture through personal and group study, the reintroduction of the spiritual priesthood of every believer, and the personal practice of holy living.

His main contribution to theological thinking which affects the understanding of authority is expressed in his epistemology. For Spener, our certainty of God and of His authority in our life is grounded in personal experience. Only those who have personally experienced the saving work of Jesus Christ (regeneration) possess real knowledge of truth. In this sense Spener distinguished between physical and spiritual knowledge. The unregenerate can attain physical knowledge, that is they can have an external knowledge of the faith without the work of the Spirit. But true knowl-

edge or spiritual knowledge only comes through the new birth affected by the Spirit. This is a completely different notion from that
held by the Reformers who believed that any insight into revealed
truth required the illuminating work of the Holy Spirit. Spener
had separated the Word and the Spirit, which in traditional Reformation thought was the seat of authority, and elevated experience
with the Word through the Spirit as his authority. In this way
Spener took one step away from the inherent authority of the Word
of God in its objective form toward an authority based on a subjective experience with the Word. Consequently, he anticipated
the modern notion of a subjective authority.

Spener's subjectivism is apparent in the whole gamut of his theological convictions. Faith is more than knowledge and confidence;
it is a living power from which the actual experience of being
"born again" is realized. Regeneration is understood as an inner
transformation which is the source of the new life. This replaces
the more classic understanding of a standing before God on the
basis of the imputation of Christ's righteousness. The whole swing,
then, of his theology is toward the inner man, toward a subjective
concept of knowledge, certainty, and authority.[5]

This movement away from the objective toward the subjective
is also found in the theology of John Wesley and the whole movement of revivalism. In his diary, Wesley confessed that he had
preached without an inward assurance of forgiveness and reconciliation with God. He diligently sought this experience until May
24, 1738. When at a gathering in Aldersgate Street through the
reading of Luther's preface to the epistle to the Romans he confessed, "I felt my heart strangely warmed. I felt I did trust in
Christ, Christ alone for salvation: and an assurance was given me,
that he had taken away *my* sins, even *mine*, and saved *me* from the
law of sin and death."

This specific experience of Wesley's, which had already been
advocated by the pietists, grew into a position of supreme importance among the revivalists and accounts for the evangelical insistence on knowing the time and place of the conversion experience as a ground for acceptance by God. This in itself illustrates

the subjective character of evangelical Christianity. Certainty and authority are grounded in experience.

For both the pietists and the revivalists subjectivity only began with the conversion experience. All of life from then on was brought under the power of this experience as it, through the Spirit, evoked a habit of good works and a life of holiness in the believer. Both the pietists and the revivalists tended to fix their experiences into normative rules and regulations for their followers. While many willingly chose to observe the rules out of a conviction of their validity, others tended to observe them for the sake of gaining the spirit they represented. In this way the authority of evangelicalism became externalized for many second-generation followers. The Spirit was not real in their lives, but they followed the rules anyway in the belief that they were the evidences of regeneration.

Although the pietists and revivalists emphasized the experience with the Word as their ground of authority, it should not be concluded that they intended to demean the external authority of the Bible. On the contrary, they espoused a high view of Scripture, regarding it as the only source of truth for faith and practice. They would not tolerate the criticisms of its statements, the questioning of its authority, or doubts about its authenticity.

While this attitude at first may appear to be a strength of evangelicalism, it turned out later to be its major weakness. It is so, simply because it elevates the *experience* with the truth of the Bible to a position of authority. The Bible is the Word of God to me because I have experienced it as true. This approach to authority produces three unhealthy results.

First, it absolutizes the conversion experience. The authority is not so much the Word as it is my experience with the Word. In turn, this attitude tends to relativize the interpretation of Scripture. Groups of sincere Christians sit around talking about what certain passages of Scripture "mean" to them without giving any thought or consideration to the life situation of the passage. Thus, without knowing the intent of the passage or its original meaning, different people conclude different things from the same passage.

Consequently its authority is not rooted in its original meaning, but in an existential experience which could vary vastly from person to person. The final result is an anti-intellectual approach to Scripture. This is exactly what happened in the nineteenth century. While the critics were tearing the Scripture to shreds, the conservatives were completely oblivious to what was going on. They had no need to discuss the origin and meaning of Scripture because they experienced it in their hearts. While this may have been sufficient for one generation, it was not for the next: A whole generation of students learned about the critical view of Scripture in the universities. For them, the experience of the pietists and revivalists could no longer be valid, because they could no longer believe the Bible to be objectively true.

SUBJECTIVISTIC RATIONALISM

The confrontation between conservative experientialism and rationalistic criticism introduces us to the second response to the rationalism of scholasticism. As we have seen, conservatism reacted to scholasticism by emphasizing the authority of experience. Another trend of thought, which came to be known as liberalism or modernism, responded to scholasticism by elevating the authority of reason and experience. Because liberalism combined both personal piety and the critical spirit toward Scripture in a most unusual way, I choose to call it an authority based on subjectivistic rationalism. This stance became most evident in the nineteenth century.

The cultural milieu of this period was revolutionary for theological studies. Just as the epistemological and cosmological revolutions affected theological thought in the eighteenth century so drastic changes occurred in the nineteenth century which affected the attitude toward authority.

For one thing, many had grown weary of the sheer objectivity of rationalism. A group known as the romantics emerged to insist that the rationalists were superficial, that truth was much deeper than the external, that religion belongs to the inner man. Fredrick Schleiermacher, often referred to as the father of modern theology, was the spokesman for this point of view in theology.

In order to appreciate the effects of Schleiermacher's subjectivism, it must be seen in its relationship to the new world view that was emerging. There are three movements in particular that shaped the mind-set of the nineteenth century.

First, the Darwinian theory of evolution. Assuming that man evolved in a series of stages from primitive to more civilized states, it was argued that his religion was also a matter subject to development from primitive ideas about God to the more complex notions of the New Testament. These opinions were foundational to the reorganization of the Old Testament into the variety of documents (JEDP) that were supposed to substantiate the development of religion from its more primitive expression to its late and elaborate priestly system.

Second, the philosopher Hegel developed a methodology of discovering truth. He insisted that behind all reality there is an absolute spirit which is manifesting itself in the world in a scheme of thesis, antithesis, synthesis. All aspects of life are therefore manifestations in time of the absolute spirit coming to self-consciousness. Because no single manifestation is adequate to express the absolute spirit, every thesis gives rise to an antithesis. Both later merge into a synthesis which in turn becomes another theses, and the process continues. Ultimately all things will unite.

This approach was soon applied to theological questions by the followers of Hegel. The Trinity, for example, was a result of this process. The thesis was the monotheism of Hebrew thought. The antithesis was the polytheism of Hellenism. The synthesis was the Trinitarian formulae hammered out at the Council of Nicea in 325. This same method was applied to the New Testament. Peter's teaching about Jesus, which emphasized Him as the fulfillment of Messianic expectations, was the thesis. Paul's description of Jesus as Divine was the antithesis. The synthesis was Jesus the God-man.

Third, literary and historical criticism was applied to the quest for the historical Jesus. At first a distinction was posed between the teaching of Jesus and the teaching of His disciples. Assuming an evolution of Jesus' simple ethical teachings into the more doctrinal teachings of His disciples, a search was conducted for what Jesus really said and did. One conclusion was that Jesus' teaching and the stories about Him were the product of literary development. Stories had been spread around about Jesus attempting to convey the wonder of this man. For example the incident that Jesus walked on the water is not a story based in fact but in an attempt to explain His greatness. Someone desiring to express his respect for Jesus could have said, "this man could walk on water." From that kernel idea developed a full-blown story that He did. Not being able to verify the facts in the story of Jesus, it soon became an issue whether Jesus ever existed at all. According to F. C. Bauer (1792-1860) the question was unanswerable and its resolve was basically indifferent to theology since the important thing is not the historicity of Jesus but the idea of Jesus.

Schleiermacher's subjectivism and the rationalism of Darwin, Hegel, and historical criticism were combined by Albert Ritschl (1822-1889) who introduced the idea that value judgments are the only important thing in religion. We may not know the exact nature of food but we understand its value. Thus we may not know the exact nature of Jesus or even whether or not He lived, but we do know His value to our lives. His monumental work, *The Christian Doctrine of Justification and Reconciliation,* is an excellent example of the subjectivistic rationalism that dominated this age. Although he used all the tools of rationalism to take apart the faith, he nevertheless did it in a spirit of reverent and personal piety toward the value of Christ in the life of His followers. The result of this combination of rationalism-subjectivism for authority suggested that authority lay squarely in the experience which each individual had in the value of Christ for his life and in his mind. Through the use of rationalism he was able to reconstruct Christian teaching to his fancy.[6] Christianity had truly reached its point of secularization.

More than one person recognized what had happened and a mad scramble to return to authority began in the nineteenth century. The most significant movement occurred in the Church of England and has come to be known as the Oxford Movement. The leaders of this group appealed to apostolic succession and apostolic tradition as their authority. John Henry Newman (1801-1890) began writing *Tracts for the Times* which created a sensation because of its defense of traditional Christian convictions. He appealed to tradition as an authoritative source for doctrine, regarded the early councils as authoritative and stressed sacramental grace. Although the group was regarded by many as too Catholic, it nevertheless produced a large following and to a certain extent revitalized the faith in England.

CONCLUSION

My stated purpose was to sketch the erosion of authority from the seventeenth through the nineteenth centuries in order to gain a perspective on the problem of biblical authority in the twentieth century. In short, I have tried to set forth a brief summary allowing us to see that the problems of our era are rooted in trends taken in the past.

The same problems still exist today. The conservative still tends to emphasize either the authority of rationalism in the orthodox scholastic sense or the authority of experience in the pietistic-revivalistic sense. The liberal still tends to emphasize the approach of subjectivistic rationalism, although the specific form of his view has taken new shape through the varying expressions of new theologies. Nevertheless, at bottom, neither the liberal nor the conservative has gone significantly beyond the morass of nineteenth century confusion.

During the last twenty years twentieth-century conservative scholarship has been slowly coming of age. It is not my purpose here to detail that movement. What I do want to suggest, though, are a few guidelines for continued thinking.

First, we must recognize that the movements from the past we have detailed are still with us. Much of contemporary conservatism is similar to orthodoxy of the seventeenth century. It is passionately concerned with proving the reasonableness of its position. As we have seen, the danger of this concern is that it opens the door to making reason more important than revelation. Unless we adopt the principle that reason must always be subject to revelation, we are likely to repeat the blunder of orthodoxy and open conservatism to rationalism. If this happens, it is likely that history will repeat itself and present-day conservatism will become a new modernism.

Second, the danger of emphasizing experience is still with us. Many pastors and untrained lay people, in our generation, have tended to elevate personal experience to a position of authority. We claim the Bible is true because we have experienced its truth in our life. Or we interpret passages of the Bible by our experience ignoring the historical background to which it relates. This method opens us up to a dogmatism based on experience and an anti-intellectualism which denies the validity of historical background and clear thinking. Like the pietists and revivalists, we may have a warm feeling about the Scripture, but we will be unable to make the biblical message intelligible to the age in which we live.

Finally, there are several considerations which should guide our thinking about biblical authority. First, we must always insist that the authority of Scriptures cannot be proved through either reason or experience. Reason may attest to its reliability, its accuracy, its dependability, but never its authority. Neither does experience prove the authority of Scripture. It may confirm that its promises are genuine and that when taken by faith it performs what it says it will do, but at best it only collaborates its message, never proves it.

Second, the authority of the Bible is inherent within it. Because it is an authority derived from God, it is rooted in the inseparable union between the Word and the Spirit. This is a presupposition about the character of Scripture that is implicit within the doctrine of inspiration. It is God's message, not man's. Even as Paul affirmed that his message was not from man, nor by man, but through God, so the authority of Scripture must rest on the premise that it is from God even though it came to us by man. Thus, God dwells in the Scripture. It was and always is God-breathed. It is not a collection of words waiting to be verified through reason or an extraordinary religious experience which makes it come true at a moment (although I would not want to deny that man can have an experience with the living Word through the written Word that makes it authoritative for *him* in his own existential experience).

Third, we ought to develop more thoroughly the relationship between the authority of the Bible and that of the church. The Scripture witnesses to the union of the Holy Spirit with the Bible, the church, and the believer. How are we to understand the correlation of these three areas of Holy Spirit activity with authority? While it is beyond the framework of this essay to explore such a question, I hope some deeper thinking about the nature of biblical authority in its relational aspect to the church and the individual will emerge among evangelicals in the near future.

Fourth, I think also we must rethink the relationship between biblical authority and apostolic tradition. The tradition of the Church, especially in the early rules of faith, the old Roman symbol, the Nicene Creed, and later the Apostles' Creed, surely suggests something about the work of the Holy Spirit progressively clarifying the salient features of the Gospel message. While the Scripture and not the creeds continue to be the authority, the creeds certainly point to a summary of the essential Gospel world view—that which is authoritative in matters of faith. Systematic theology then, becomes the attempt to explain what the Scriptures and the church proclaim in matters of faith and practice. Thus, the proclamation and not the explanation is authoritative, freeing us therefore to think creatively in our theology, bound by the Scripture and guided by the conclusions of the early Church.

Fifth, granted that the Scriptures are a proclamation about life, the authority of Scripture is precisely that it tells the truth about life, about the human situation. It proclaims a truthful world view. It tells the truth about the origin, the meaning, and the destiny of all things. It tells the truth about man, his fallenness and the potential for renewal through faith in Jesus Christ who by His life, death, and rising again recreates man. It tells the truth about the human situation—how, because of man's separation from God, he directs culture away from God in keeping with the powers of evil. It tells the truth about the situation of the new man in Christ in the world—how he is to live as an individual and how he is to live in the community of the Church. Thus the Bible is authoritative not just because it says it is, but because it tells the truth about life and this truth corresponds with reality.

And finally it should be asserted once again that the Bible is an authority in matters of faith and practice. The Bible is not primarily a book on history or science or geography. It is a Book with a message, a vehicle for the living Word who pardons our sin, comforts us, and makes us acceptable to the Father. It is a Book which therefore declares a way of life, and calls us to action. When we make the Bible anything else it becomes a dead letter, a book to be debated and proved or rejected. When we allow this to happen, we miss the main point. The Bible does not demand proof of our experience, simply action. When we learn to act on what it says, individually and collectively in the Church, we will discover that it has not led us astray.

11

On the Limitations of Hermeneutics

by Herbert Jacobsen

I HAVE THOUGHT of making a motto of the following sentence:

> Interpretation used to be so easy,
> and then someone called it hermeneutics.

I do not know that substituting the word *hermeneutics* for the word *interpretation* automatically alters the kind of work that an interpreter does, but I have seen the naive confidence of many individuals, usually first-year college students, suddenly shattered when I have introduced the word in the biblical context as "the science of studying the Scriptures." A new sense of seriousness and care replaces a somewhat frivolous and smug attitude toward understanding the Bible. For these people the Bible becomes a new book, an adventureland that previously they had seen only from a very great distance. Now they search it diligently as though its precious truths had never been seen before.

This is the way I have seen some students begin a more mature study of the Scriptures. When they heard the word *hermeneutics* it was as though the spirit of Hermas suddenly invaded their psyche, prompting them to a new love of eloquence and truth.

It has pleased me to observe these changes in attitude toward biblical studies, but rarely have I found a person who learned how to interpret the Bible by simply changing his attitude. There were many tools, e.g., languages, history, that he would have to master if he desired to become proficient, and there were many misconceptions that would need correcting. Of course, it is to be expected

217

of the beginning student of Scripture that he will falter on occasion.

In my experience I have usually found one misconception significantly more common among my students than any other. They surmise that any differences between the way one person conceives and implements a hermeneutic and the way another does it is largely, or sometimes solely, a matter of skill. In some measure they are correct. Certainly skill is important, but to see skill as the only way in which interpreters may differ is a misconception.

Perhaps their misconception is a result of a naive view of life in which everything is subject to rigid "scientific law." Perhaps it is the result of an immature understanding of science. Whatever the cause, we can favorably acknowledge the desire for an interpreter to be skillful. Just as we prefer an automobile mechanic who knows the appropriate procedures for replacing defective fuel pumps and who has the requisite tools for the job to one who lacks the knowledge and the tools, so we prefer a biblical interpreter who knows the rules and guidelines of hermeneutics and who has the tools for interpretation to one who lacks them. This is not to say one could not interpret the Scriptures correctly without such knowledge, but rather that one should not be encouraged to interpret them in this fashion.

While many people have such skill, the lack of it among some Christians makes them easy prey to the teachings of various cultic groups. Occasionally I have illustrated to my students how skill in hermeneutics may help them to avoid the false teachings of the various cults. For example, Mormons, who believe in the existence of many gods, sometimes use the references in the King James Version to the Holy Spirit and to the Holy Ghost to suggest that these are two gods, not one. It is helpful to know that in the Greek texts there is one word, *pneuma*, which the King James Version translates as both *Spirit* and *Ghost*. The Bible teaches that there are three persons in the Holy Trinity, not four or more as the Mormons claim.

A similar approach is taken by the Jehovah's Witnesses. They are anxious to prove that the absence of the definite article in John 1:1 means that the indefinite article is implied. Hence, instead of translating the passage "in the beginning was the Word and the Word was God," they suggest that "the Word was a god." They argue for the deity of Jesus, but not for a Trinity. For them, Jesus is a secondary deity created by the one true Jehovah who alone is uncreated. In this instance it helps to know the rules of Greek grammar. The absence of a definite article before "God" does not mean one is justified in translating the phrase as "a God." This is especially the case if the word *God* follows an intransitive verb. Here "God" follows "was" and functions in the sentence as a predicate nominative, not a direct object. The Word, which becomes flesh, is God. I do not pretend fully to understand the Trinity, but I do know that the biblical descriptions of God leave no other alternative.

On the basis of these examples, I have explained to my students that a knowledge of Greek is important at times, and at other times a knowledge of grammar is equally important. On yet other occasions, I tell them just to listen carefully to what words are used. For example, when the Jehovah's Witnesses refer to Colossians 1:15 in their translation of the Bible, *The New World Translation,* they conveniently insert the word "other" on several occasions so that the passage implies that Jesus is one of the created beings. No Greek text supports this translation, ironically not even the *Emphatic Diaglott,* which is a Greek interlinear text published by the Jehovah's Witnesses. A more accurate translation can be acquired by reading any of several good English translations.

From these illustrations there can be no doubt of the value of skill and expertise in hermeneutics. One must respect the person who desires this skill and admire the individual whose expertise is so finely honed that even small insights require extensive study and concentration. It is easily understood that a talent so valuable, yet so painstakingly achieved, will receive major attention by those interested in furthering the science of hermeneutics. Many people have devoted themselves to this task.

When I introduce the subject of hermeneutics, these are the kinds of explanations and illustrations that I often use. To be sure they are only introductory remarks, so I warn the student that there are many more facets to hermeneutics than these. Therefore

I tell him that he should not think that hermeneutics is simply a matter of language study and grammar. I invite him to examine the evidence from the history of the Christian church. Church history indicates that skill in these areas always seems to take place within larger parameters of interpretation. There are two models that I ask him to consider.

First I present the Alexandrian model which is represented by Origen, a church scholar of the second and third centuries. Origen suggests that hermeneutics must proceed on three levels of interpretation: the historical, the typological, and the spiritual. These three levels are the result of Origen's tremendous synthesis of Platonism and Christianity. According to his model, a biblical narrative such as Abraham's attempt to sacrifice Isaac will have a historical meaning, a reference by typology to the character of God the Father, and a reference to the behavior expected of "the sons of Abraham." Occasionally a fourth interpretation was added, the eschatological. In this sense, for example, passages talking about Jerusalem may be referring to: 1) the city itself; 2) the Church; 3) the human soul; and 4) the heavenly dwelling place of God. Obviously this tradition emphasizes allegorizing the Scriptures.

There is an attractiveness to this view for it allows the interpreter a tremendous latitude in applying biblical passages to contemporary issues. However, the basis of its attractiveness is also the root of its danger. Freedom is often taken to be license and the result of this freedom has been an extensive distortion of Scripture. When Martin Luther saw the distortions, especially on matters of salvation by grace through faith, he was persuaded to develop an altogether different hermeneutic.

Luther's hermeneutic is an amalgamation of nominalism and Christianity, rather than Platonism and Christianity, and it suggests that proper interpretation must be primarily historical, and beyond that, Christocentric. Unless otherwise indicated in the Bible itself, a description of Jerusalem is just that; a description of Jerusalem.

Luther was not alone in rejecting Origen's hermeneutic and replacing it with one of his own making. Many reformers have done the same throughout the history of the church, with both

Origen's and Luther's views. Consequently there abound many different hermeneutics in church history. While it would be interesting and informative to compare more of these approaches, our purposes require the recognition of only two. Nearly any two would do if, like these two, they substantiate that their differences are not simply technical. This point alone warrants a more careful study of the subject of hermeneutics.

There are, of course, other philosophical and theological reasons for studying hermeneutics. For example, if one agrees with William Hordern[1] that twentieth-century theology is wrestling with the concept of revelation in the same manner as early Christian theology wrestled with Christology, he will conclude that questions concerning the interpretation of revelation will be of paramount importance.

For those who suppose they can unravel the truths of Scripture through a simple reply to the question: "What does this verse mean to me?" an introduction to hermeneutics as a science of interpretation proves quite unsettling. They quickly realize the value of language study, grammar, and historical context, and how interpretation may depend upon a theological and cultural perspective. For them it is true:

> Interpretation used to be so easy,
> and then someone called it hermeneutics.

The new difficulties involved in interpretation are welcomed by them because the rewards are a clearer understanding of God and of man. However, correctly "dividing the Word of Truth" occasionally blurs our vision of why we interpret the Scriptures. To return to the person who naively fields the question, "What does the Bible mean to me?" We note he may have overlooked the fact that God revealed His Word in an historical setting which requires a concern for the language and the culture of those times, but he senses correctly that interpretation does not stop there. From these two thoughts we may say that the subject of hermeneutics should satisfy at least two purposes. First it has a historical dimension, and second, a personal one. I think that a third dimension could also be added, one which I call the interpersonal dimension. Now the previous chapters have, for the most part, elaborated on the significance of Scripture as a historical document and drawn several guidelines for the Bible student. Consequently I shall treat this dimension rather succinctly and then press on to the other two dimensions.

1

A good hermeneutic must be concerned with the matter of getting at the truth-claims in Scripture. Evangelical theology has been, and continues to be, keenly sensitive to these truth-claims and to the related subjects of revelation and interpretation. When the integrity of the apostles and the truth of God's revelation were being challenged in the nineteenth century by searches for the historical Jesus and naturalistic theories about man's religious evolution, the Bible was considered by many liberal scholars to be merely a history of the Jews wrestling with their identity and their destiny. In other words, they believed that the Jews predicated a divine being for reasons such as adding motivation to otherwise seemingly arbitrary values or explaining deeply moving psychological experiences in "pre-psychological" terminology. Hence the propositions were subject to all kinds of possible distortions and needed demythologizing before their teaching could be called truth. The church was fortunate in those days to have men like J. Gresham Machen to defend its historic faith in God and its historic position that God also reveals Himself in propositional form. During years that followed the early confrontation of liberal and orthodox theologians in the modernist-fundamentalist controversy, all of the doctrines of the church were challenged and nearly subverted. Subsequent history has pointed out the vacuity of much of liberal theology, especially its view of man's innate goodness. For the orthodox theologians the basic doctrines or fundamentals all depended upon a commitment to the Bible as God's revelation to man.

This commitment is not an easy one to maintain in light of the many criticisms from philosophy, science, and psychology. Even more difficult is explaining how the Bible is the inerrant Word of God. Some have argued for what amounts to a dictation theory while others such as Donald Grey Barnhouse, have argued for a "paradox" view. In this view the mystery of how the Bible can be God's Word and at the same time man's word is seen as secondary to the mystery that Jesus is wholly God and wholly man. The mystery of the incarnation is the greatest, but if the Lordship of Christ is accepted, then the secondary mysteries that He endorses must be accepted too. On the basis of Jesus' Lordship, the believer argues that he can entertain no less a view of the Bible than his Lord held, and Jesus taught that the Bible is God's Word. Whatever the accompanying difficulties to this view of the Bible may be, the evangelical Christian is committed to a respect for the historical dimension of hermeneutics.

2

The personal dimension I have in mind is expressed by the apostle John near the end of his gospel.

> And many other signs truly did Jesus in the presence of his disciples, which are not written in this book; but these are written that ye may believe that Jesus is the Christ, the Son of God; and that believing ye might have life through his name (Jn 20:30-31).

To be sure, one could devote a whole lifetime of study to the historical interpretation of John's gospel. Who is the Word? How does He enlighten every man? Is enlightenment by man's reason, moral abilities, or some other way? What are the meanings of the "I am" passages? How does one interpret the "signs"? Why is this Gospel so different from the synoptics? Surely these questions are profitable and could involve a great deal of study. However, they miss the point of John's questions which are directed to the reader: How do I get Life? How do I believe?

This personal dimension to hermeneutics causes a great problem for most scholars. It is the problem of the seminarian or pastor who has spent all day wrestling with the text and as the day draws to a close tries to reverse his procedure by allowing the text to wrestle with him. In many ways this problem is far more difficult to handle than the internal problems and questions raised by the text. It always seems easier to understand something outside oneself than to understand oneself. Jesus recognized this difficulty when He

asked, "Why do you look for the splinters in your brother's eye
when there is a log in your own?" In the Bible, finding oneself,
difficult as it may be, is offered as the highest reward for righteous
living. Jesus said, "He who loses himself for my sake and the gospel's, that same man shall find himself." There are several persons
outside of the biblical record who also understand the magnitude
of discovering one's identity. No less a figure than Socrates also
advised knowing oneself.

Unfortunately, knowing oneself is never easy. It requires hard
work, a sensitive spirit, a critical mind, and great resolve just to get
started. To complete the task, the Bible states that it requires
God's grace. To this end God has provided man with His Holy
Scriptures. The Bible is not merely a book written about God and
man as though they were beings in some mystical Narnia. The
Bible talks about me and my relationship to the Living Word,
Jesus, the Son of God. I must let it speak to me for it tells me both
who I am, and who, by God's grace and His Holy Spirit, I ought to
be. A hermeneutic which claims to be complete but fails to acknowledge the necessity of bringing oneself into a dynamic relationship with God the Father through Jesus Christ has missed its
most important purpose.

It puzzles me at times that the literature on hermeneutics, at
least in the Protestant tradition, does not deal more extensively
and seriously with this personal dimension. When the Reformation began, there seemed to be a much more balanced approach to
hermeneutics than there is today. Since then, several Protestants
have tended to elevate the importance of biblical unity and integrity significantly above the personal dimension. Some even elimi-
nate the personal aspect altogether. For an example of one who
held these two dimensions in dynamic tension consider Martin
Luther, the founder of the Reformation. Although he saw no clear
divine authority outside the Bible, if he had to defend either the
integrity of the Bible or the value of the Gospel, he would defend
the Gospel. It is not Scripture, but the proclamation of Scripture,
that brings a man before God.

The rationale behind this thinking is evidenced in the following quotation in which Luther argues for the superiority of John's Gospel over the synoptics.

> If I had to do without one or the other—either the works or the preaching of Christ—I would rather do without the works than without His preaching. For the works do not help me, but His words give life, as He Himself says. John 6:63[2]

Luther follows this advice admirably. The Word of God which "overcomes sin, death, and hell, and gives life, righteousness, and salvation," is to be proclaimed. The church which preaches this Gospel is the true church. The church that does not preach this Gospel, even if it does preach the inerrancy of the Bible, is not the true church, but a self-righteous and pharisaical imitation. The words are strong, and for Luther they have to be. The true church must be self-critical if it wishes to give glory to God alone.

Fortunately, the personal dimension is not completely forgotten by everyone. A. Berkeley Mickelsen realizes its importance and devotes a helpful chapter to it in his book, *Interpreting the Bible*.[3] While the chapter lacks the forcefulness of Luther's view, it nevertheless presents the problems in a forthright manner. He is aware that when a believer studies the Bible "to hear what God has to say to him," he faces a not all-too-easy task. Indeed, he may use the same passage to justify two or more different actions. How does he find the right interpretation for himself?

Bernard Ramm, in his book, *Protestant Biblical Interpretation*, is another theologian who has not lost sight of the individual. Like Mickelsen, he devotes a chapter to the problem of the personal dimension in hermeneutics which offers some general advice for the interpreter to follow. "The Bible," he writes, "is a spiritual book. . . ." Hence, "an interpreter must have the same Spirit that inspired the Bible as the *sine qua non* for interpreting the Bible. . . ."[4]

Finally, we may look to James M. Gray. While his book, *Synthetic Bible Studies*, is not a text on hermeneutics, Gray is conscious of the personal dimension when he recommends that we read the Bible prayerfully. He supports this claim with two reasons that are similar to the two dimensions that have been given above for hermeneutics. He says that "in the first place, the Bible can not be

studied just like any other book, because it is unlike every other
book in the world. It is God's own book."[5] Here we have the first
dimension to hermeneutics that is acknowledged above. Gray
continues:

> But the other reason is this: Do we not desire our Bible study to
> be something more than a feast of intellect? Do we not desire
> Him whom our soul loveth to tell us where He feeds His flock,
> where He maketh them to rest at noon? . . . Do we not wish to lie
> down in the green pastures and be led by the still waters? Do we
> not desire a rich blessing in our souls? But how can this be with-
> out the power of the Holy Ghost through the Word, and how shall
> we obtain this power except as we ask?[6]

The Christian is encouraged to study the Bible because it brings
him into contact with the living Word of God. These two cannot
be separated without distorting the unity of the Christian message.
Without Christ, arguments for biblical authority result in a meaningless biblicism. Without the Bible, Christ is reduced to whatever
one subjectively wishes Him to be. The two must go hand in hand.
In the words of John Edward Carnell, "The living Word is the soul
of the written Word."[7]

We have already agreed that there are guidelines to follow if one
wants to understand the text of the Bible and have referred the
reader to earlier chapters in the festschrift. Are there also any
guidelines to follow if one wants to understand himself? As I ask
this question I know full well that there are hundreds of persons
who earn their living by helping hundreds of others to discover
and to accept themselves. I know too, that hundreds of books,
pamphlets, and sermons are written on this topic by psychologists
and pastors. Probably everyone has asked the question, "Who am
I and how do I discover my identity?" at least once.

The question of identity is no doubt important and many of the
answers are no doubt helpful, but how many of the answers are
given either from a biblical perspective or toward the end of aiding
biblical hermeneutics? There is an abundance of material in both
of these areas, although far more in the area of biblical or theological statements about man than on how a theology of man affects

hermeneutics. It is because this aspect of hermeneutics, so important, is so neglected that I enter the plea to correct the imbalance by increasing dialogue in this area. As bare essentials to dialogue on the personal dimension, I would like to suggest three guidelines.

The first of these I refer to as humility, although I might just as well call it growth. The basis for this guideline results from a recognition of God's sovereignty and man's limitations. As a man proceeds in this life, he often becomes more and more conscious of how far God's thoughts are above his own. This seems to be the case for the Apostle Paul who describes himself in three successive passages as further and further removed from God's holiness. He says he is the least of the apostles, then the very least of the saints, and finally he remarks he is the chief of sinners.[8] Each of the assertions is true, but taken serially they suggest a growing awareness in the apostle that Christ must increase while he must decrease. Some philosophers and theologians, like Sören Kierkegaard and Karl Barth, take this principle to an extreme. They presuppose that there is an infinite qualitative difference between God and man. While I am unprepared to go this far, I do wish to argue that man differs from God on both intellectual and moral levels. Of course there are other differences, but these two specific differences have a direct bearing on hermeneutics.

On the intellectual level one must be prepared to admit that much of what the Bible teaches escapes us because we lack the ability to understand it. I recall a minister who concluded his sermons by saying, "This is as far as I have come." In a very real sense all of us must conclude our study in the same way. The message speaks to us at our level, but it also transcends us. We see the Truth, but its visage is blurred as though it were behind a darkened glass. When we recognize this ever present limitation in our ability to understand Scripture, we will prayerfully ask God to forgive our misconceptions and deliver us from evil. We must also trust that someday God will make the message clear.

The moral level is a little more difficult to handle. Let me begin with a biblical story that bothers me. I have often wondered why the Jewish scribes who knew that the Messiah would be born in Bethlehem did not join the wise men in worshiping Him. I have supposed that they were too committed to Herod to find room in their hearts for an incarnation. It is a sad experience to read of these men and to find others who knew the words of the Bible, but never really heard its message. Gaining knowledge is important, but not sufficient. Confession and forgiveness are also necessary. In the beatitudes Jesus promised that those who are pure in heart will see God, and that those who hunger and thirst after righteousness will be filled. There are some people who never had the opportunity to attend seminary or engage in professional training but nevertheless have a tremendous insight into the spiritual teaching of the Bible which seems to flow from their thirst for righteousness. What accounts for this intuitive ability? I do not claim to know the full answer to this question. Perhaps the answer can come only in time to an individual who sincerely humbles himself and thirsts for God's righteousness. If this is true, then perhaps the text on hermeneutics ought to instruct the reader to seek righteousness and to wait for the biblical insights until he has had sufficient experience with life.

The second guideline is a generally accepted one in Protestant hermeneutics. How much it is followed is another matter. Mickelsen puts it this way:

> Personal application involves the working out from the passage *a principle* that is true for anyone who belongs to God or a principle for individuals in parallel situations.[9]

Discovering these principles requires a great sensitivity to the intent of the text, but it also requires a sensitivity to oneself. Consider the situation of the young church member who justifies his reprimanding of the minister solely on the basis that Paul once rebuked Peter. Arguing that no one, not even the minister, is above rebuke, he condones his behavior toward the minister. What this person does not ask is, "Am I sufficiently sensitive to my wishes to rebuke him as well as his well-being once it is done?" All too often it seems, we use scriptural principles for our ends without suitable discussion or thought as to whether the principle really applies to our situation. If one shirks this aspect of his responsibility, he is likely to use the Bible in a proof-texting manner to satisfy his own righteousness. Such persons are more like the Pharisee whose prayer was a list of accomplishments rather than like the publican who went home justified. The Pharisee never really knew who he was, so he was never able to capitalize on what God had for him.

Part of this guideline includes working on the development of a systematic biblical theology. Many verses in Scripture can be viewed as contradicting others if they are taken out of context. Therefore a systematic approach seems essential. One should wrestle with descriptions of God and man and also with the various ways in which God seeks to restore man to health. One way to begin work on this guideline is to define what the image of God in man is. Is the image of God man's reason, emotion, morality, social nature, independence, creativity, or something else? Answers to questions like this come in part from our experience, so articulation of them helps to answer who we are and what our situation is. They help us to find the principles in the Bible.

A third guideline for knowing oneself is a little more elusive than the preceding ones. It is important for a Christian to engage other Christians in critical dialogue. In other words one should belong to a church. In the church God has ordained some to be teachers, and some to be prophets. Of course, belonging to a church will not guarantee enlightenment on all of the passages in the Bible. It will help, however, and probably check false interpretations. Participating in such a group of like-minded individuals is a partial admission that one is not thoroughly able to comprehend God's Word by oneself. Furthermore, if God has provided such aid, it would be foolish to flaunt it.

Let us summarize these guidelines. First, we have suggested that humility as a factor in personal development is necessary for a sane hermeneutic because people are born neither omniscient nor omnibenevolent. Secondly, we have suggested that each person must know who he is if he is to apply biblical principles properly. While some principles apply to everyone, there are several that apply to people only if they are in a given situation. We must know that situation. Thirdly, we have suggested that participation in a Christian community is a great help in understanding both oneself and the biblical text.

3

Now let us consider the interpersonal dimension of hermeneutics. Matthew concludes his gospel with the following words of Jesus:

> All authority in heaven and on earth has been given unto Me. Go therefore and make disciples of all nations, baptizing them in the name of the Father and the Son and the Holy Spirit, teaching them to observe all that I have commanded you; and lo, I am with you always, even to the end of the age (Mt 28:18-20, NASB).

To those who have heard the good news that righteousness before God is available to those whose trust is in Jesus, this commission comes less as a command and more as an invitation to enter into the joyful service of the Lord. Ever since the first century these words have inspired Christian men to proclaim the Gospel to others who have not heard it. Their work as missionaries has brought them great personal reward and furthered the expansion of God's Kingdom several hundredfold. The work, however, has not been without its challenges and dangers. Explaining the Christian faith to someone who lacks the Jewish heritage for understanding it is not as easy as it might seem. It is in this challenge that I find the final dimension of hermeneutics. When a person interprets the Bible for someone else, he must also develop a sensitivity to his audience, or else he runs the risk of preaching a message that is irrelevant to the needs of his hearers.

While all of the possible difficulties that may be encountered in meeting this challenge are not included in the Bible, the Bible does anticipate some of these problems. The Bible also illustrates the kinds of problems that Christians will face as they engage in the task of preaching the Gospel. Undoubtedly the greatest anticipation is contained in the Great Commission quoted above. In the same quotation the best reason for witnessing and the best aid in witnessing are also found. Witnessing is commanded by Jesus who also says, "I am with you." Jesus also anticipates the difficulties one can encounter in preaching the Gospel when He intercedes in the high priestly prayer for those who believe through the words of the apostles. We need divine assistance.

Another significant indication of the importance of preaching the Gospel is in the extensive training that Jesus gives His disciples before they are commissioned as apostles to establish His church. The very word "apostle" suggests this communicating function and it is from the activity of the apostles that we get our illustrations of this dimension to hermeneutics.

Our primary source for information about this interpersonal dimension is the book of Acts. Here, Luke records the expansion of the Christian message in the first century. It is not a full history of the church, but a more than sufficient one to indicate the sensitivity for which I am calling.

The apostles were called upon to preach the Gospel to the world. In terms of the structure of the book of Acts, the world is represented by three communities; the Jewish community, the Greco-Roman community, and a group of persons associated with mystery religions. As the apostles spoke to these people they could not, indeed would not, change the story of Jesus or shirk the responsibility of condemning sin when they found it. They found, however, that their audiences had preconceived notions of the Christian faith and preset ideas on what it should offer a believer if it were true. So the apostles adjusted their proclamation of the message of the Gospel according to the mind-set of their audience.

For example, compare Peter's sermon on the Day of Pentecost (Ac 2:14-36) with Paul's sermon on Mars' Hill (Ac 17:22-31). Peter's basic message is that God has raised Christ Jesus from the dead and that Jesus is therefore God and Lord. The basic response he desires is that the Jews will repent. Beyond these basics, Peter encourages the Jews to understand this message in terms of prophecy and miracles. He quotes the prophets Joel (once) and David (three times) to explain the Day of Pentecost and the person of Christ. The miracles he refers to are first those performed by Jesus in the presence of the Jews, and then the miracle of Jesus' resurrection. These miracles which he has witnessed he claims can only be the work of Almighty God.

Paul's message also depends upon God's resurrection of Christ, which threatens the Greek with the thought that failure to repent will result in a moral judgment by God. However, he never encourages the Greek to understand this message by quoting the prophets of Israel or by listing the miracles of Christ. The evidence he offers is drawn from an understanding of the Greek cultural background. Paul appeals to reason and to the Greek poets. How can the God who made this world live in a shrine made by man, or demand human service to fulfill His needs? The gods worshiped by the Greeks are too small. The poets, according to Paul, had a clearer conception of God than the priests when they wrote, "In him we live and move and have our being," and also, "For we are indeed his offspring."

The point illustrated in these sermons implies the same principle of common sense that virtually every parent follows in rearing his children. The parent who is sensitive to the abilities of a child's mind in handling concrete and abstract information will try to teach that child accordingly.

In the task of hermeneutics, if we sense the calling to explain our faith to our neighbor, it seems to me that we are obliged as good stewards to understand our non-Christian man and to put the Gospel into his terms as much as possible. We must understand that we don't necessarily lose the faith by putting it into terms that the poorly educated can understand any more than we would lose it if it is translated into a sophisticated philosophical system. We must also understand that we would lose our audience if we insisted upon preaching in technical or philosophical terms to the poorly educated, and that we would probably bore the intellectual if we did not.

From the illustrations of Peter and Paul's sermons, as well as from Jesus' expectations in the High Priestly Prayer and the Great Commission, we may discern two biblical principles to support further study of the interpersonal dimension of hermeneutics. The first principle is that of servanthood. Each person who acknowledges Jesus as his Lord is also acknowledging himself as Jesus' servant. The responsibilities of servanthood as taught in the Holy Scriptures are frequently and probably primarily discharged in interpersonal relations and not God-man relations. Consider the evaluation which Jesus made about those who served Him, "Not every one who says to Me, 'Lord, Lord,' will enter the kingdom of heaven; but he who does the will of my Father, who is in heaven" (Mt 7:21, NASB). The question then, is "how does one do the will of the Father?" The answer given by Jesus consists in loving God fully and in loving your neighbor. The apostle Paul emphatically explains that the interpersonal social responsibilities contained in these commands are fulfilled simply if you love your neighbor. Consider also that when Jesus was asked by John the Baptist whether He was the Messiah or not, His entire response was given in social terms, "the blind receive sight and the lame walk, the lepers are cleansed and the deaf hear" (Mt 11:5).

Jesus loved His neighbor and expects His servants to do the same. This is a beautiful thought although there is something in Jesus' response to John the Baptist that we often miss. Jesus gave sight to the blind not simply because He had the authority to restore sight but also because someone lacked sight. I am familiar with an inner-city church that has appealed to wealthier suburban churches for aid in clothing and food. Initially both were problems but at present a large room is overstocked with clothing and the pantry is empty. Many people who continue to answer this appeal feel they are genuinely helping when they send only shirts and trousers to this church. Perhaps they cannot give anything other than clothing, yet it seems to me that there ought to be a greater awareness of matching the gift with the needs. After all, the gift of God toward us was in terms of our needs.

The second principle is that of stewardship. While servanthood and stewardship ideally are wedlocked, I suppose the difference between them is the emphasis that stewardship places on the wise and fruitful use of one's talents. At least this is Jesus' explanation of the parable of the faithful servant.

> And that slave who knew his master's will and did not get ready or act in accord with his will, shall receive many lashes, . . . And from everyone who has been given much, shall much be required; and to whom they entrusted much, of him they will ask all the more (Lk 12:47-48, NASB).

Given, then, the privileges of servanthood and the call to wise and faithful stewardship, how can we neglect being sensitive to the interpersonal dimension of hermeneutics?

To say that we should be sensitive to our culture is one thing, but to learn how to be sensitive is another. This task takes far more time than talent. One needs to meet and to talk with people. One needs to be friendly and to make friends. One needs to listen. I suppose that of these time-consuming responsibilities, the greatest is learning to listen.

How do we listen? Perhaps it is as an acknowledgment of the difficulties of listening that the Scripture so often concludes its comments with the following words: Let him who has ears to hear, hear.

Again, how do we listen? This is a great question that I, for one, have only begun to answer. In no way, then, do I judge myself to have arrived at such an understanding of how one listens that I am prepared to instruct others in the art. However, I should like to present one thought that I find to be increasingly helpful. The thought may be simply put: Listening is far more than aural awareness.

I recall a student who insisted, in Feuerbachian fashion, that God and religion were only extensions of one's relationship to one's father. In large measure, this is true. Each father has the responsibility of training up his child in the ways of God. Yet religion consists in more than this human projection. At first I argued that if this were all he wished religion to be then his lack of religion was evidence of a lack of a relationship to his father and said nothing about God's existence. He violently disagreed with the counter-argument, and it soon became apparent that he would not agree with any argument for religion. He was not really saying God was a projection of the father image but "I don't want God." He said it, not by the words he uttered but in his belligerence and vehemence.

Another kind of "listening," and one which I enjoy, is listening to commercials. Usually I learn more about the people who buy the product than about the product itself. I have very little knowledge, for example, of what makes toothpaste even though I have read or heard hundreds of advertisements. I do know, however, that some people who buy toothpaste are concerned about a decay preventive, while many others hope for a magical love experience. I suppose it is true that some people in our society purchase toothpaste, not to clean their teeth, but to find acceptance with other people. I believe each of us has a need to be accepted, but seldom will we openly confess that need. We "say" to others we want acceptance by the clothes we wear, the way we act, and who knows how many other nonverbal statements. If we wish to be accepted we must learn to accept and this will involve developing sensitivity to nonverbal communications.

There are many books available to help develop awareness in these areas. Recently, I turned to Paul Tournier who salts his books quite liberally with case studies. In *The Weak and the Strong* he explains several behavioral attitudes and even some physical illnesses that "say something" about the character of the person with those traits. Tournier claims that a person whose reactions are

> depression, despondency, sadness, self-pity, self-reproach, weariness of life, exaggerated self-criticism, panic, escapism, withdrawal into one's shell, silence, and [or] torpor, is generally a "weak" person. Among strong reactions are exhilaration, euphoria, gaiety, condescension, self-satisfaction, optimism, exaggerated criticism of others, rashness, aggressiveness, buoyancy, glibness of tongue, and excitability.[10]

The point I wish to establish is that the people to whom we speak are not blank pages onto which we may write "God is love" but living human beings with many experiences and ideas. We need to be sensitive to them and, conversely, sensitive to what our verbal and nonverbal sentences are saying.

Consider the parents who wish to provide strong Christian education for their five children. They send them to private schools in the fall, winter, and spring and to Christian camps in the summer. It is not an uncommon episode in this family for communication to be stifled. Imagine the last day of camp and all five rush at the first sight of mother and father to share their experiences. The jumble is too much for the parents who order silence, respect,

and obedience. "We can't hear if you all talk at once, don't you
have any manners? We'll talk later when things are quieter, go get
your things and let's pack the car." Unwittingly the well-intentioned parents are telling their children that packing the car is
more important than the experiences of camping that they said
they wanted their children to have.

Some time ago I was visited by two Mormon elders. They said
that they were not proselytizing but sharing their faith; but they
never once asked me who I was or what I did to earn a living, or
how many children I had. When I tried to ask them these types
of questions they dismissed them curtly and got into their programmed presentation in almost a mechanical fashion. What were
they "saying" to me?

In the interpersonal dimension of hermeneutics this is the im-
portant question. What do I "say" to someone when I explain the
Gospel and what does he "say" he is prepared to hear from the
Gospel?

This interpersonal dimension is the most neglected area of hermeneutics. This is the instance of the minister who knows his Bible
but does not know his church; this is the missionary who scratches
where people do not itch; this is the church that doesn't see that
her demands on its priests are suffocating the human being who is
the priest. It is perhaps appropriate to conclude with a quotation
from the apostle Paul who was probably the most influential missionary the church has ever seen. In the following quotation he
demonstrates what I consider to be the integrity of the interpersonal dimension to hermeneutics.

> For though I am free from all men, I have made myself a slave to
> all, that I might win the more. And to the Jews I became as a Jew,
> that I might win Jews; to those who are under the Law, as under
> the Law, though not being myself under the Law, that I might
> win those who are under the Law; to those who are without law,
> as without law, though not being without the law of God but un-
> der the law of Christ, that I might win those who are without law.
> To the weak I became weak, that I might win the weak; I have
> become all things to all men, that I may by all means save some.

And I do all things for the sake of the gospel, that I may become a fellow-partaker of it (1 Co 9:19-23, NASB).

The person who knows the Gospel is truly free to know his neighbor and to serve him well for the sake of the Gospel.

12

Bibliographic Tools of Biblical Interpretation

by Steven Barabas

A Bibliography of Theological Bibliographies

THE AVERAGE CLERGYMAN and Christian scholar who wants to find his way among religious books faces almost hopeless bewilderment and frustration. Of the hundreds of religious books published each year only a few will be read a year later, and a still smaller number will survive the test of time and continue to be read. But the serious student wants to know what are the best books of the past and the present. With time so limited, one should read only the best. One should steer by the stars.

But how is a person to know what are the stars in the firmament of religious literature? How can he distinguish them from the meteors which flash brilliantly for a brief time and then burn out? For this, guidance from experts is needed. Fortunately, the person who earnestly wants to distinguish the basic books will find published helps to guide him. This section of this chapter deals with the most important of these.

All clergymen should carefully read and make constant use of three books written especially for their benefit: *Minister's Library Handbook* (Boston: Wilde, 1958, 148 pp.), by Jay J. Smith; *The Pastor and His Library* (Chicago: Moody, 1953, 160 pp.), by Elgin S. Moyer, who was for many years a teacher and a librarian at the Moody Bible Institute; and *The Minister's Library* (Grand Rapids: Baker, 1974, 376 pp.), by Cyril J. Barber, Associate Professor

238

and Director of the Library at the Rosemead Graduate School of Psychology. Mr. Smith's book offers no specific recommendations of books; it attempts to show the various kinds of books that should be a part of a well-balanced pastor's library. Mr. Moyer, in a chapter on "Selecting Books for Your Library," provides helpful lists of recommended evangelical books and authors. Mr. Barber's book is the fullest and most valuable of the three. The major part of the volume consists of a well-annotated list of the best expository literature and aids available, both old and new.

Ella V. Aldrich and Thomas E. Camp have put all seminarians in their debt with their book, *Using Theological Books and Libraries* (Englewood Cliffs, N.J.: Prentice-Hall, 1963, 119 pp.). Although intended primarily to equip students to do research on their own, without the assistance of a librarian, it is of great value to ministers and serious students of the Bible in general. The book, packed with information, is worth its weight in gold. The user of this book should save himself endless hours of searching for information on almost any subject in the religious area. It not only lists but describes all the basic reference and research tools in a theological library: the different indexes—theological, general, and special; the general and theological dictionaries and encyclopedias; the various yearbooks and directories; the Bible versions, commentaries, and atlases; the biographical material, both theological and general; indeed, just about anything a Bible scholar may want to know. It is true that not many clergymen have access to a theological library. Almost all, however, live in the neighborhood of a public library, and the average good public library would have on its reference shelves the majority of the books listed in this handbook. Moreover, it also tells him what basic reference books he needs for his own library.

Two books which all serious students of the Bible will find indispensable are *Tools for Bible Study* (Richmond: Knox, 1956, 159 pp.), edited by Balmer H. Kelly and Donald G. Miller, of Union Theological Seminary, Richmond, Virginia, and *Multi-Purpose Tools for Bible Study* (St. Louis: Concordia, 1960, 289 pp.), by Frederick W. Danker, of Concordia Theological Seminary. The eleven chapters of the first of these two books originally appeared as articles in the theological quarterly, *Interpretation,* and were so widely acclaimed that it was decided to publish them together in one volume. They were written by seminary professors from various institutions, each one an expert in his field, and describe the books of fundamental value in all the important areas of biblical study. The following are the chapter headings of the book: 1. Concordances, 2. New Testament Lexicons, 3. Bible Dictionaries and Encyclopedias, 4. Grammars of the Greek New Testament, 5. Archaeology, 6. Hebrew Grammars and Lexicons, 7. Biblical Geographies and Atlases, 8. Commentaries, 9. The Versions of the New Testament, 10. Works on Biblical Preaching, and 11. The Rabbinic Writings. Danker's book was written entirely by himself and shows a phenomenal acquaintance with basic literature pertaining to the Bible. The two books naturally overlap in many of the subjects treated, but they supplement rather than duplicate one another. Danker includes chapters on subjects not covered in the other book.

Some of the leading seminaries in the country, aware that students are often at a loss in trying to determine what are the standard religious works and that their alumni require assistance in selecting the most helpful books for their own libraries, have tried to meet these needs by publishing bibliographies, prepared by their various departments, which are periodically revised so as to bring them up to date. Some of these are well over one hundred pages in length.

Princeton Theological Seminary has produced three such bibliographies: *A Bibliography of Bible Study for Theological Students* (Princeton: Theological Seminary Library, 1948, 85 pp.; rev. ed., 1960, 107 pp.) ; *A Bibliography of Systematic Theology for Theological Students* (Princeton: *Theological Seminary Library,* 1949, 44 pp.) ; and *A Bibliography of Practical Theology* (Princeton: Theological Book Agency, 1949, 71 pp.) . The first of these bibliographies covers books on the whole Bible, the Old Testament, the New Testament, and linguistic aids to exegesis. The second lists books under about twenty-five different headings, such as revelation and inspiration, the Trinity, Providence and the problem of evil, the Atonement, eschatology. The third lists books under two main headings: homiletics and related subjects (such as public worship, church music, public speaking, religious radio) and Christian education and related subjects. These bibliographies are restricted to books in the English language except for original texts, dictionaries, and grammars, where the use of foreign languages is unavoidable.

The following institutions have produced similar bibliographies: Andover Newton, *Theological Bibliographies, Essential Books for a Minister's Library* (Andover Newton Quarterly, September 1963, 138 pp.), edited by Norman K. Gottwald, and a 16-page supplement for books appearing in 1964-66 (Andover Newton Quarterly, March 1966); Southwestern Baptist, *A Bibliography for Pastors and Theological Students* (Fort Worth: Southwestern Baptist Theological Seminary, n.d., 140 pp.; a revised edition, with the title, *Essential Books for Christian Ministry* (129 pp.) came out in 1972); Union (New York City), *A Basic Bibliography for Ministers* (New York: Union Theological Seminary, 1960, 139 pp.); Union (Richmond, Va.), *Essential Books for a Pastor's Library: Basic and Recommended Works* (Richmond: Union Theological Seminary, 1960, 71 pp.). G. S. Glanzman, S. J., and J. A. Fitzmyer, S. J., of Woodstock College, a Roman Catholic institution, have prepared *An Introductory Bibliography for the Study of Scripture* (Westminster: Newman, 1962, 135 pp.) in which Catholic works are indicated by an asterisk. All of these bibliographies are up to date, authoritative, and comprehensive, although sometimes failing to list books of real worth by evangelical scholars. The annotations in some of them are often the most helpful parts of the lists.

Two Fuller Theological Seminary faculty members have brought out more specialized bibliographies: William S. LaSor, *A Basic Semitic Bibliography* (Wheaton: Van Kampen, 1950, 56 pp.) and Wilbur M. Smith, *A Preliminary Bibliography for the Study of Biblical Prophecy* (Boston: Wilde, 1952, 44 pp.). Both are fully annotated. The LaSor book is number 1 of the Fuller Theological Seminary Bibliographical Series, but no subsequent volumes have been published. Wilbur Smith says that his bibliography is not intended to be exhaustive, or to include works of an extremely critical nature, but is constructed for those who hold to a tradi-

tional, conservative view of Scripture. Among its titles are many
books published in the last century, even the first half of it.

Newly-established seminaries, Bible colleges, and Bible institutes require, for accreditation, libraries that will meet certain ex-
acting standards. To assist in the choosing of the proper books, two
bibliographies have been prepared. The Accrediting Association
of Bible Institutes and Bible Colleges has brought out, in mimeographed form (141 pp.), *A List of Books for Theological Libraries*
(no place of publication or date is given, but it was apparently
done in the early 1950s, as I purchased a copy c. 1955). The Fuller
Library Bulletin (October 1955-March 1956, nos. 28-29, p. 12) says
of it that it was "prepared by a number of educators in this country
and put together by Professor Terrelle B. Crum of the Providence
Bible Institute." Mr. Crum was then Secretary of the Accrediting
Association of Bible Institutes and Bible Colleges.

The other bibliography was produced by the Theological Education Fund of the International Missionary Council to assist theological seminaries and colleges in the churches of Africa, Asia, and
Latin America. It is called *A Theological Book List* (Naperville,
Ill.: Allenson, 1960, 242 pp.) and was edited by Robert P. Morris.
It lists 5,400 basic titles which are grouped under the four main
areas of theological study: Bible, church history, doctrine, and practical theology. Two supplements to this bibliography, listing books
in English, French, German, Portuguese, and Spanish, were published in 1963 (184 pp.) and 1968 (170 pp.). These bibliographies, although prepared for institutional libraries, are naturally
of great use to students of the Bible in helping them determine
what are the most worthwhile books in the various categories of
biblical and theological study.

The last few years have seen the appearance of a number of
guides for Old Testament and New Testament exegesis. Dallas
Theological Seminary brought out, in mimeographed form, *Bibliography for Old Testament Exegesis and Exposition* (1970, 38
pp.), by Kenneth L. Barker and Bruce K. Waltke, and *Bibliography for New Testament Exegesis and Exposition* (n.d., 23 pp.).
These are intended for pastors with small libraries and in most
cases the theological point of view of the books is indicated. David

M. Scholer, of Gordon-Conwell Theological Seminary, brought out, in 1971, *A Basic Bibliographic Guide for New Testament Exegesis* (South Hamilton: Gordon-Conwell Bookcentre, 56 pp.; just republished by Eerdmans). Most helpful for New Testament students is *A Bibliography of New Testament Bibliographies* (New York: Seabury, 1966, 75 pp.), compiled by J. C. Hurd, Jr., of the Episcopal Theological Seminary of the Southwest, Austin, Texas. It would be wonderful if something like this were done for the Old Testament too.

Inter-Varsity Fellowship in England has published several guides to Christian reading. The first of these was *A Guide to Christian Reading: A Classified List of Selected Books* (1952, 120 pp.). The editor's name is not given. A second edition, entirely revised (160 pp.), edited by A. F. Walls, was published in 1961. A similar book, with the title, *Encounter with Books* (1970, 262 pp.), was edited by H. D. Merchant with the assistance of seventy evangelical scholars. The annotations make this a very helpful work.

The Banner of Truth Trust (London) published in 1968 *The Best Books: A Guide to Christian Literature* (175 pp.), edited by W. J. Grier, who for over forty years was connected with the Evangelical Bookshop, in Belfast, Ireland. It too has helpful annotations.

Dr. Wilbur M. Smith, for many years Professor of English Bible at Fuller Theological Seminary and Trinity Evangelical Divinity School, has brought out an excellent book in which he lists what he regards as the most important books for a Bible student's library. The second half of this book, *Profitable Bible Study* (Boston: Wilde, 1939, 214 pp.), has the subtitle, "The First One Hundred Books for the Bible Student's Library." At the end of his list he adds fifteen books which he says are more or less indispensable. The book has been twice revised, in 1951 and 1963.

How shall one find one's way among the multitude of religious books which are coming from the presses today? Chiefly by reading book reviews in the best religious periodicals. Reviewers do not always agree in their estimates of a book, but there is usually consensus regarding the really good ones.

"Read the best books first, or you may not have a chance to read them at all," said Thoreau a hundred years ago. Life is too short to waste time reading what is second-rate when it is possible, with the help of the many excellent guides available, to steer by the stars.

BIBLIOGRAPHY OF BOOKS USEFUL IN BIBLICAL EXEGESIS

APOCRYPHAL AND APOCALYPTIC LITERATURE

Charles, R. H. *The Apocrypha and Pseudepigrapha of the Old Testament in English with Introductions and Critical and Explanatory Notes to the Several Books.* 2 vols. Oxford: Clarendon, 1913. A monumental work, the only one containing so large a number of pseudepigraphic works. It is old and needs revision, but it has not been superseded.

Hennecke, E. *New Testament Apocrypha.* Ed. Schneemelcher. English trans. ed. R. McL. Wilson. 2 vols. Philadelphia: Westminster, 1963, 1965. The best edition of the New Testament Apocrypha, although the one edited by M. R. James, published by Oxford, is good too.

Metzger, B. M. *Introduction to the Apocrypha.* New York: Oxford, 1957. Based on the RSV. The most useful introduction to the Old Testament Apocrypha.

Metzger, B. M., ed. *The Oxford Annotated Apocrypha: The Apocrypha of the Old Testament, Revised Standard Version.* New York: Oxford, 1965. The most helpful translation now available; has good introductions, notes, etc.

Russell, D. S. *The Method and Message of Jewish Apocalyptic 200 B.C.-A.D. 100.* Philadelphia: Westminster, 1964. Reviews the most important Jewish apocalyptic writings, Daniel, and some Dead Sea Scroll material.

ARCHAEOLOGY

The Whole Bible

Albright, W. F. *The Archaeology of Palestine.* Rev. ed. Baltimore: Penguin, 1954. Somewhat dated, but still standard.

Finegan, J. *Light from the Ancient Past.* 2d ed. rev. Princeton: Princeton U., 1959. Moderately conservative; profusely illustrated.

Frank, H. T. *Bible, Archaeology, and Faith.* Nashville: Abingdon, 1971.

Kenyon, K. M. *Archaeology in the Holy Land.* New York: Praeger, 1971. Somewhat liberal.

Thompson, J. A. *The Bible and Archaeology.* Grand Rapids: Eerdmans, 1962. Conservative.

Wright, G. D. *Biblical Archaeology.* Rev. ed. Philadelphia: Westminster, 1962. By a competent scholar, although somewhat liberal; well illustrated.

Old Testament Archaeology

Albright, W. F. *Archaeology and the Religion of Israel.* Rev. ed. Baltimore: John Hopkins, 1946. By the foremost biblical archaeologist of our time.

Pritchard, J. B., ed. *The Ancient Near East in Pictures Relating to the Old Testament.* Princeton: Princeton U., 1954. A companion volume to the author's *Ancient Near Eastern Texts.* Has over 700 pictures. Great.

Pritchard, J. B., ed. *Ancient Near Eastern Texts Relating to the Old Testament.* Rev. ed. Princeton: Princeton U., 1955. Monumental.

Pritchard, J. B., ed. *The Ancient Near East: Supplementary Texts and Pictures Relating to the Old Testament.* Princeton: Princeton U., 1969.

Thomas, D. W., ed. *Documents from Old Testament Times.* New York: Nelson, 1958. Good collection of texts from Near Eastern countries which shed light on Israel's history and customs.

Unger, M. J. *Archaeology and the Old Testament.* Grand Rapids: Zondervan, 1954. Conservative.

New Testament Archaeology

Blaiklock, E. M. *The Archaeology of the New Testament.* Grand Rapids: Zondervan, 1970. Readable; written by a competent evangelical scholar.

Bruce, F. F. *Second Thoughts on the Dead Sea Scrolls.* Grand Rapids: Eerdmans, 1956. By a world-famous evangelical scholar.

Deissmann, G. A. *Light from the Ancient East.* 2d ed. rev. London: Hodder & Stoughton, 1922. A great work by a pioneer papyrological scholar.

Finegan, J. *The Archaeology of the New Testament: The Life of Jesus and the Beginning of the Early Church.* Princeton: Princeton U., 1969. Fine.

LaSor, W. S. *The Dead Sea Scrolls and the New Testament.* Grand Rapids: Eerdmans, 1972.

Unger, M. J. *Archaeology and the New Testament.* Grand Rapids: Zondervan, 1962.

ATLASES

Aharoni, Y., and Avi-Yonah, M. *The Macmillan Bible Atlas.* New York: Macmillan, 1968. Has some very unique features.

Grollenberg, L. H. *Atlas of the Bible.* London: Nelson, 1956. Of the many fine Bible atlases published in recent years this is one of the best; has magnificent maps and over 400 illustrations.

Wright, G. E., and Filson, F. V. *The Westminster Historical Atlas to the Bible.* Philadelphia: Westminster, 1946. Has fewer illustrations than Grollenberg, but the text may be better.

BACKGROUND OF THE BIBLE

Barrett, C. K., ed. *The New Testament Background: Selected Documents.* London: S.P.C.K., 1956. Provides Greek, Roman, and Jewish texts that illuminate the New Testament.

Bouquet, A. C. *Everyday Life in New Testament Times.* New York: Scribner, 1955.

De Vaux, R. *Ancient Israel, Its Life and Institutions.* New York: McGraw-Hill, 1962. An authoritative study of Israel's family, civil, and religious institutions.

Forster, W. *Palestinian Judaism in New Testament Times.* Edinburgh: Oliver & Boys, 1964.

Heaton, E. W. *Everyday Life in Old Testament Times.* New York: Scribner, 1956.

National Geographic Society. *Everyday Life in Bible Times.* Washington, D.C.: Nat. Geog. Soc., 1950. A magnificently illustrated work.

Pedersen, J. *Israel: Its Life and Culture.* 4 vols. in 2. New York: Oxford, 1926-40. An outstanding contribution to the study of Hebrew life and thought.

Schurer, E. *A History of the Jewish People in the Time of Jesus Christ.* 2d ed. 5 vols. New York: Scribners, 1886-1890. A classic work, now being revised.

BIBLE: HISTORY OF ITS TRANSMISSION

Ackroyd, P. R., et al. *The Cambridge History of the Bible.* 3 vols. Cambridge: Cambridge U., 1963, 1969, 1970.

From the Beginnings to Jerome. Ed. P. R. Ackroyd & C. F. Evans. Vol. 1, 1970.

The West from the Fathers to the Reformation. Ed. G. W. H. Lampe. Vol. 2, 1969.

The West from the Reformation to the Present Day. Ed. S. L. Greenslade. Vol. 3, 1963. There is nothing else in English so complete and useful.

Kenyon, F. K. *Our Bible and the Ancient Manuscripts*. Rev. A. W. Adams. London: Eyre & Spottiswoode, 1958. By a world-famous expert on biblical manuscripts.

CHARACTERS OF THE BIBLE

Whyte, A. *Bible Characters*. 6 vols. London: Oliphants, n.d. A classic work by one of Scotland's greatest preachers. Beautifully written.

CANON

Green, W. H. *General Introduction to the Old Testament: The Canon*. New York: Scribner, 1898. A standard work by a great Princeton scholar.

Gregory, C. R. *Canon and Text of the New Testament*. New York: Scribners, 1912. Fine treatment.

Harris, R. L. *Inspiration and Canonicity of the Scriptures*. Grand Rapids: Zondervan, 1957. Fine study by a very able Old Testament scholar.

Westcott, B. F. *Canon of the New Testament*. 6th ed. London: Macmillan, 1889. By one of the famous Cambridge triumvirate of New Testament scholars. A classic.

CHRIST: LIFE AND TEACHING

Andrews, S. J. *The Life of Our Lord upon the Earth*. New York: Scribner, 1893. Especially good on the chronology of Christ's life.

Bruce, A. B. *The Parabolic Teaching of Christ*. London: Hodder & Stoughton, 1882.

Edersheim, A. *The Life and Times of Jesus the Messiah*. 2 vols. New York: Longmans, Green, 1883. The best of all life of Christs.

Jeremias, J. *The Parables of Jesus*. New York: Scribner, 1955. The most influential recent book on the subject.

Machen, J. G. *The Virgin Birth of Christ*. New York: Harper, 1930. Perhaps the best treatment of the subject in any language.

Major, H. D. A.; Manson, T. W.; and Wright, C. J. *The Mission and Message of Jesus* (N.Y.: Dutton, 1938). A classic work.

Morgan, G. C. *The Teaching of Christ*. New York: Revell, 1913. By one of the outstanding exegetes in recent times.

Smith, D. *The Days of His Flesh*. 8th ed. rev. New York: Doran, 1910. Very good.

Trench, R. C. *Notes on the Parables of Our Lord*. London: Macmillan, 1882. A classic.

COMMENTARIES

One-Volume Bible Commentaries on the Whole Bible

Guthrie, D.; Motyer, J. A.; Stibbs, A. M.; and Wiseman, D. J. *The New Bible Commentary*. Rev. ed. Grand Rapids: Eerdmans, 1970. This is a completely revised and rewritten edition of a previous work with the same title edited by F. Davidson, A. M. Stibbs, and E. F. Kevan. The best there is.

Pfeiffer, C. F., and Harrison, E. F. *The Wycliffe Bible Commentary*. Chicago: Moody, 1962. A scholarly work by evangelicals.

Multi-Volume Commentaries on the Whole Bible

Buttrick, G. A., ed. *The Interpreter's Bible*. 6 vols. Nashville: Abingdon, 1957. Liberal in theology and uneven in quality.

Cooke, T. C., ed. *The Bible Commentary*. 10 vols. New York: Scribner, 1890. First appeared in 1871-88; Anglican; conservative; Westcott on John is included.

Ellicott, C. J., ed. *The Bible Commentary for English Readers*. London: Cassell, n.d. [1877-1884]. Good; conservative.

Henry, M. *Exposition of the Old and New Testaments*. This first appeared in 1708-10 and has been published in many different editions since then. George Whitefield is said to have read it four times, the last time on his knees.

Jamieson, R.; Fausett, A. R.; and Brown, D. A. *A Commentary Critical, Experimental, and Practical on the Old and New Testaments*. 6 vols. Chicago: Moody, 1945. One of the best nineteenth century commentaries. First appeared in 1868.

Kirkpatrick, A. F., and Perowne, J. J. S., eds. *The Cambridge Bible for Schools and Colleges*. 56 vols. Cambridge: Cambridge U., 1877-1909. A good exegetical commentary, but some of the Old Testament volumes must be used cautiously.

Lange, J. B., ed. *Commentary on the Holy Scriptures.* 24 vols. Grand Rapids: Zondervan, n.d. Learned, detailed, sound in exegesis; first appeared in 1868-1913.

Maclaren, A. *Expositions of Holy Scripture.* 25 vols. London: Hodder & Stoughton, 1910. A rich exposition by a great nineteenth century preacher.

Nicoll, W. R., ed. *The Expositor's Bible.* Grand Rapids: Eerdmans, n.d. This has been published in a number of editions: 6 volumes, 25 volumes, and 50 volumes. The volumes vary in quality; some are very rich.

Wiseman, D. J., and Tasker, R. V. G., eds. *Tyndale Bible Commentaries.* Grand Rapids: Eerdmans, and Downer's Grove: Inter-Varsity, 1958-. So far, most of the New Testament volumes have been completed, but not many of the Old Testament ones. An outstanding commentary; evangelical.

Multi-Volume Commentaries on the Old Testament

Keil, C. F., and Delitzsch, F. J. *Biblical Commentary on the Old Testament.* 25 vols. Edinburgh: Clark, 1866-90. Conservative, careful study of the Hebrew text.

Young, E. J., ed. *The New International Commentary on the Old Testament.* Grand Rapids: Eerdmans. Of the thirty-two volumes projected only three (on Isaiah, by E. J. Young) have so far been published.

Multi-Volume Commentaries on the New Testament

Barclay, W. *The Daily Study Bible.* 17 vols. Edinburgh: Saint Andrew, 1953-. Always helpful and stimulating, but must be used with caution.

Bengel, J. A. *Gnomon of the New Testament.* 3 vols. Edinburgh: Clark, 1850. Originally published in Latin in 1742. A real classic.

Lenski, R. C. H. *The Interpretation of the New Testament.* 11 vols. Columbus, Ohio: Wartburg, 1943. By an outstanding conservative Lutheran scholar.

Nicoll, W. R., ed. *The Expositor's Greek Testament.* 5 vols. London: Hodder & Stoughton, 1897-1910. Some of these are exceptionally good, some not.

Perowne, J. J. S.; Parry, R. S.; and Robinson, J. A., eds. *Cambridge Greek Testament for Schools and Colleges.* 18 vols. Cambridge: Cambridge U., 1880-. Concise; excellent for exegetical study.

Stonehouse, N. B., and Bruce, F. F. *The New International Commentary on the New Testament.* Grand Rapids: Eerdmans, various dates. So far, most of the eighteen volumes projected have been published. Nothing better being done today.

Commentaries on Books of the Old Testament

GENESIS

Kidner, D. *Genesis.* Chicago: Inter-Varsity, 1967. Excellent.
Leupold, H. C. *Exposition of Genesis.* Grand Rapids: Baker, 1949. Very good.
Thomas, W. H. G. *Genesis: A Devotional Commentary.* Grand Rapids: Eerdmans, 1946. Valuable.

EXODUS

Betteridge, W. R. *Exodus.* Philadelphia: Amer. Bapt. Pub. Soc., 1914.
Cole, R. A. *Exodus.* Chicago: Inter-Varsity, 1973.

LEVITICUS

Bonar, A. *A Commentary on the Book of Leviticus.* Grand Rapids: Zondervan, 1959. A reprint of a commentary published in 1846. A great commentary.
Genung, G. F. *The Book of Leviticus.* Philadelphia: Amer. Bapt. Pub. Soc., 1906.

NUMBERS

Genung, G. F. *The Book of Numbers.* Philadelphia: Amer. Bapt. Pub. Soc., 1906.
Greenstone, J. H. *Numbers with Commentary.* Philadelphia: Jewish Pub. Soc. of America, 1939.

DEUTERONOMY

Betteridge, W. R. *The Book of Deuteronomy.* Philadelphia: Amer. Bapt. Pub. Soc., 1915.
Reider, J. *Deuteronomy with Commentary.* Philadelphia: Jewish Pub. Soc. of Amer., 1937.

JOSHUA, JUDGES, RUTH

Cundall, A. E., and Morris, L. *Judges and Ruth.* London: Tyndale, 1969.
Garstang, J. *Joshua-Judges.* London: Constable, 1931.

1 AND 2 SAMUEL

Blaikie, W. G. *The First Book of Samuel.* New York: Armstrong, 1888.
Blaikie, W. G. *The Second Book of Samuel.* New York: Armstrong, 1888.

1 AND 2 KINGS

Gray, J. *I and II Kings: A Commentary.* 2d ed. rev. Philadelphia: Westminster, 1971.
Montgomery, J. A. *A Critical and Exegetical Commentary on the Books of Kings.* New York: Scribners, 1951. Not conservative, but contains much of value.

1 AND 2 CHRONICLES

Keil, C. F. *Chronicles.* Edinburgh: Clark, 1872.
Myers, J. M. *II Chronicles.* Garden City, N.Y.: Doubleday, 1965.

EZRA, NEHEMIAH, ESTHER

Keil, C. F. *Ezra, Nehemiah and Esther.* Edinburgh: Clark, 1893.
Myers, J. M. *The Books of Ezra and Nehemiah.* Garden City, N.Y.: Doubleday, 1965.

JOB

Davidson, A. B. *The Book of Job.* Cambridge: Cambridge U., 1903.
Gibson, E. C. S. *The Book of Job.* 3d ed. London: Methuen, 1919.

PSALMS

Kidner, D. *Psalms 1-72.* Chicago: Inter-Varsity, 1973.
Leupold, H. C. *Exposition of the Psalms.* Columbus, Ohio: Wartburg, 1959.

PROVERBS

Greenstone, J. H. *The Holy Scripture with Commentary: Proverbs.* Philadelphia: Jewish Publ. Soc., 1950. By a conservative Jewish scholar.
Kidner, D. *Proverbs.* London: Tyndale, 1964.

ECCLESIASTES

Leupold, H. C. *Exposition of Ecclesiastes.* Grand Rapids: Baker, 1966.

SONG OF SOLOMON

Ginsburg, C. D. *Choeleth and Song of Songs*. New York: Ktav, 1968.

ISAIAH

Alexander, J. A. *Commentary on the Prophecies of Isaiah*. London: Oliphants, 1953. Originally published in 1846. Outstanding.

Young, E. J. *The Book of Isaiah*. 3 vols. Grand Rapids: Eerdmans, 1966-72.

JEREMIAH AND LAMENTATIONS

Harrison, R. K. *Jeremiah-Lamentations*. Chicago: Inter-Varsity, 1973.

Laetsch, T. *Jeremiah*. St. Louis: Concordia, 1952. Includes Lamentations.

EZEKIEL

Ellison, H. L. *Ezekiel: The Man and His Message*. Grand Rapids: Eerdmans, 1956.

Taylor, J. *Ezekiel*. Chicago: Inter-Varsity, 1967.

DANIEL

Walvoord, J. F. *Daniel: The Key to Prophetic Revelations*. Chicago: Moody, 1971.

Young, E. J. *The Prophecy of Daniel*. Grand Rapids: Eerdmans, 1949.

THE TWELVE MINOR PROPHETS

Laetsch, T. *The Minor Prophets*. St. Louis: Concordia, 1956.

Orelli, C. von. *The Twelve Minor Prophets*. Edinburgh: Clark, 1893.

Pusey, E. B. *The Minor Prophets with a Commentary*. London: Nisbet, 1885.

Smith, G. A. *The Book of the Twelve Prophets*. 2 vols. New York: Armstrong, 1908.

HOSEA

Morgan, G. C. *Hosea: The Heart and Holiness of God*. New York: Revell, 1935.

JOEL

Kapelrud, A. S. *Joel Studies*. Uppsala: Lundquistka, 1948.

AMOS

Cripps, R. S. *A Critical and Exegetical Commentary on the Book of Amos.* London: S.P.C.K., 1929.

OBADIAH

Watts, J. D. W. *Obadiah: A Critical, Exegetical Commentary.* Grand Rapids: Eerdmans, 1969.

JONAH

Martin, H. *The Prophet Jonah.* London: Banner of Truth Trust, 1958. First published in 1866.

MICAH

Copass, B. A., and Carlson, E. L. *A Study of the Prophet Micah.* Grand Rapids: Baker, 1950.

NAHUM

Maier, W. A. *The Book of Nahum: A Commentary.* St. Louis: Concordia, 1950.

HABAKKUK

Lloyd-Jones, D. M. *From Fear to Faith.* Chicago: Inter-Varsity, 1953.

ZEPHANIAH

Davidson, A. B. *Nahum, Habakkuk and Zephaniah.* Cambridge: Cambridge U., 1896.

HAGGAI, ZECHARIAH, MALACHI

Baldwin, J. *Haggai, Zechariah, Malachi.* Chicago: Inter-Varsity, 1972.
Baron, D. *The Visions and Prophecies of Zechariah.* London: Marshall, Morgan & Scott, 1908.
Leupold, H. C. *Exposition of Zechariah.* Grand Rapids: Baker, 1975.
Morgan, G. C. *Studies in Malachi.* London: Marshall, Morgan & Scott, n.d.

Commentaries on Books of the New Testament

MATTHEW

Hendricksen, A. *The Gospel of Matthew.* Grand Rapids: Baker, 1973. By an outstanding conservative exegete.

Plummer, A. *An Exegetical Commentary on the Gospel according to St. Matthew.* New York: Scribner, 1908. Exegetical commentary based on the Greek text.

MARK

Lane, W. L. *Commentary on the Gospel of Mark.* Grand Rapids: Eerdmans, 1974. Really good; very thorough; conservative.

Swete, H. B. *The Gospel according to St. Mark.* London: Macmillan, 1902. A classic commentary, based on the Greek text.

Taylor, V. *The Gospel according to St. Mark.* New York: St. Martin's, 1955. By a very able New Testament scholar; based on Greek text.

LUKE

Geldenhuys, J. N. *Commentary on the Gospel of St. Luke.* Grand Rapids: Eerdmans, 1951. A work of massive scholarship.

Plummer, A. *A Critical and Exegetical Commentary on the Gospel according to St. Luke.* Edinburgh: Clark, 1906. Fine commentary based on Greek text.

JOHN

Barrett, C. K. *The Gospel according to St. John.* London: S.P.C.K., 1955. Fine; based on the Greek text.

Morris, L. *Commentary on the Gospel of John.* Grand Rapids: Eerdmans, 1971. By one of the ablest living evangelical New Testament scholars.

ACTS

Bruce, F. F. *Commentary on the Book of Acts.* Grand Rapids: Eerdmans, 1954. Bruce has two commentaries on Acts, one on the English text, the other on the Greek text. Both are first-rate.

Rackham, R. B. *The Acts of the Apostles.* London: Methuen, 1906. One of the best.

ROMANS

Murray, J. *The Epistle to the Romans.* 2 vols. Grand Rapids: Eerdmans, 1959, 1966. By a very able American theologian; conservative.

Sanday, W., and Headlam, A. C. *A Critical and Exegetical Commentary on the Epistle to the Romans.* Edinburgh: Clark, 1902. The best based on the Greek text.

1 CORINTHIANS

Barrett, C. K. *A Commentary on the First Epistle to the Corinthians.* New York: Harper & Row, 1968.

Grosheide, F. W. *The First Epistle to the Corinthians.* Grand Rapids: Eerdmans, 1953.

2 CORINTHIANS

Barrett, C. K. *A Commentary on the Second Epistle to the Corinthians.* New York: Harper & Row, 1967.

Hughes, P. E. *Paul's Second Epistle to the Corinthians.* Grand Rapids: Eerdmans, 1961.

GALATIANS

Burton, E. D. *A Critical and Exegetical Commentary on the Epistle to the Galatians.* Edinburgh: Clark, 1921.

Lightfoot, J. B. *St. Paul's Epistle to the Galatians.* 19th ed. London: Macmillan, 1896. A monumental commentary by one of the Cambridge triumvirate.

EPHESIANS

Hendricksen, W. *Exposition of Ephesians.* Grand Rapids: Baker, 1967.

Robinson, J. A. *The Epistle of Paul to the Ephesians.* London: Macmillan, 1909.

PHILIPPIANS

Hendricksen, W. *Exposition of Philippians.* Grand Rapids: Baker, 1962.

Lightfoot, J. B. *The Epistle of St. Paul to the Philippians.* London: Macmillan, 1885.

COLOSSIANS AND PHILEMON

Hendricksen, W. *The Epistles to the Colossians and Philemon.* Grand Rapids: Baker, 1964.

Lightfoot, J. B. *St. Paul's Epistles to the Colossians and to Philemon.* 3d ed. London: Macmillan, 1879.

1 AND 2 THESSALONIANS

Milligan, G. *St. Paul's Epistles to the Thessalonians.* London: Macmillan, 1908.

Morris, L. *The First and Second Epistles to the Thessalonians.* Grand Rapids: Eerdmans, 1959.

THE PASTORAL EPISTLES

Guthrie, D. *The Pastoral Epistles.* Grand Rapids: Eerdmans, 1957.
Hendricksen, W. *I and II Timothy and Titus.* Grand Rapids: Baker, 1957.

HEBREWS

Bruce, F. F. *Commentary on the Epistle to the Hebrews.* Grand Rapids: Eerdmans, 1964.
Westcott, B. F. *The Epistle to the Hebrews.* London: Macmillan, 1909. A classic commentary; based on the Greek text.

JAMES

Mayor, J. B. *The Epistle of St. James.* London: Macmillan, 1892.
Ross, A. *The Epistles of James and John.* Grand Rapids: Eerdmans, 1954.

PETER AND JUDE

Mayor, J. B. *The Epistle of St. Jude and the Second Epistle of St. Peter.* London: Macmillan, 1907.
Selwyn, E. G. *The First Epistle of St. Peter.* London: Macmillan, 1947.

EPISTLES OF JOHN

Findlay, G. G. *Fellowship in the Life Eternal: An Exposition of the Epistles of St. John.* Reprint. Grand Rapids: Eerdmans, 1955.
Westcott, B. F. *The Epistles of St. John.* London: Macmillan, 1892.

REVELATION

Beckwith, I. T. *The Apocalypse of John.* New York: Macmillan, 1919. Historical treatment.
Ladd, C. E. *A Commentary on the Revelation of John.* Grand Rapids: Eerdmans, 1972. Posttribulational premillennarian.
Walvoord, J. F. *The Revelation of Jesus Christ.* Chicago: Moody, 1966. Dispensational.

CONCORDANCES

English Bible

Ellison, J. W., comp. *Nelson's Complete Concordance of the Revised*

Standard Version Bible. New York: Nelson, 1957. Does not list such monosyllabic words as "a," "an," "the."

Strong, J. *The Exhaustive Concordance of the Bible.* New York: Methodist Book Concern, 1890. Lists every word in the KJV, including common articles.

Young, R. *Analytical Concordance to the Holy Bible.* Rev. ed. New York: Funk & Wagnalls, 1902. The twenty-second edition, published by Eerdmans, has a supplement on the canon of the Bible by R. K. Harrison and E. F. Harrison. Includes all words in the KJV except monosyllabic articles.

Hebrew Old Testament

Mandelkern, S. *Veteris Testamenti Concordantiae Hebraicae atque Chaldaicae.* Jerusalem & Tel-Aviv: Sumptibus Schocken, 1964. The most complete concordance of the Hebrew Old Testament. The basic definitions are in Latin, but it can be used without a command of the language.

Greek New Testament

Moulton, W. F., and Geden, A. S. *A Concordance to the Greek Testament.* Rev. ed. Edinburgh: Clark, 1963. The best available concordance for the Greek New Testament.

Smith, J. B. *Greek-English Concordance to the New Testament: A Tabular and Statistical Greek-English Concordance Based on the KJV with an English-to-Greek Index.* Scottdale, Pa.: Herald, 1955. Useful for comparative statistical analysis.

CRITICISM: BIBLICAL

Allis, O. T. *The Old Testament: Its Claims and Its Critics.* Grand Rapids: Baker, 1972. By a master of Old Testament scholarship; the fruit of a lifetime of study.

Broomall, W. *Biblical Criticism.* Grand Rapids: Zondervan, 1957. Deals with both the Old and the New Testament.

Hunter, A. M. *Interpreting the New Testament, 1900-1950.* London: S. C. M., 1951. Brief, but packed with helpful information.

Kraeling, E. *The Old Testament Since the Reformation.* New York: Harper, 1955.

Kümmel, W. G. *The New Testament: The History of Investigation of Its Problems.* Nashville: Abingdon, 1972. By a liberal scholar, but nevertheless valuable.

Neill, S. *The Interpretation of the New Testament 1861-1961*. London: Oxford, 1964. Deals with all the major issues of biblical criticism.

DEAD SEA SCROLLS

Burrows, M. *The Dead Sea Scrolls*. New York: Viking, 1955. One of the best accounts.

Burrows, M. *More Light on the Dead Sea Scrolls*. New York: Viking, 1958. Supplements the above work by Burrows.

Cross, F. M. *The Ancient Library of Qumran and Modern Biblical Studies*. Rev. ed. Garden City: Doubleday, 1961. Regarded as the best work on the Dead Sea Scrolls.

La Sor, W. S. *The Dead Sea Scrolls and the New Testament*. Grand Rapids: Eerdmans, 1970.

Vermes, G. *The Dead Sea Scrolls in English*. Baltimore: Penguin, 1962. Fine translation.

DICTIONARIES AND ENCYCLOPEDIAS

Buttrick, G., ed. *The Interpreter's Dictionary of the Bible*. 4 vols. Nashville: Abingdon, 1962. Valuable, but often nonconservative.

Davis, J. D., ed. *A Dictionary of the Bible*. Philadelphia: Westminster, 1898. Later revised and rewritten editions by H. S. Gehman and published under the title *The Westminster Dictionary of the Bible* and *The New Westminster Dictionary of the Bible* are less conservative in the Old Testament section.

Douglas, J. A., ed. *The New Bible Dictionary*. London: Inter-Varsity, 1962. The best one-volume Bible dictionary, but has few illustrations.

Ferm, V., ed. *An Encyclopedia of Religion*. New York: Philosophical Library, 1945.

Hastings, J., ed. *Dictionary of the Bible*. Rev. F. C. Grant and H. H. Rowley. New York: Scribners, 1963. Nonconservative, but often helpful.

Hastings, J., ed. *A Dictionary of the Bible*. 5 vols. Edinburgh: Clark, 1898-1904. Must be used with caution because of its frequent nonconservative positions.

Hastings, J., ed. *A Dictionary of Christ and the Gospels*. 2 vols. New York: Scribners, 1906-1908. Usually very good.

Hastings, J., ed. *A Dictionary of the Apostolic Church*. 2 vols. New York: Scribners, 1916-1919. Usually very good.

Jackson, S. M., ed.; Sherman, C. C.; and Gilmore, G. W. *The New Schaff-Herzog Encyclopedia of Religious Knowledge, Embracing Biblical, Historical, Doctrinal, and Practical Theology, and Biblical, Theological, and Ecclesiastical Biography from the Earliest Times to the Present Day.* 13 vols. New York: Funk & Wagnalls, 1908-1914. A uniquely valuable work.

Loetscher, L. A., ed. *Twentieth Century Encyclopedia of Religious Knowledge.* 2 vols. Grand Rapids: Baker, 1955. Brings the above work by Jackson up to date.

McClintock, J., and Strong, J., eds. *Cyclopaedia of Biblical, Theological, and Ecclesiastical Literature.* 10 vols. New York: Harper, 1867-1881. A later edition appeared in 1894 and a two-volume supplement in 1885-1887. Old, but still very valuable.

Orr, J., ed. *The International Standard Bible Encyclopaedia.* Rev. 5 vols. Chicago: Howard-Severance, 1929. The best conservative Bible dictionary; in process of revision.

Tenney, M. C., ed. *Zondervan Pictorial Bible Dictionary.* Grand Rapids: Zondervan, 1963. Written for the lay Bible student; evangelical; excellently illustrated.

Tenney, M. C., ed. *Zondervan Pictorial Bible Encyclopedia.* 5 vols. Grand Rapids: Zondervan, 1974. Best.

DICTIONARIES: HEBREW

Brown, F.; Driver, S. R.; and Briggs, C. A. *A Hebrew and English Lexicon of the Old Testament.* Rev. ed. Oxford: Oxford U., 1952. Standard; the words are not arranged in alphabetical order but according to consonantal roots.

Koehler, L., and Baumgartner, W., eds. *Lexicon in Veteris Testamenti Libros.* Leiden: Brill; Grand Rapids: Eerdmans, 1958. A supplement was published in 1958.

DICTIONARIES: GREEK

Bauer, W. *A Greek-English Lexicon of the New Testament and Other Early Christian Literature.* Trans. W. F. Arndt and F. W. Gingrich. Chicago: U. of Chicago, 1957. The standard lexicon for the Greek New Testament and the Apostolic Fathers.

Moulton, H. J., and Milligan, G. *The Vocabulary of the Greek New Testament: Illustrated from the Papyri and Other Non-Literary Sources.* London: Hodder & Stoughton, 1914-1930. Not a complete lexicon of the Greek New Testament, lists only those words found in the papyri. Very valuable.

GEOGRAPHY OF THE BIBLE

Aharoni, Y. *The Land of the Bible: A Historical Geography.* Philadelphia: Westminster, 1967.

Avi-Yonah, M. *The Holy Land from the Persian to the Arab Conquests (536 B. C. to A. D. 640). A Historical Geography.* Grand Rapids: Baker, 1946.

Baly, D. *The Geography of the Bible.* New York: Harper, 1957. First-rate work.

Dalman, G. *Sacred Sites and Ways: Studies in the Topography of the Gospels.* New York: Macmillan, 1935. A classic work.

Smith, G. A. *The Historical Geography of the Holy Land, in Relation to the History of Israel and of the Early Church.* 26th ed. London: Hodder & Stoughton, 1931. Old, but still very helpful; fascinatingly written.

GRAMMARS: HEBREW

Gesenius, H. F. W. *Gesenius' Hebrew Grammar.* Ed. E. Kautzsch; 2d English ed. A. E. Cowley. Oxford: Clarendon, 1910. The best reference grammar.

Weingreen, J. *Practical Grammar for Classical Hebrew.* Oxford: Clarendon, 1950.

GRAMMARS: GREEK

Blass, F., and Debrunner, A. *A Greek Grammar of the New Testament and Other Early Christian Literature.* Chicago: U. of Chicago, 1961. Most useful grammar.

Moulton, J. H. *A Grammar of New Testament Greek.* Vol. 1, *Prolegomena.* Vol. 2, *Accidence and Word-Formation with an Appendix on Semitisms in the New Testament,* by J. H. Moulton and W. F. Howard. Vol. 3, *Syntax,* by N. Turner. Edinburgh: Clark, 1908, 1929, 1963.

Robertson, A. T. *A Grammar of the Greek New Testament in the Light of Historical Research.* Nashville: Broadman, 1934. Monumental; the result of twenty-six years of research by America's greatest New Testament Greek scholar.

HISTORY: OLD TESTAMENT

Bright, J. *A History of Israel.* Philadelphia: Westminster, 1959. Follows the Albright school of Old Testament thought.

Harrison, R. K. *Old Testament Times.* Grand Rapids: Eerdmans, 1970. Excellent.

Pfeiffer, C. F. *Old Testament History.* Grand Rapids: Baker, 1973. Contains eight previous books by the author.

HISTORY: NEW TESTAMENT

Bruce, F. F. *New Testament History.* Garden City: Doubleday, 1971. The best.

Tenney, M. C. *New Testament Times.* Grand Rapids: Eerdmans, 1965. A companion volume to the author's *New Testament Survey.*

INTERPRETATION OF THE BIBLE

Farrar, F. W. *History of Interpretation.* London: Macmillan, 1885. Written from a somewhat liberal standpoint, but has much valuable material.

Mickelsen, A. B. *Interpreting the Bible.* Grand Rapids: Eerdmans, 1963. Best evangelical work on the subject.

Ramm, B. *Protestant Biblical Interpretation.* Boston: Wilde, 1950. Simply written; conservative.

Terry, M. S. *Biblical Hermeneutics.* 2d ed. New York: Phillipa & Hunt, 1885. Old, but still very valuable; a classic.

Wood, J. D. *The Interpretation of the Bible: A Historical Introduction.* London: Duckworth, 1958. Brief but valuable history of Bible interpretation.

INTERTESTAMENTAL PERIOD

Charles, R. H. *Religious Development between the Old and the New Testaments.* New York: Holt, 1914. Brief; shows changes in Jewish theology in this period.

Reicke, B. *The New Testament Era: The World of the Bible from 500 B. C. to A. D. 100.* Philadelphia: Fortress, 1968.

INTRODUCTION: OLD TESTAMENT

Archer, G. A. *A Survey of Old Testament Introduction.* Rev. ed. Chicago: Moody, 1974. A thoroughly conservative and scholarly study of the Old Testament canon and text and special introduction.

Geisler, N. L., and W. E. Nix. *A General Introduction to the Bible.* Chicago: Moody, 1968. Covers both testaments.

Harrison, R. K. *Introduction to the Old Testament.* Grand Rapids: Eerdmans, 1969. Most complete work of its kind in English by a conservative scholar. Covers every phase of Old Testament study: canon, text, history, theology, special introduction.

Rayne, J. B., ed. *New Perspectives on the Old Testament.* Waco, Tex.: Word, 1970. Seventeen papers by as many scholars on important aspects of Old Testament study. Thoroughly evangelical.

Young, E. J. *An Introduction to the Old Testament.* Grand Rapids: Eerdmans, 1949. Conservative; less technical than Archer and Harrison; deals only with special introduction.

INTRODUCTION: NEW TESTAMENT

Feine, P., and Behm, J. *Introduction to the New Testament.* Ed. W. G. Kümmel. 14th ed. Nashville: Abingdon, 1966. Standard liberal introduction.

Guthrie, D. *New Testament Introduction.* 3 vols. Grand Rapids: Eerdmans, 1962-65. Finest special introduction in English. Conservative. Now available in one volume.

Harrison, E. F. *Introduction to the New Testament.* Grand Rapids: Eerdmans, 1964. Covers canon, text, special introduction; scholarly, conservative.

JUDAICA

Daube, D. *The New Testament and Rabbinic Judaism.* London: U. of London, 1956. Describes points in common between the Judaism of Jesus' day and Christianity.

Finkelstein, R. L. *The Pharisees: The Sociological Background of Their Faith.* 2d ed. 2 vols. Philadelphia: Jewish Publ. Soc., 1940. A classic.

Josephus, F. *The Works.* A number of different editions are available of this first-century Jewish historian, who is indispensable for the Maccabean period and first century A. D.

Montefiore, C. G. *Rabbinic Literature and Gospel Teachings.* New York: Macmillan, 1930.

Montefiore, C. G. *Synoptic Gospels.* 2 vols. 2d ed. New York: Macmillan, 1927. This writer shows how rabbinic writings illuminate the teachings of Jesus.

Moore, G. F. *Judaism in the First Centuries of the Christian Era: The Age of Tannaim*. 3 vols. Cambridge: Harvard, 1927-30. A monumental work.

Strack, H. L. *Introduction to the Talmud and Midrash*. Philadelphia: Jewish Pub. Soc. of Amer., 1931. By an outstanding Talmud scholar.

LINGUISTIC AIDS: GREEK

Barclay, W. *A New Testament Wordbook*. London: S.C.M., 1955. This book and the next one are designed for those who know little or no Greek. Fascinating. Both are now available in one volume.

Barclay, W. *More New Testament Words*. New York: Harper, 1958.

Bridges, R., and Weigle, L. A. *The Bible Word Book*. New York: Nelson, 1960. Concerning obsolete or archaic words in the King James Version of the Bible. Does not go into the Greek; very useful to users of the KJV of the Bible.

Cremer, H. *Biblico-Theological Lexicon of New Testament Greek*. 4th ed. Edinburgh: Clark, 1895. Not a mere lexicon, but a theological dictionary like Kittel's, though less complete.

Kittel, G., and Friedrich, G., eds. *Theological Dictionary of the New Testament*. 9 vols. Grand Rapids: Eerdmans, 1964-74. An indispensable work, produced by many German scholars, although many of them liberal.

Trench, R. C. *Synonyms of the New Testament*. Grand Rapids: Eerdmans, 1948. A reprint of a classic work that first came out in 1880 before the discovery of papyri that have done so much to illuminate the meaning of Greek New Testament words.

Vine, W. E. *Expository Dictionary of New Testament Words*. 4 vols. London: Oliphants, 1939-41. Very helpful for those with no knowledge of Greek.

LINGUISTIC AIDS: HEBREW

Girdlestone, R. B. *Synonyms of the Old Testament*. Grand Rapids: Eerdmans, 1953. Originally appeared in 1897. A work similar to Trench's on New Testament synonyms.

PAUL: LIFE

Farrar, F. W. *The Life and Work of St. Paul*. London: Cassell, Petter, Calpin, 1883. Old, but still very valuable.

Moe, O. E. *The Apostle Paul.* Vol. 1, *His Life and Work.* Vol. 2, *His Message and Doctrine.* Minneapolis: Augsburg, 1950, 54. By a fine evangelical scholar.

Smith, P. *The Life and Letters of St. Paul.* New York: Harper, 1932. Standard.

Wood, T. C. *The Life, Letters, and Religion of St. Paul.* Edinburgh: Clark, 1925. Very good.

PAUL: TEACHING

Barclay, W. *The Mind of St. Paul.* London: Collins, 1959. Makes Paul's thought live.

Bruce, A. B. *St. Paul's Conception of Christianity.* Edinburgh: Clark, 1894.

Deissmann, A. *St. Paul: A Study in Social and Religious History.* London: Hodder & Stoughton, 1912. A classic.

Hayes, D. A. *Paul and His Epistles.* New York: Methodist Book Concern, 1915. Excellent; can be used by the layman; vividly written.

Machen, J. B. *The Origin of Paul's Religion.* Grand Rapids: Eerdmans, 1925. Has been called "the best book on Paul by any American writer."

Ramsay, W. M. *The Teaching of Paul in Terms of the Present Day.* London: Hodder & Stoughton, 1913. By a great New Testament archaeologist and expert on Paul.

Scott, C. A. A. *Christianity according to St. Paul.* Cambridge: Cambridge U., 1927. First-rate treatment of Paul's theology.

Stewart, J. S. *A Man in Christ; the Vital Element of St. Paul's Religion.* London: Hodder & Stoughton, 1935. Paul's teaching on union with Christ; a fine work.

SCIENCE AND THE BIBLE

American Scientific Affiliation. *Modern Science and the Christian Faith.* Grand Rapids: Eerdmans, 1949. A symposium by Christian scientists.

Mixter, R. L., ed. *Evolution and Christian Thought Today.* Grand Rapids: Eerdmans, 1959.

Ramm, B. *The Christian View of Science and Scripture.* Grand Rapids: Eerdmans, 1954.

SEPTUAGINT

Hatch, E., and Redpath, H. *A Concordance to the Septuagint and Other Greek Versions of the Old Testament, Including the Apoc-*

ryphal Books. 3 vols. Oxford: Clarendon, 1897-1906. The standard concordance for the Septuagint.

Jellicoe, S. *The Septuagint and Modern Study.* Oxford: Clarendon, 1968.

Rahlfs, A., ed. *Septuaginta.* 2 vols. Stuttgart: Württembergische Bibelanstalt, 1935. Most useful edition of the Septuagint.

Swete, H. B. *An Introduction to the Old Testament in Greek.* 2nd ed. rev. Cambridge: Cambridge U., 1914. Best introduction to the text of the Septuagint.

SURVEY OF THE BIBLE

Gundry, R. H. *A Survey of the New Testament.* Grand Rapids: Zondervan, 1970.

Schultz, S. J. *The Old Testament Speaks.* 2d ed. Harper & Row, 1970. The best Old Testament survey.

Tenney, M. C. *New Testament Survey.* Grand Rapids: Eerdmans, 1961.

THEOLOGY: DICTIONARIES

Harrison, E. F., ed. *Baker's Dictionary of Theology.* Grand Rapids: Baker, 1960. Contains over 850 brief articles on theological terms; evangelical.

Richardson, A., ed. *Theological Word Book of the Bible.* New York: Macmillan, 1951. Not as conservative as Harrison's book.

THEOLOGY: HISTORY

Fisher, G. P. *History of Christian Doctrine.* New York: Scribner, 1923. Good survey.

Hughes, P. E., ed. *Creative Minds in Contemporary Theology.* 2d ed. Grand Rapids: Eerdmans, 1968. Careful exposition and evaluation of fourteen modern theologians.

Mackintosh, H. R. *Types of Modern Theology: Schleiermacher to Barth.* London: Nisbet, 1937. On Schleiermacher, Hegel, Ritschl, Troeltsch, Kierkegaard, Barth.

Neve, S. L., and Heick, O. W. *A History of Christian Thought.* 2 vols. Philadelphia: Muhlenberg, 1946. Covers the whole field, but with special emphasis on the period from 1700 to the present. An excellent study.

Seeberg, R. *Textbook of the History of Doctrines.* 2 vols. in 1. Grand Rapids: Baker, 1952. A standard survey; encyclopedic.

THEOLOGY: SYSTEMATIC

Berkhof, L. *Systematic Theology.* 2d ed. Grand Rapids: Eerdmans, 1941. Written from a strong Calvinistic position.

Brunner, E. *Dogmatics.* 3 vols. Philadelphia: Westminster, 1950-62. Neo-orthodox, but very stimulating.

Miley, J. *Systematic Theology.* 2 vols. New York: Eaton & Mains, 1892-1894. Arminian.

Thiessen, H. C. *Lectures in Systematic Theology.* Grand Rapids: Eerdmans, 1949. Dispensationalist.

THEOLOGY: OLD TESTAMENT

Davidson, A. B. *The Theology of the Old Testament.* New York: Scribners, 1904. Good.

Oehler, C. T. *Theology of the Old Testament.* 2d ed. New York: Funk & Wagnalls, 1884. Old, but still very good.

Payne, J. B. *The Theology of the Older Testament.* Grand Rapids: Zondervan, 1962. The best Old Testament theology; thoroughly evangelical.

Schultz, S. J. *The Gospel of Moses.* New York: Harper & Row, 1974.

THEOLOGY: NEW TESTAMENT

Kümmel, W. G. *The Theology of the New Testament.* Nashville: Abingdon, 1973. Not thoroughly conservative.

Ladd, G. E. *A Theology of the New Testament.* Grand Rapids: Eerdmans, 1974.

Richardson, A. *An Introduction to the Theology of the New Testament.* New York: Harper, 1959. Somewhat neo-orthodox.

Ryrie, C. C. *Biblical Theology of the New Testament.* Chicago: Moody, 1959. Dispensationalist.

THEOLOGY, DOCTRINAL: ATONEMENT

Crawford, T. J. *The Doctrine of Holy Scripture Respecting the Atonement.* Edinburgh: Blackwood, 1874. A classic.

Morris, L. *The Cross in the New Testament.* Grand Rapids: Eerdmans, 1965. By one of the ablest living New Testament scholars.

THEOLOGY, DOCTRINAL: CHRISTOLOGY

Cullmann, O. *The Christology of the New Testament.* Rev. ed. Philadelphia: Westminster, 1963. A classic.

Lidden, H. P. *The Divinity of Our Lord and Saviour Jesus Christ.* London: Rivingtons, 1867. Unsurpassed study.

Mackintosh, H. R. *The Doctrine of the Person of Jesus Christ.* Edinburgh: Clark, 1912. Thorough historical study.

Warfield, B. B. *The Person and Work of Christ.* Philadelphia: Presbyterian & Reformed, 1950. By one of the great Princeton theologians.

THEOLOGY, DOCTRINAL: DEMONOLOGY

Nevius, J. L. *Demon Possession and Allied Themes.* New York: Revell, 1894. A classic study by a missionary in China for forty years.

THEOLOGY, DOCTRINAL: DISPENSATIONALISM

Bass, C. B. *Backgrounds to Dispensationalism: Its Historical Genesis and Ecclesiastical Implications.* Grand Rapids: Eerdmans, 1960. Non-dispensationalist.

Ryrie, C. C. *Dispensationalism Today.* Chicago: Moody, 1965. An attempt to correct misconceptions regarding dispensationalism by a Dallas dean.

THEOLOGY, DOCTRINAL: GOD

Bavinck, H. *The Doctrine of God.* Grand Rapids: Eerdmans, 1951. By a great modern Reformed theologian.

THEOLOGY, DOCTRINAL: HOLY SPIRIT

Kuyper, A. *The Work of the Holy Spirit.* New York: Funk & Wagnalls, 1900. By one of the greatest modern Dutch theologians.

Smeaton, G. *The Doctrine of the Holy Spirit.* Edinburgh: Clark, 1882. Thorough study.

THEOLOGY, DOCTRINAL: SECOND ADVENT

Brown, D. *Christ's Second Coming: Will It Be Premillennial?* Rev. ed. Edinburgh: Clark, 1849. The classic statement of the postmillennial view.

Hamilton, F. E. *The Basis of Millennial Faith.* Grand Rapids: Eerdmans, 1942. Presents the amillennial position.

Walvoord, J. F. *The Millennial Kingdom.* Findlay, Ohio: Dunham, 1959. Dispensationalist.

Reese, A. *The Approaching Advent of Christ*. London: Marshall, Morgan & Scott, 1937. Argues for posttribulational premillennial position.

THEOLOGY, DOCTRINAL: SIN

Berkouwer, G. C. *Sin*. Grand Rapids: Eerdmans, 1971.

Orchard, W. E. *Modern Theories of Sin*. London: Clark, 1909.

Tulloch, J. *The Christian Doctrine of Sin*. Edinburgh: Blackwood, 1876.

TEXTS OF THE BIBLE

Kittel, R., and Kahle, P., eds. *Biblia Hebraica*. Stuttgart: Privilegierte Württembergische Bibelanstalt, 1937. The most useful edition of the Hebrew text.

Nestle, E., and Aland, K., eds. *Novum Testamentum Graece, zum apparatus critico*. 25th ed. Stuttgart: Privilegierte Württembergische Bibelanstalt, 1963. Available in various editions and sizes. Most handy Greek Testament.

TEXTUAL CRITICISM

Metzger, B. M. *The Text of the New Testament: Its Transmission, Corruption, and Restoration*. 2d ed. New York: Oxford, 1968. There is nothing better.

Roberts, B. J. *The Old Testament Texts and Versions*. Cardiff: U. of Wales, 1951. Necessary to the advanced student.

Wurtheim, E. *The Text of the Old Testament: An Introduction to Kittel-Kahle's Biblia Hebraica*. New York: Macmillan, 1957. Has value as a guide to the use of the critical notes in Kittel-Kahle's Biblia Hebraica.

SUGGESTIONS FOR USING BIBLIOGRAPHY IN BIBLE STUDY AND EXEGESIS

The purpose of Bible study and exegesis is to understand what God has to say to us through His Word. For this it is necessary to know what the writer of the book said to the original recipients of the book and then to determine what it says to our modern situation—personally, economically, psychologically, anthropologically, etc. Understanding what the author says involves a considerable amount of knowledge of the background—historical, cultural, and contextual.

Christians sometimes mistakenly think that Bible study requires nothing more than the illuminating work of the Holy Spirit and that they can dispense with human helps. The truth is, however, that the Holy Spirit does not impart information about things we can find out for ourselves; for example, about the city of Ephesus or Herod Agrippa I. We must, moreover, be humble enough to realize that the Holy Spirit has revealed spiritual truths in His Word to other Bible students before us. There is no more reason for a Bible student to begin from scratch in the study of the Bible than there is for a person wanting to know physics to dispense with all previous discoveries, with the expectation of finding out everything for himself.

What Bible study involves.

1. An understanding of the development of the author's thought and of the broad sweep of his teaching in the book.

2. A careful study of the words of the text. This involves the use of lexicons, word study books, and scholarly commentaries.

3. A careful study of syntax. If the text studied is the original Hebrew or Greek, grammars should always be at hand.

4. A knowledge of the cultural and historical setting of the times when the book was written.

5. A knowledge of the context of the book or passage being studied.

6. A knowledge of introduction, both general and special. This includes an understanding of textual criticism, so that an intelligent choice can be made where there are variant readings in the text (the appendix of Mark, for example), and of problems of authorship, date, place of writing, destination, purpose, and the particular circumstances that led to the writing of the book.

7. A knowledge of the general and special rules of biblical hermeneutics.

8. The illumination of the Holy Spirit. This comes only through complete dedication to Christ; freedom from theological prejudices, various forms of pride, and wrong religious conditioning;

and a willingness to do some intensive research and hard thinking in understanding the book.

The tools necessary for exegesis.

1. A good sound text of the Bible—Hebrew, Greek or English. If the original text is used, be sure to get an edition, like Kittel's Hebrew Old Testament or Nestle's Greek New Testament, with a good critical apparatus; that is, with variant readings of the text at the bottom of the page. If the English text is used, at least two translations should be used: a rather literal one, like the New American Standard Bible, and a paraphrase, like *The Living Bible,* for rapid reading. If the KJV is used, it should be done with *The Bible Word Book,* by R. Bridges and L. A. Weigle, which explains over 800 words in the KJV which have changed in meaning since the KJV was printed in 1611. Students not thoroughly versed in the Greek will find helpful a Greek Testament with an English translation on the opposite page, like the one put out by the American Bible Society, which has an excellently edited Greek text on one side and *Today's English Version* on the other.

2. The best available dictionary of Hebrew or Greek. Those who cannot use Greek will find very helpful W. E. Vine's *Expository Dictionary of New Testament Words with Their Precise Meanings for English Readers.*

3. Hebrew and Greek grammars, especially those with an index of references showing where in the grammar difficult passages are discussed.

4. A dictionary of theology, like E. H. Harrison's *Baker's Dictionary of Theology.*

5. Word study books, of which there are a number of very helpful ones, like G. Kittel's *Theological Dictionary of the New Testament Greek* and its Old Testament counterpart, G. J. Botterweck and H. Ringgren's *Theological Dictionary of the Old Testament,* of which only the first volume has so far appeared.

6. A good unabridged concordance: Hebrew, Greek, or English.

7. Bible dictionaries and encyclopedias. There are many of these, in one or more volumes. These have articles on everything men-

tioned in the Bible and are usually well-illustrated and have good maps of Bible lands.

8. Commentaries. There are several kinds of these—some based on the original text and some on the English, some exegetical and some expository, some scholarly and critical (not necessarily in a bad sense) and some popular. There are commentaries on the whole Bible in one volume, and some on one book of the Bible in several volumes. They come in sets or as individual commentaries.

How exegesis proceeds.

How exegesis actually proceeds depends to some extent on whether the passage is studied in the original or the English language. The study of it in the original language is naturally preferable and leads to a more accurate understanding of it, but the study of a passage in English can be reasonably accurate in its results.

1. Read through, several times, the Bible book containing the passage being exegeted, not with the idea of understanding the meaning of every word but to get the sweep of the author's argument and the place of the passage in that argument.

2. Read some material, as much as time allows, on the background of the book, for it cannot be understood apart from this knowledge. This background material should deal with the basic questions of introduction: authorship, date, destination, purpose, place of writing, circumstances leading to the writing of the book, the cultural and historical milieu of the book, the distinctive features of the book, problems of the Hebrew or Greek text, problems of the book's acceptance into the canon. Material on these subjects may be found in a variety of sources, books on Old and New Testament introduction, Bible dictionaries, and the introductory sections of scholarly commentaries.

3. Read the text carefully with the purpose of understanding precisely what the author tried to get across to the recipients of the book. For this the student must make constant use of all available aids: dictionaries, concordances, grammars, word study books, Bible dictionaries and encyclopedias, commentaries. Bible dictionaries, encyclopedias, and commentaries must be read with discre-

tion, since they necessarily reflect the theological biases of the authors: Calvinist, Arminian, Neo-Orthodox, Dispensationalist, Liberal, etc. Scholars, moreover, do not always agree in their interpretation of particular passages in the Bible, sometimes because they have honest differences and sometimes because they are influenced by their theological views. Apply the principles of hermeneutics in trying to understand the text.

4. Once the author's message to the recipients of the book is clearly understood, try to determine the application of his message to us today. The Bible should have more than a historical interest for us; it is a living book, and its message is relevant to every aspect of life today. Ask, What does God have to say to us today? Exegesis is not complete until that question is answered.

Notes

CHAPTER 1

1. Tertullian, *de Anima* 20; cf. Lactantius (quoting Seneca), *Divine Institutes* 6. 25.
2. E. O. James, *The Tree of Life: An Archaeological Study* (Leiden: Brill, 1966).
3. Ibid., p. 69.
4. For an extended discussion of this practice see Frazer, "The Scapegoat," in *The Golden Bough,* part 4 (New York: Macmillan, 1930).
5. W. F. Albright, *From the Stone Age to Christianity* (Baltimore: John Hopkins, 1940), pp. 203-4.
6. Ibid., pp. 206-7.
7. R. K. Harrison, *Introduction to the Old Testament* (Grand Rapids: Eerdmans, 1969), p. 351.
8. E. O. James, *The Ancient Gods* (New York: Capricorn Books, 1960), p. 69. Cf. statements denying the existence of such stages in Henry Frankfort, *Ancient Egyptian Religion* (New York: Harper & Row, 1961), pp. 8, 14; and S. H. Hooke, *Babylonian and Assyrian Religion* (Norman, Okla.: U. of Oklahoma, 1963), p. 14.
9. See discussion in Siegfried Morenz, *Egyptian Religion* (Ithaca, N.Y.: Cornell U., 1973). The Egyptologists Junker and Kees both held this view. Morenz thinks the "unity" was monolatry, not monotheism.
10. E. A. Wallis Budge, *The Gods of the Egyptians* (New York: Dover, 1969), 1:117-20.
11. James, *The Ancient Gods,* p. 70.
12. S. J. Schultz, *The Old Testament Speaks* (New York: Harper & Row, 1970), p. 147.
13. James, *The Ancient Gods,* pp. 87-92.
14. Ibid.

CHAPTER 2

1. C. L. Barnhart, ed., *The American College Dictionary* (New York: Random, 1950).
2. *Encyclopedia Britannica* (Chicago: William Benton, 1972), 2:223.
3. O. R. Gurney, *The Hittites* (Baltimore: Penguin, 1954). One of the better books dealing with these findings.
4. H. V. Hilprecht, ed., *Recent Research in Bible Lands* (Philadelphia: Wattles, 1896), p. 28.
5. A. T. Clay, *Light on the Old Testament from Babel* (Philadelphia: Sunday School Times, 1907), p. 21f.
6. R. A. Torrey, *Difficulties in the Bible* (Chicago: Moody, 1907), p. 23.
7. A. Berkeley Mickelsen, *Interpreting the Bible* (Grand Rapids: Eerdmans, 1963), p. 164.

8. See G. Ernest Wright, *Biblical Archaeology* (Philadelphia: Westminster, 1962), chapter 8.
9. See Jack Finegan, *The Archeology of the New Testament* (Princeton: Princeton U., 1969), pp. 198-202.
10. W. F. Albright, "Toward a More Conservative View," *Christianity Today,* January 18, 1963, p. 3.
11. Ibid., p. 5.
12. Ibid., p. 3.
13. W. F. Albright, "Archaeological Discovery and the Scriptures," *Christianity Today,* June 21, 1968, pp. 3-5.
14. Merrill F. Unger, *Archeology and the Old Testament* (Grand Rapids: Zondervan, 1956), pp. 146-48.
15. Kathleen M. Kenyon, *Archaeology in the Holy Land* (New York: Praeger, 1970), chapter 8.
16. J. A. Thompson, *The Bible and Archaeology* (Grand Rapids: Eerdmans, 1962), p. 4.
17. Bernard Ramm, *Protestant Biblical Interpretation* (Boston: Wilde, 1956), p. 98.
18. See Thompson, chapter 7, for both Omri and Ahab.
19. E.g., Yigael Yadin, *Masada* (New York: Random, 1966).
20. See W. M. Ramsay, *The Cities of St. Paul* (New York: Hodder & Stoughton, 1907).
21. See H. G. May and R. M. Engberg, *Material Remains of the Megiddo Cult* (Chicago: U. of Chicago, 1935), plate 12. The 1973 season at Beersheba uncovered the largest horned altar yet found.
22. James B. Pritchard, ed., *The Ancient Near East in Pictures Relating to the Old Testament* (Princeton: Princeton U., 1954).
23. Yigael Yadin, *The Art of Warfare in Biblical Lands* (New York: McGraw-Hill, 1963), 1:9f.
24. James B. Pritchard, ed., *Ancient Near Eastern Texts Relating to the Old Testament,* 2d ed. (Princeton: Princeton U., 1955).
25. Wright, p. 23.
26. W. F. Albright, *The Archaeology of Palestine* (Baltimore: Penguin, 1960), p. 234.
27. The three texts used for the following discussion are: Pritchard's *Ancient Near Eastern Texts Relating to the Old Testament; Ancient Iraq* by Georges Roux (Baltimore: Penguin, 1964); and *The Greatness That Was Babylon* by H. W. F. Saggs (New York: Mentor, 1962).
28. Albright, *Archaeology,* p. 219.
29. Ibid.
30. Ibid., p. 220.
31. Edwin M. Yamauchi, *The Stones and the Scriptures* (Philadelphia: Lippincott, 1972).
32. R. K. Harrison, *Introduction to the Old Testament* (Grand Rapids: Eerdmans, 1969), p. 61.

CHAPTER 3

1. G. Larue, *Old Testament Life and Literature* (Boston: Allyn & Bacon, 1968), p. 31.
2. J. Lindblom, *Prophecy in Ancient Israel* (Philadelphia: Fortress, 1962), pp. 47-48.
3. Ibid., p. 95.
4. Jay G. Williams, *Understanding the Old Testament* (New York: Baron's Ed. Ser., 1972), pp. 193-95.
5. J. K. West, *Introduction to the Old Testament* (New York: Macmillan, 1971), pp. 269-71.
6. R. H. Pfeiffer, *Introduction to the Old Testament* (New York: Harper, 1941), pp. 415-48.

7. R. K. Harrison, *Introduction to the Old Testament* (Grand Rapids: Eerdmans, 1969), p. 741. See also H. E. Freeman, *An Introduction to the Old Testament Prophets* (Chicago: Moody, 1968).
8. Cf. S. J. Schultz, "The Religion of Israel," in *The Old Testament Speaks* (New York: Harper & Row, 1970), pp. 57-74.
9. Meredith Kline, *Treaty of the Great King* (Grand Rapids: Eerdmans, 1963), pp. 1-45.
10. ———, "Canon and the Covenant Community," in *The Structure of Biblical Authority* (Grand Rapids: Eerdmans, 1972), pp. 76-93.
11. For a discussion of the Pentateuch as essentially Mosaic, see R. K. Harrison, pp. 495-541.
12. Cf. S. J. Schultz, *The Prophets Speak* (New York: Harper & Row, 1968), pp. 68ff, and *The Gospel of Moses* (New York: Harper & Row, 1974), pp. 95ff.
13. Gerhard von Rad, *Old Testament Theology* (New York: Harper & Row, n.d.), 2:194.
14. J. Bright, *History of Israel* (Philadelphia: Westminster, 1959), p. 257.
15. F. F. Bruce, ed., *Israel and the Nations* (Grand Rapids: Eerdmans, 1963), pp. 55-57.
16. Jacques Ellul, *The Politics of God and the Politics of Men* (Grand Rapids: Eerdmans, 1972), p. 157.
17. Charles H. Troutman, "Evangelism and Social Action in Biblical Perspective," *Evangelical Missions Quarterly* 9(Winter 1973): 103.

CHAPTER 4

1. Midrash Exodus Rabbah 42. 8; Babylonian Talmud, Megilloth 14a.
2. *Prolegomena*, p. 489.
3. Peter R. Ackroyd, "The Interpretation of the Exile and Restoration," *Canadian Journal of Theology* 14(January 1968): 10.
4. Paul Humbert, "La Logique de la perspective nomade chez Osée et l'unite d'Osée 2, 4-22," in *Vom Alten Testament, Karl Marti zum Siebzigsten Geburtstage* (Giessen: Verlag von Alfred Töpelmann, 1925), pp. 164-65.
5. G. E. Ladd, *A Commentary on the Revelation of John* (Grand Rapids: Eerdmans, 1972), p. 22.

CHAPTER 5

1. See Nigel Turner, "Syntax" in *Grammar of New Testament Greek*, by J. H. Moulton (Edinburgh: T. & T. Clark, 1963), 3:325f.
2. Eusebius, *Ecclesiastical History* 3. 39. 4.
3. Cf. D. A. Hagner, *The Use of the Old and New Testaments in Clement of Rome* (Leiden: Brill, 1973), pp. 303-12.
4. See T. W. Manson, "The Argument from Prophecy," *Journal of Theological Studies* 46(1945): 136. Cf. K. Stendahl, *The School of St. Matthew*, 2d ed. (Philadelphia: Fortress, 1968).
5. See especially B. Gerhardsson, *Memory and Manuscript* (Lund: Gleerup, 1961).
6. See P. Kahle, *The Cairo Geniza*, 2d ed. (New York: Praeger, 1960). Especially important for New Testament study is the Palestinian targum of the Pentateuch as reflected in Codex Neofiti, and partially in Pseudo-Jonathan and the Fragment targum. Cf. M. McNamara, *Targum and Testament* (Grand Rapids: Eerdmans, 1972).
7. See F. M. Cross, Jr., *The Ancient Library of Qumran and Modern Biblical Studies*, rev. ed. (Garden City, N. J.: Anchor, 1960), pp. 168-94.
8. Cf. R. Laird Harris, who refers to the "represtination" of the Septuagint text in "The Dead Sea Scrolls and the Old Testament Text," in *New Perspectives on the Old Testament*, ed. J. Barton Payne (Waco, Tex.: Word, 1970), pp. 201-11.

9. For an excellent and detailed summary of the extent of septuagintal quotations in the New Testament, see H. B. Swete, *An Introduction to the Old Testament In Greek*, 2d ed. (Cambridge: Cambridge U., 1902), pp. 381-405.
10. Ibid., pp. 462-77.
11. R. H. Gundry, "The Language Milieu of First-Century Palestine," *Journal of Biblical Literature* 83(December 1964): 404-8.
12. See McNamara, pp. 91-169.
13. These examples are borrowed from F. F. Bruce, *The Books and the Parchments*, 3d ed. rev. (London: Pickering & Inglis, 1963), p. 138.
14. See J. R. Harris, *Testimonies*, vols. 1-2 (Cambridge: Cambridge U., 1916-20).
15. R. H. Gundry, *The Use of the Old Testament in St. Matthew's Gospel* (Leiden: Brill, 1967), pp. 172ff.
16. E. E. Ellis, *Paul's Use of the Old Testament* (London: Oliver & Boyd, 1957), pp. 139ff.
17. See *Gesenius' Hebrew Grammar*, ed. E. Kautzsch and A. E. Cowley, 2d ed. (Oxford: Clarendon, 1910), p. 312f.
18. See especially R. E. Brown, *Sensus Plenior of Sacred Scripture* (Baltimore: St. Mary's U., 1955).
19. For a standard introduction, see G. W. H. Lampe and K. J. Woollcombe, *Essays on Typology* SBT 22 (London: SCM, 1957).
20. An outstanding discussion of this subject can be found in R. N. Longenecker's article, "Can We Reproduce the Exegesis of the New Testament?" *Tyndale Bulletin* 21(1970): 3-38. Longenecker's answer to the question is carefully balanced. See also his *Biblical Exegesis in the Apostolic Period* (Grand Rapids: Eerdmans, 1975).
21. See H. M. Wolf, "A Solution to the Immanuel Prophecy in Isaiah 7:14–8:22," *Journal of Biblical Literature* 91(1972), pp. 449-56. Wolf argues that *Maher-shalal-hash-baz* is the prophesied child, and thus another name for Immanuel. He allows that a fuller sense of the passage applies to the birth of Jesus.
22. Cf. A. Berkeley Mickelsen, *Interpreting the Bible* (Grand Rapids: Eerdmans, 1963), p. 300; B. Ramm, *Protestant Biblical Interpretation* (Boston: Wilde, 1956), pp. 233-34.
23. For an excellent discussion of Jesus' use of the Old Testament (as distinct from the evangelists' use of it), see R. T. France, *Jesus and the Old Testament* (London: Tyndale, 1971).
24. See the discussion in J. G. Baldwin, *Haggai, Zechariah, Malachi*, Tyndale Bible Commentary (London: Tyndale, 1972), pp. 190ff.

CHAPTER 6

1. See Adolf Deissmann, *Light from the Ancient East* (Grand Rapids: Baker, 1965), pp. 146-245; especially pp. 228-45.
2. W. R. Ramsay, *The Letters to the Seven Churches of Asia* (New York: A. C. Armstrong, 1905), p. 24.
3. A. M. Hunter, *Introducing the New Testament*, 2d ed. (London: SCM, 1957), p. 157.
4. R. P. C. Hanson, *Second Corinthians* (London: SCM, 1954), p. 7.
5. Ernst Haenchen, *The Acts of the Apostles: A Commentary* (Philadelphia: Westminster, 1971), p. 41.
6. Martin Dibelius, *Studies in the Acts of the Apostles* (London: SCM, 1956), p. 122.
7. J. Jeremias, *Rediscovering the Parables* (New York: Scribner, 1966).
8. See, e.g., G. E. Ladd, "Why Not Prophetic-Apocalyptic?" *Journal of Biblical Literature* 76(1957): 192-200; G. W. Barker, W. L. Lane, and J. R. Michaels, *The New Testament Speaks* (New York: Harper & Row, 1969), pp. 362-84.
9. See especially John Wick Bowman, *The First Christian Drama* (Philadelphia: Westminster, 1955).
10. Berkeley Mickelsen, *Interpreting the Bible* (Grand Rapids: Eerdmans, 1963), p. 303.

CHAPTER 7

1. Cf. James D. Smart, *The Strange Silence of the Bible in the Church: A Study in Hermeneutics* (Philadelphia: Westminster, 1940).
2. Robert M. Grant, *A Short History of the Interpretation of the Bible*, rev. ed. (New York: Macmillan, 1966), p. 88.
3. George E. Ladd, *The New Testament and Criticism* (Grand Rapids: Eerdmans, 1966), chaps. 1-2; Simon Kistemaker, *The Gospels in Current Study* (Grand Rapids: Baker, 1973).
4. J. M. Houston, "An Environmental Background to the New Testament"; Harold H. Rowdon, "The Historical and Political Background and Chronology of the New Testament"; "The Religious Background of the New Testament (Pagan)"; and H. L. Ellison, "The Religious Background of the New Testament (Jewish)," in *A New Testament Commentary*, ed. G. C. D. Howley, F. F. Bruce, and H. L. Ellison (Grand Rapids: Zondervan, 1969).
5. F. F. Bruce, *New Testament History* (Garden City: Doubleday, 1971); Floyd V. Filson, *New Testament History* (Philadelphia: Westminster, 1964); Merrill Tenney, *New Testament Times* (Grand Rapids: Eerdmans, 1965); J. Jeremias, *Jerusalem in the Time of Jesus* (Naperville, Ill.: Allenson, 1969).
6. Clark Pinnock, *Biblical Revelation* (Chicago: Moody, 1971), chaps. 1-2, 4.
7. E. Earle Ellis, "The Role of the Christian Prophecy in Acts," in *Apostolic History and the Gospel*, ed. W. Ward Gasque and Ralph P. Martin (Grand Rapids: Eerdmans, 1970), p. 60.
8. John Alexander, "The Authority of Scripture," and editorial in *The Other Side* (January-February 1973): 1ff. The author briefly and persuasively faces the question of interpretation of the Bible and political implications for evangelicals.
9. Cf. Louis Lutzbetak, *The Church and Cultures* (Divine Word, 1970) for a helpful introduction to cultural anthropology which can throw a great deal of light on understanding a culture or a people's mind and customary ways; Marvin Mayers, *Christianity Confronts Culture* (Grand Rapids: Zondervan, 1974); Eugene Nida, *Message and Mission* (New York: Harper, 1960).
10. Ronald M. Enroth, Edward E. Erickson, and C. Breckenridge Peters, *The Jesus People* (Grand Rapids: Eerdmans, 1972), p. 97.
11. Gerhard Kittel, ed., *Theological Dictionary of the New Testament* (Grand Rapids: Eerdmans, 1964-71), 3:679-81, s. v. *kephale*.
12. Cf. Richard Bube, *The Encounter Between Christianity and Science* (Grand Rapids: Eerdmans, 1965), pp. 96-97.
13. D. Flusser, "Blessed Are the Poor in Spirit," *Israel Exploration Journal* 10(1960): 2.
14. 1QA 18:14-15; 1QA 14:3; 1QM 14:7; all cited by Flusser, ibid., pp. 3ff.
15. Cf. Norman Snaith, *The Distinctive Ideas of the Old Testament* (New York: Schocken, 1964), p. 180.
16. A good example is the recent *Commentary on the Gospel of John* by Leon Morris (Grand Rapids: Eerdmans, 1971) which combines faithfulness to the integrity of Scripture as the Word of God with excellent historical and cultural understanding.
17. J. Jeremias, *The Parables of Jesus*, rev. ed. (New York: Scribner, 1971), p. 147. We do not have to follow Jeremias all the way to profit greatly from his historical and cultural insight.
18. Ibid., pp. 188-89.
19. Paul L. Maier, *Pontius Pilate* (Garden City: Doubleday, 1968), pp. 364-65.
20. Cf. the excellent help in C. K. Barrett, *The New Testament Background: Selected Documents* (New York: Harper & Row, n.d.), pp. 139-72; see also for rabbinic backgrounds S. Safrai and M. Stern, eds., *The Jewish People in the First Century* (Philadelphia: Fortress, 1974); David Daube, *The New Testament and Rabbinic Judaism* (New York: Arno, 1973); J. Jeremias, *Jerusalem in the Time of Jesus* (Naperville, Ill.: Allenson, 1969); G. G. Montefiore and H. Lowe, *A Rabbinic Anthology* (New York: Schocken, 1974).

21. Cited by William S. LaSor, *The Dead Sea Scrolls and the New Testament* (Grand Rapids: Eerdmans, 1973), p. 240.
22. Cf. C. H. Dodd, *The Parables of the Kingdom*, rev. ed. (New York: Scribner, 1961).
23. Cf. Jeremias, *Parables*, pp. 66ff.
24. Cf. Barrett, *Documents*, p. 148f.
25. E.g., Bruce Metzger, *The New Testament: Its Background, Growth and Content* (Nashville: Abingdon, 1965), chap. 2.
26. E.g., Jeremias, *Jerusalem*, chap. 11; Jacob Neusner, *From Politics to Piety: The Emergence of Pharasaic Judaism* (Englewood Cliffs, N. Y.: Prentice-Hall, 1973).
27. Metzger, *New Testament*, p. 39.
28. Ibid., p. 41.
29. Hugh Schonfield, *The Passover Plot* (New York: Bantam, 1971); Haim Cohn, *The Trial and Death of Jesus* (New York: Harper & Row, 1971).
30. Cf. Emil Schurer, *The Literature of the Jewish People in the Time of Jesus* (New York: Schocken, 1972). One must also use the extensive text and translations of this literature found in R. H. Charles, *The Apocrypha and Pseudepigrapha of the Old Testament*, 2 vols. (London: Oxford, 1913).
31. Cited by Martin McNamara, *Targum and Testament, Aramaic Paraphrases of the Hebrew Bible: A Light on the New Testament* (Grand Rapids: Eerdmans, 1973), p. 147. This volume provides many other cases of New Testament parallels to targum materials.
32. For the best help available on these linguistic possibilities in the New Testament, see the newly translated nine-volume *Theological Dictionary Of the New Testament*, ed. G. Kittel (Grand Rapids: Eerdmans, 1964-74). Also helpful but technical is J. H. Moulton and George Milligan, *The Vocabulary of the Greek New Testament* (Grand Rapids: Eerdmans, 1959).
33. Cf. Harold Mattingly, *Christianity in the Roman Empire* (New York: Norton, 1967), p. 35f.
34. F. F. Bruce, *New Testament History* (Garden City: Doubleday, 1972), pp. 340-41.
35. Cf. Barrett, *Documents*, p. 146.
36. Cited by McNamara, *Targum*, p. 73.
37. Cf. Snaith, *Ideas*, chaps. 4, 8; Leon Morris, *The Apostolic Preaching of the Cross* (Grand Rapids: Eerdmans, 1956), chaps. 7-8.
38. Edwin Yamauchi, *Pre-Christian Gnosticism* (Grand Rapids: Eerdmans, 1973).
39. Cf. Barrett, *Documents*, pp. 227ff.
40. G. E. Ladd, "Why Not Prophetic-Apocalyptic?" *Journal of Biblical Literature* 86(1957): 192-200; also, "The Revelation and Jewish Apocalyptic," *Evangelical Quarterly* 29(1957): 94-100; also, "Apocalyptic," in *The New Bible Dictionary*, ed. J. D. Douglas (Grand Rapids: Eerdmans, 1962). See also Leon Morris, *Apocalyptic* (Grand Rapids: Eerdmans, 1972).
41. J. Julius Scott, Jr., "Paul and Late-Jewish Eschatology—a Case Study, 1 Thessalonians 4:13-18 and 2 Thessalonians 2:1-12," *Journal of Evangelical Theological Society* 15 (1972): 133-43.
42. Cited by L. Paul Trudinger, "Some Observations Concerning the Text of the Old Testament in the Book of Revelation," *Journal of Theological Studies* 17(1966): 88.
43. A. DuPont-Sommer, *The Essene Writings from Qumran* (Meridian, 1961), p. 208.
44. Trudinger, "Observations," p. 87.
45. Richard B. Norton, "The Importance of Imperial Roman Backgrounds for Interpreting the Revelation," (M.A. Thesis, Wheaton College Graduate School of Theology, 1949), pp. 14ff.
46. F. F. Bruce, *History*, pp. 412-13.

CHAPTER 8

1. Wilhelm Vischner, *The Witness of the Old Testament to Christ* (London: Lutterworth, 1949), p. 156.
2. James Wood, *The Interpretation of the Bible* (London: Duckworth, 1958), p. 7.
3. Ibid., p. 11.
4. Allan Stibbs, *Understanding God's Word* (London: Inter-Varsity, 1962), p. 32.
5. A. Berkeley Mickelsen, *Interpreting the Bible* (Grand Rapids: Eerdmans, 1963), p. 85.
6. F. W. Farrar, *History of Interpretation* (New York: Dutton, 1886), p. 295.
7. Wood, *Interpretation*, p. 87.
8. Ernest Renan, *The Life of Jesus* (New York: Carleton, 1864), p. 184.
9. Walter Rauschenbusch, *Christianity and the Social Crisis* (New York: Harper & Row, 1964), pp. 48, 68.
10. Harry Emerson Fosdick, *The Man from Nazareth* (New York: Harper, 1949).
11. See Albert Schweitzer, *The Quest of the Historical Jesus* (New York: Harper & Row, 1956).
12. Daniel Callahan, ed., *The Secular City Debate* (New York: Macmillan, 1966), p. 194.
13. See Rudolph Bultmann, *Jesus and the Word* (New York: Scribner, 1958).
14. For representative works by Heidegger, see his *Being and Time* (New York: Harper & Row, 1962), and *Existence and Being* (Chicago: Regnery, 1949). For helpful paperback treatments of existentialism, consult the anthology compiled by Walter Kaufmann, *Existentialism from Dostoevsky to Sartre* (Cleveland: World, 1956), and J. Rodman Williams's analysis in *Contemporary Existentialism and Christian Faith* (Englewood Cliffs, N. J.: Prentice-Hall, 1965). For an interchange between Bultmann and his critics, review *Kerygma and Myth* (New York: Harper & Row, 1961). A brief statement of the necessity of interpreting faith in existential fashion is found on pp. 15-16.
15. Stauffer's definitive work in this connection is *Jesus and His Story* (New York: Knopf, 1960).
16. Hugh Anderson, ed., *Jesus* (Englewood Cliffs, N. J.: Prentice-Hall, 1968), p. 20.
17. Günther Bornkamm, *Jesus of Nazareth* (New York: Harper, 1960), p. 158.
18. C. H. Dodd, *The Founder of Christianity* (New York: Macmillan, 1970), pp. 22-23.
19. For a more extensive bibliography of the recent biographies of Jesus, see Hugh Anderson's "Bibliographical Note," in *Jesus*, pp. 175-79. To sense something of the transition from existential concern with Christ to the new quest, consider the following rigorous studies: Maurice Goguel, *The Life of Jesus* (New York: Macmillan, 1933), and Charles Guignebert, *Jesus* (New York: University Books, 1956).
20. See especially Dietrich Bonhoeffer, *Act and Being* (New York: Harper, 1962); *Christology* (London: Collins, 1966); *The Cost of Discipleship* (New York: Macmillan, 1949).
21. Bonhoeffer, *Christology*, p. 51.
22. For further elaboration of this viewpoint, see Morris Inch, "Jesus Is Lord," *Journal of the Evangelical Theological Society* 14(1972): 173-80.

CHAPTER 9

1. George H. Williams, *Spiritual and Anabaptist Writers*, Library of Christian Classics, vol. 25 (Philadelphia: Westminster, 1957); and *The Radical Reformation* (Philadelphia: Westminster, 1962).
2. William C. Robinson, *The Reformation: A Rediscovery of Grace* (Grand Rapids: Eerdmans, 1962), pp. 1-36.
3. Philip Schaff, *The Creeds of Christendom* (New York: Harper, 1877), 2:79-80.

4. Robert M. Grant, *A Short History of the Interpretation of the Bible* (New York: Macmillan, 1963), pp. 128-29.
5. John Calvin, *Institutes of the Christian Religion,* Library of Christian Classics, ed. John T. McNeill (Philadelphia: Westminster, 1960), 20:74-75.
6. Williams, *Writings,* pp. 151-52.
7. Calvin, *Institutes,* 21:1084.
8. Ibid., p. 93.
9. Jaroslav Pelikan, ed., *Luther's Works* (St. Louis: Concordia, 1967), 30:166.
10. H. T. Kerr, *A Compend of Luther's Theology* (Philadelphia: Westminster, 1966), pp. 3-20.
11. Williams, *Writers,* pp. 22-23, 30ff.
12. Robert L. Ferm, *Readings in the History of Christian Thought* (New York: Holt, Rinehart & Winston, 1964), pp. 528-35.
13. Williams, *Writers,* p. 51.
14. B. Ramm, *Protestant Biblical Interpretation* (Boston: W. A. Wilde, 1956), p. 55.
15. Emil Brunner, *Revelation and Reason* (Philadelphia: Westminster, n.d.), p. 276; R. C. Johnson, *Authority in Protestant Theology* (Philadelphia: Westminster, n.d.), pp. 36-39.
16. J. M. Reu, *Luther and the Scriptures* (Waverly, Ia.: Wartburg, n.d.), pp. 44-45.
17. Calvin, *Institutes,* 20:76.
18. Ibid.
19. Ramm, *Interpretation,* pp. 53-57; see also E. F. Klug, *From Luther to Chemnitz* (Grand Rapids: Eerdmans, 1972), pp. 1-114.
20. Will Durant, *The Story of Civilization,* vol. 6, *The Reformation* (New York: Simon & Schuster, 1957), pp. 477, 849.
21. Otto W. Heick and J. L. Neve, *A History of Christian Thought* (Philadelphia: Fortress, 1965), 1:269.
22. Ramm, *Interpretation,* p. 57.
23. Calvin, *Institutes,* 21:1155.
24. Ibid., p. 95.
25. Johnson, *Authority,* pp. 42-57.
26. H. J. Forstman, *Word and Spirit: Calvin's Doctrine of Biblical Authority* (Stanford, Calif.: Stanford U., n.d.), p. 78.
27. Brunner, *Reason,* pp. 127-28.
28. W. Neisel, *The Theology of Calvin* (Philadelphia: Westminster, n.d.), p. 31.
29. *Works of Martin Luther* (n. p.: Holman & Castle), 3:16.
30. Paul J. Achtemeier, *An Introduction to the New Hermeneutic* (Philadelphia: Westminster, 1969), p. 116.

CHAPTER 10

1. For a more elaborate development of this thesis see my contribution to Marvin K. Mayers, *Reshaping Evangelical Higher Education* (Grand Rapids: Zondervan, 1972), chaps. 1-5.
2. For a specific debate about Scripture see *Translating Theology into the Modern Age,* ed. Robert W. Funk with Gerhard Ebeling (New York: Harper, 1965), chap. 2.
3. Some illustrative documents of this period appear in *Reformed Dogmatics,* ed. John W. Beardslee III (New York: Oxford, 1965).
4. Pertinent quotes from these authors appear in *A History of Christianity,* ed. Clyde L. Monschreck (Englewood Cliffs, N. J.: Prentice-Hall, 1964), chap. 5.
5. See F. Ernest Stoeffler, *The Rise of Evangelical Pietism* (Leiden: Brill, 1965).
6. For examples of this stance see James C. Livingston, *Modern Christian Thought: From the Enlightenment to Vatican Two* (New York: Macmillan, 1971), chaps. 6-9.

CHAPTER 11

1. William Hordern, *The Case for a New Reformation Theology* (Philadelphia: Westminster, 1959), p. 66.
2. Martin Luther, *"Preface to the New Testament,"* in *Selected Writings of Martin Luther,* ed. Theodore G. Tappert (Philadelphia: Fortress, 1967), 4:398.
3. A. Berkeley Mickelsen, *Interpreting the Bible* (Grand Rapids: Eerdmans, 1963), pp. 356-66.
4. Bernard Ramm, *Protestant Biblical Interpretation* (Boston: Wilde, 1950), p. 7.
5. James M. Gray, *Synthetic Bible Studies* (New York: Revell, 1906), p. 10.
6. Ibid.
7. John Edward Carnell, *The Case for Orthodox Theology* (Philadelphia: Westminster, 1959), p. 34.
8. Compare 1 Co 15:9, Eph 3:8, and 1 Ti 1:15.
9. Mickelsen, *Bible,* p. 357.
10. Paul Tournier, *The Strong and the Weak* (Philadelphia: Westminster, 1963), p. 97.

Date D